What to Say . . . How to Say It

What to Say . . . How to Say It

Improving Your Image by Mail, on the Phone, in Person

Compiled and edited by
N. H. and S. K. Mager

William Morrow and Company, Inc.
New York   1980

Library of Congress Cataloging in Publication Data

Main entry under title:

What to say . . . how to say it.

   1. Communication.   I. Mager, Nathan H. (date)
II. Mager, Sylvia K. (date)
P90.W445   001.54   79-19873
ISBN 0-688-03571-X

Printed in the United States of America

First Edition
1 2 3 4 5 6 7 8 9 10

Book Design by Michael Mauceri

Acknowledgments

The editors express sincere appreciation to the scores of writers whose ideas helped form this guide and particularly to Alexander Hamilton Institute; Alexander Marketing Services; American Express Company; American Express Publishing Corporation; American Kidney Fund; American Preservation; Amnesty International USA; Antique Monthly; Apartment Life; Apollo Publications, Inc.; Architectural Digest; Robert Seckel and Arco Publishing Company, Inc.; Art in America; Automatic Data Processing, Inc.; Baldwin Cooke Company; Berkshire Life Insurance Company; Paul J. Bringe; Business Week; Paul Butterworth; Changing Times; Chase Manhattan Bank; The Children's Aid Society; Cole's Metropolitan Housing Directory; Coleman Folding Tables; Connecticut Mutual Life Insurance Co.; Connoisseur; Direct Marketing; Donnelley Marketforce Ltd.; Nelson Doubleday, Inc.; V. W. Eimicke Associates, Inc.; Bruce W. Eberle & Associates, Inc.; Eliot Books; Federal Envelope; Filmack Studios, Inc.; Forbes Magazine; General Motors Acceptance Corporation; Gift & Decorative Accessories; Alan Glazer Associates; Grumman Flxible Corporation; Gulf Oil Corp.; Leon Henry, Inc.; Henry Hoke; JS&A National Sales Group; Idea Art; Andrew S. Linick; Informative Computer Services Ltd.; Investment Dealers' Digest; Lauren R. Januz; Kelly Girl; Kentucky Electric Steel Company; Kiplinger Washington Editors, Inc.; Krause Publications, Joseph A. Kreuger Associates; Liberty List Co.; Liberty Federal Savings; McDonald's; Mail-O-Graph Co.; Mail Marketing Minnesota; Shirley Mariachin; Stanley Morantz; National Data Corp.; Theodore Reade Nathan; National Taxpayer's Union; New York Association for the Blind; New York Life Insurance Company; Norann Mail

Specialties; Pitney Bowes; Planned Parenthood Federation of America; Playboy Enterprises; Police Athletic League; Publisher's Clearing House; Rapistan Inc.; Reader's Digest; Russ Reid Company; Reply-O-Letter Company, Inc.; Sig Rosenblum; Sales Marketing Management; Sanger & Harris; Richard Silverman; Smithsonian Magazine; Society for Animal Rights; Sperry & Hutchinson Company; Standard Rate & Data Service; State University at Buffalo; Stauffer Chemical Company; Texas Monthly; Ticor Mortgage Insurance; The Translation Company of America, Inc.; Travelers Aid Society of New York; Travel & Leisure; Tufts University; U.S. News & World Report; Wells Fargo Investment Advisors; Wells Fargo Bank; West Publishing Company; Western Union; Xerox Education Publication; YMCA Camping Services of Greater New York; Vital Speeches; Wolf Envelope Company; World Coin News; Xerox Education Publications.

Complaint-handling material is copyright 1977 by Sperry and Hutchinson Company. Material in the telephone chapter is from "Profitable Telephone Sales Operations" by Robet Steckel, by permission of Arco Publishing Company, Inc. Goodwill and service letters are from "Agents Guide to Letter Writing," Connecticut Life Insurance Co., by permission.

Contents

What to Say . . . How to Say It

Chapter 1

Communicating with Impact

Communication is an all-embracing function of living. It is part of the training of children and of the chatter of teenagers on the telephone, the smoke signals of the Indians and the musical background of television commercials. It is body talk and sometimes even silence. Most, but not all, of our everyday, adult communication is by conversation (direct and by telephone) and by writing.

This book is designed to help you make that communication easier and more effective. This is not always accomplished by the simple imperative: "Please get the job done." It involves an understanding of how and why people react as they do. Two examples of effective communication are cited in a recent media newsletter:

> The director of a school for boys sought a way to make his students tuck in their shirttails. Talk was ineffective. Lace sewn on the shirttail produced results.

> A New York policeman told me: "If you're ever attacked in a building, don't yell 'Help'—yell 'Fire.'"

The process of communication is one of transferring an idea from your brain to another's. Let your reader see the picture, visualize what you are describing.

There is, of course, no sure-fire way to be effective every time you want to say something. Each message must be tailored to the situation and the personalities involved. We present here some general rules, based on much experience, and some samples that will suggest an approach to the more common problems.

For most people, speaking is the "easy" way. Most conscious communication is verbal. But all of us communicate in other ways: in our attitudes, dress, gestures, body tone, eyes, facial expressions—and even in the ways we perceive what others are saying. Even sitting impassively communicates. Nonverbal communication may be very ambiguous. A smile, for example, may convey lack of assurance, agreement, friendliness, superiority, disdain, victory, or just a private joke in reverie. Of course, even verbal comments can be ambiguous. A "yes" said coldly or with a turning away may be a "no" or a reluctant "yes."

Writing is the difficult way, not only because we are inhibited by the physical act of putting words on paper but also because there is a subconscious restraint on what we commit to a writing.

Nevertheless, writing is the universal method in important person-to-person communication. Because writing represents a more considered message, it is taken far more seriously than a telephone conversation or a tête-à-tête. And rightfully so. For this reason letters and letter writing form a very basic part of our lives—to express emotions to friends and to the unfriendly, to report, to hold relationships, and to get and to break them, to announce, to record, to ask for things, and to say thank you. All these are part of everyday living.

Even more important to many of us is the correspondence aspect of business, which performs on a more formal scale but with similar functions: selling ideas, merchandise, reputations; accepting, complaining, and adjusting; and sometimes just calling attention to ourselves, our products, or our services.

There are two approaches to personal communication. For many, what is said is a means of expression, of emotional release, of "getting it off my chest." For others it is a means of obtaining a response, a means of affecting the audience in the desired way.

Those cumbersome emotions

In our personal relations most of the things we say are designed to express our own emotions. In business, most of the things we say are designed to affect the other person, to induce a response, to make an employee or a superior enthusiastic, to justify an action, and so forth.

When you are angry, worried, disappointed, envious, sometimes just feeling bad—in personal life and often in business—there is a strong impulse to sit down and write a letter. Emotionally this is often a relief from tension. It gets something off your chest. For your mental health, this may be a wise thing to do.

Then tear the letter up.

If it is written under high emotion, the letter will probably be a source of regret to you when you have calmed down.

There is, of course, no fence that divides the two approaches. To say anything most effectively requires that you assume, even momentarily, the condition of the communicatee. For a time this was called "assuming the you attitude." The polite compliment, the greeting, even "how are you," when you don't care a bit, are social amenities we live with all the time. And for most sophisticated adults the "effect" approach is a normal, habituated way of communication, with emotional outbursts limited to a private expression at appropriate time and place, perhaps to a secretary or a spouse.

Using honey

Often you will find that becoming angry in order to get something done is a waste of emotion: that understanding and explanation are more helpful. "You catch more flies with honey than with vinegar," the old saw notes.

Without ignoring the beneficial effects of an emotional outburst, this commentary leans to the "honey" side of communication. It assembles some of the ways used to accomplish necessary, sometimes difficult ends in a nice and easy way.

The essence of what you *say* to others in the course of the day is what creates their estimation of you—whether they like you or don't like you, whether they think you are bright or mediocre. The man or woman who responds brusquely, negatively, or pleasantly builds up impressions at each encounter.

If you really want to know what your image is, sum up at the end of each day the conversations you have had with each person. Rate what you said in terms of impression on the other person: pleasant, unpleasant, neutral. Convert this into units of minutes or sentences for each contact. Then you can take a look at yourself as others see you.

You have an ego, and so does everyone you know. You also have a built-in resistance to compliments that seem to be flattery, sycophancy, buttering up. Many people who receive a nice word respond: "What does he want from me now?"

For this reason, sending a compliment—even a sincere one—is both useful and difficult, especially when the recipient is unsentimental and the occasion is equivocal. Yet such letters can massage the ego, make or solidify friendships, and prove most effective toward a general or a specific purpose. The art of praising is the beginning of the fine art of pleasing.

The "you" approach

The job of a salesman is not merely to talk to a customer, but to induce him or her to buy a product or service. The principal job of a letter writer is not to write a letter but to accomplish the purpose of a letter.

Some people may see the "you" approach as being cynical and self-centered. The first thought is that a letter or even conversation should spring from the heart, in all sincerity, without thought of who might be hurt by it, or what the reaction will be.

This is fine for a child who cannot understand the effect of a cruel word or a tactless remark. Adults are more willing to find something to compliment rather than to criticize, to tell little white lies to spare feelings, to consider what words will do to others rather than how much personal emotion they can relieve.

They do this unconsciously, having trained themselves early in life to consider others and to assume responsibility for the effects of what they say. Tact in communication becomes a subliminal restraint, not a conscious thinking out for each sentence. Carried further, it becomes a way of framing a letter—or a sentence—with some thought of whom it will help or hurt, and how.

Humor

Humor has an important place in setting the climate for communication. It breaks the ice. It makes an audience more receptive. So the public speaker starts with a few funny stories. A letter starts with a bright anecdote. An advertiser evokes a pleasant image. There are exceptions, of course.

Timing

When you say something is often as important as what you say. An apology, a thank you (sometimes), condolences—indeed, any letter that responds to a negative emotional expression—should come quickly. Such a letter long delayed serves only to reawaken a feeling that you were gauche, ungrateful or unsympathetic. And in many cases, delay only reawakens a feeling of the original hurt. Difficult situations should usually be disposed of quickly and forgotten.

On the other hand, where there is no solution to a "difference" it is often wise to delay—and perhaps delay again. Emotions do cool off. Time can therefore be an aid when you don't have your emotion under control. Often it is possible to laugh off a dispute that seemed a matter of life and death when the argument occurred.

Don't wait until writing a letter is a today imperative. Find a reason to write a letter just as you might want to pick up a telephone to talk. And there are many reasons—an occasion or a nonoccasion—just to say hello, or to reminisce or to ask for a favor or offer an unsolicited favor. For the shut-in, for the man or woman away from home, for someone you know who may be unhappy, or even for someone who has been blessed with good fortune, a letter is uplifting, a personal pleasantness that makes life a little better for you and for your correspondent.

Getting started

A major deterrent to most letter writers is the start-up blank: "What should I say?" "How do I start?"

The answer is simple: picture the audience and write as you would talk. Start with something you have in common. Then "chat."

It is almost always a good idea, before you start to say or write something, to decide just what you want to accomplish. The few exceptions occur when you want to convey a personal emotion which long consideration or reasoning may dissipate. In such a situation, write first, then monitor your words when you calm down.

One way to keep your eye on the objective is to start by writing down what you want the letter to do:

> I want to make a friend of Mr. Johnson.

> I want to get Mr. Johnson to send me a check.

> I want Mr. Johnson to buy seven gross of Whatzits.

When you have finished a written communication, place yourself in the position of the reader. Read what you have written and ask yourself: How would I respond emotionally? What facts does the communication assume I know that I don't know? (You can't ask questions of a letter.) Is the reasoning understandable and convincing? Are the authorities I quote acceptable, known to the person I'm writing to, friendly or unfriendly?

Chapter 2

Getting and Keeping Customers

LETTERS THAT SELL

The unsolicited sales letter is probably the most demanding letter you will write in the normal course of doing business. It must stand by itself and either accomplish the objective or be a total waste. And the result will be evident in dollars and cents.

Good writing, fine sentence structure, even good grammar are irrelevant. The appeal, the argument, the response are all that matters. So it is a good idea before you write to list (1) why the customer should buy and (2) why he thinks he or she shouldn't. Work out your letter to explain (1) and eliminate (2). Write as if the customer were in front of you, putting yourself in the reader's place and speaking the reader's language.

Every letter, like every letter writer, has a personality. You should make your letter natural, friendly, sincere. Here the "you" attitude, the approach from the reader's point of view, is particularly important:

> *Not:* Our Whatzit is the best on the market.
> *But:* You'd gladly pay twice the price when you need our Whatzit.

Eliminate excess words or unnecessary thoughts. The shorter the letter, the greater the readership. Be specific:

> *Not:* Our Whatzit is a fine product with more capacity than any other on the market.
> *But:* You'll find the Whatzit does 180 revolutions a minute and so does almost twice the work of any other model.

In the course of much analysis, a great many factors have been tested and certain elements have generally been found to be vital to effective business communication. The problems have been classified:

1. To get the "package" opened.
2. To get and hold attention until the message is reached.
3. To get the message across.
4. To create desire.
5. To convince.
6. To close the sale.

Although the customer at the end of a mail route might deny it, when anyone receives a lot of mail the first reaction is to get rid of as much as possible. It is estimated that 98 percent of all the bulk mail that comes into a business office is not read. Most of it is never opened. A first objective, therefore, is to get your letter opened and read.

If you picture the package of periodicals, circulars, and first-class mail that comes to an ordinary business which has been around for a while, you will understand why most of it is thrown away unread. Each time you order anything by mail, your name goes onto a mailing list to be used over and over again by the vendor. In addition, the list will probably be rented to other vendors for other products or services. After a few years, your morning delivery may consist of pounds of bulk mail mixed with only a few pieces of regular first-class mail. The first-class mail gets your attention. The rest may get a glance before it is thrown out or put aside for later study.

Getting your letter opened involves several techniques, as we shall see. Thereafter, the problem is to get the letter read.

A basic factor of effective direct mail is its personal quality. Perception of the mail message is totally different from perception of a magazine ad, a TV commercial, a radio spot. A letter is a "class" medium as opposed to a "mass" medium. It is written to a selected person from a selected list. A direct-mail piece talks to *one* person. It can be, and should be, very personal.

This is the way to do it:

1. The emphasis in any good piece of selling mail is placed

on the reader. The word "you" is one of the best words you can use. But from time to time you have to refer to yourself. When you do, use "I" instead of "we."

A company cannot write a letter. Only a person can. "I" will automatically make your mailing a personal visit.

> I want to send you one of these new pens and let you use it yourself for a whole month. If you like it, keep it. If you don't, simply return the pen and I'll give back every cent you paid for it even though it's personalized with your initials. You can't possibly lose!

If the writer of this guarantee had used "we," look what the result would have been:

> We want to send you one of these new pens.

> We will refund your money if you are not happy, etc.

Of course you sometimes must use the word "we." Your letter may sound conceited or egotistical otherwise. For example, "I have been in business for over twenty years" versus "We have been in business for over twenty years."

2. Have your own name placed on the return card or envelope. This is more personal than your company name. Have your name typed in, not printed. This will create the impression that all mail comes straight to your desk for your personal and prompt attention.

3. Sometimes it is effective to put your picture in the mailing—perhaps as a part of your letterhead. It satisfies some customers that they know whom they're doing business with.

4. You may fill in the letter so that it appears to be directed toward *one* person and one person only. Generally speaking, obvious fill-ins are not good, but they are better than printed forms. The mag-card-typed (or auto-typed) letter is much better. This kind of letter looks like a genuine personal message.

5. Sign every letter you can. If you can't, use a processed facsimile signature—preferably in a different-color ink. The signature personalizes the letter and increases its effectiveness.

6. Before a letter is even read, it conveys an impression that could determine its effectiveness. Just as an interviewer makes an immediate judgment—sometimes subconsciously—when an applicant or a salesman walks into a room, so a letter creates an immediate impression. Some factors that create good or bad first impressions in letters:

> The paper—color, texture, size.
> The type—handwritten, typed, offset, Xeroxed, printed.
> The length.
> The layout—paragraphing, headings.
> The overall neatness.

That is not to say that the most effective letter is printed on fine paper in four colors. For each situation, a different technical style—sometimes a combination of styles—is most effective. A printed letter turns some people off because it appears to be for a mass readership. But a printed personal name at the head of a printed letter has great impact. A handwritten letter demands readership, but not necessarily respect. In between these styles are scores of devices that have varying attention-getting effect and influence.

7. "Keep it short" is a keynote for good letter writing. A long letter turns people off—especially professional people. True, there are situations where a lot of detail is necessary. In a few instances the detail is essential to the effectiveness of the letter. However, in most instances, the detail can be in the form of an attached memorandum or other selling aid.

The rule of thumb is this: If the material is of intense interest to the reader, assume he or she will read every word. If the material is important to prove *your* point, but of only supplementary interest to the reader, keep it as an addendum or an insert.

In many situations, requesting a response written right on the letter saves time for you and for the reader.

> The marginal notations in response to your letter help us get an answer to you more quickly. If you find it necessary to write again, please return this letter.

A photocopy preserves the correspondence for the files.

An initial sales letter should be brief—only long enough to make the point. An answer to an inquiry can be longer. The answer to a prospects problem can be as long as it takes to explain.

8. Repeat your story at the end.

9. Make it easy to respond.

10. Have the four elements that make a mailing effective: letter, circular, reply card, and reply envelope.

11. Don't be abstract:

> *Not:* A repeat order from you would be advisable at this time.
> *But:* Send in your order now, before the price goes up.

12. Preface your writing by answering some questions. What do you want to accomplish? What approaches are available? What do you specifically want the audience to do?

13. Sometimes you may ask yourself: What is the best approach? Letter? Telephone? Call and speak personally? Ask someone else to speak for you? Combine them?

For each alternative, evaluate what can be accomplished toward your end.

Before you begin to create a sales package, give thought to:

a. How is your product or service different—and better than others'?

b. What does the buyer want or expect? Does your product or service fill this expectation?

c. What is distinctive about your audience?

d. What is the competition doing?

e. How does your price structure compare with competitors? with the expectations of the customer? with the values you produce?

f. Can you make payment simpler by credit? use of a credit card? a check? time payments?

g. Is the price payable by a business or personally?

h. Do you expect multiple sales? repeat sales? gift sales?

i. How is the product best presented? By graphics? description? color?

j. How big is your reachable market? What distinguishes

it? Men? Women? Economic status? Urban? Age level?
Domestic? Export?

    k. Is the market seasonal? Is this the right season?

    l. Should your mail go first class? Third class? Mailgram?

    m. If you are flooded with orders can you fill them all?

Business communications are more consciously analyzed
and more realistically appraised than personal and social
communications. The objective is clear; some ethical re-
straints are released; the methods are viewed as technical
applications of the science of human behavior. There are
only two basic inhibitions: legal requirements (particularly
about the truth) and effectiveness in making the sale.

14. Obviously a personal letter is the most effective you can
send. When you have many letters you should try to get the
nearest thing to a personal letter you can get. Automatically
typed letters are the nearest thing to individual letters, at
least in appearance. An offset letter with name and address
filled in can pass muster. (The whole operation can be done
automatically with new word-processing devices.)

Computer technology also makes possible "personal
notes" in response to letters or even unsolicited mailings to
special groups or those who contributed time, money, or
ideas. Politicians use the new word-processing equipment to
respond to letters on many subjects or to adapt appeals for
mass mailings. Computers now handle 80 percent of all
letters from some congressional offices. Forty Senate offices
are wired into a $3 million computer system. These pro-
cessed letters, often signed to duplicate a legislator's signature, look like personal letters in every way. Letters are
composed from stock paragraphs, perhaps several hundred
of them, that are stored in a memory bank. A letter may be
composed of paragraphs 1, 7, 14, 21, and 27.

15. What type of postage you will use depends on the size of
the list and the mark-up of the product or service you are
selling. Rates change from time to time. First-class mail (with
a stamp affixed) is most effective. Inasmuch as most large
mailings are metered, the appearance of a metered first-class
letter and a metered third-class letter (about 40 percent less
expensive) is not usually worth the difference. If time is of

the essence, the cost difference may be worthwhile. Third-class mail may take ten to twenty days to arrive. The best way to evaluate the difference is to test two mailings and compute the net profit on each. Enclosing a business reply card or envelope adds substantially to the return.

The List

A business that wants to obtain prospects for its services or products or leads for its salesmen may compile names of prospects. One method of accomplishing this is through the bait-piece technique, using a premium to have prospects identify themselves.

Your mailing list is often the most important factor in the success of a mailing. If your customers have been satisfied, they are your best prospects for repeat or related products or services. Names of people who have bought similar products from others usually prove next best.

Timing

Timing of mail is often important. Mail received Mondays and Fridays or Saturdays is at a disadvantage. It faces shortages of executive time and interest. Similarly, holidays, Christmas season, and vacation time are nonreceptive periods.

The time you mail a broadcast letter is important. February is the worst month. March, September, October, and November usually bring 15 to 20 percent better response than other months. April brings a 12 percent response. Avoid the first and fifteenth days of a month when you compute the time your letter will be best received. These are "bill" days and especially busy for some people.

Return envelopes

Enclosing a return envelope which requires no postage generally increases responses substantially.

Testing

No matter how savvy you think you are, you cannot be infallible about the effectiveness of a mass mailing. Many factors enter into the results: the offer, the list, the copy, production, timing. Alternatives exist for all of these, and you should check in advance as many of the alternatives as possible. Sometimes a small change in the offer—three months to pay, or C.O.D., a color in the response card, a detail in the copy—may change results dramatically.

Test by sending out relatively few letters first to learn the response. If a mailing is to go to 25,000 people, a test mailing to 2,000 will reveal its basic effectiveness, what kind of questions and responses the letter elicits, and possibly some area for improvement. A letter to twenty-five persons can be tested by sending it to two or three prospects. The feedback—responses, questions, arguments, etc.—enables you to make corrections on the other letters. Sometimes you may find you are addressing the wrong person, e.g., the advertising manager instead of the sales manager. Sometimes a letter brings more questions about something you forgot to mention, cutting back results.

Test various lists, offers, and copy. Use part of a large list for a test, so that the result will be meaningful and can be followed up with additional mailings.

If a mailing is designed to bring in inquiries or a trial subscription, you will not know the true effectiveness until the trial orders are converted to regular orders. So plan to test early if you have a two- or three-step campaign.

BEGINNINGS THAT LEAD ON

The outer envelope is often the most important element in your mailing. It is the first thing the prospect sees. It is a hurdle. At that initial glance the prospect determines whether to open the envelope and read further or to toss the letter away. All your efforts can be wasted in that split-second glance. In a sense the envelope is the equivalent of a headline in an advertisement.

What options do you have with a simple envelope? Many. You may try to make it unimpressive and pass it as a business communication. Or you may put teaser copy or a photograph or a testimonial or even a whole message on the outside. You may use standard number ten or number six envelopes, or oversized or undersized, or Kraft envelopes or colored envelopes. (But note that postal regulations now discourage irregualr-size envelopes.) You may carry a return address or a special return address or a sponsor's address (e.g., The White House) or none at all.

You may simulate a bank or a government envelope or a bill. You may use a window envelope or a front and rear window or a standard one. You may use a precanceled stamp, a metered stamp, a foreign or United Nations stamp, a commemorative stamp. Or you can also put a teaser message on the "other side" of the envelope, the side that your reader will see before he opens it.

Getting the letter read

Assuming you have induced your prospect to open your letter, how do you keep him or her from glancing at it and tossing it into the wastebasket? The most reliable way of reaching a reader is a personal, first-class letter. A good imitation is the personalized form letter in an envelope that looks as if it has been sent first class, with the postage metered. Mail that is clearly "circular mail" gets delayed reaction or none at all. How some mailers get past the opening hurdle is shown below.

First, the salutation itself should be as distinctive as you can make it for the list you select.

> Dear Handyman,
>
> Dear AAA Member,
>
> To my customers and friends (and others I would like to call friends),
>
> Dear Intelligent Reader,
>
> To the Parents of Sidney Dirkson,

Or begin:

> I'm not sure, Don Brown . . .
>
> It's a delight, Steve Miller.

Or you may begin directly with a headline, either as part of the salutation or in some form of layout—a circle, a box, any special identifiable shape.

In a selling letter, the same five elements are involved as in

all advertising. Get attention, create interest, arouse desire, convince, get action—usually in that order.

Getting and holding attention is the function of the beginning of a letter. It is difficult to get people to read perceptively or even really to listen to what they "hear." This difficulty applies even after you have induced your prospect to look at a letter and read on. Basic emotional appeals must be awakened. But before you get to use them you need a grabber. Many writers use the "you are special" approach. Others use a special offer. Some find an area of agreement. Others pick a problem they think you have and offer a solution. The simplest are blatant appeals to profit, comfort, vanity, or a special interest.

The beginning of any communication must achieve perceptive attention and must draw the reader or listener into the subject. It sets the tone for an emotional response. And it clarifies the subject to be covered. Thus, it arouses attention, creates interest, sets the tone and parameters of your letter. Sometimes the beginning tells why you are writing to the particular individual.

We now have a reader. Go on to make your direct mail as personal, as "me-to-you-ish," as you can make it. One way of getting the person-to-person approach is to interject the name of the receiver into the body of the letter:

> I want you to know, John, that I did everything possible.

> There is nothing, Mr. Johnson, that our company wouldn't do to provide the special service J & J needs to market your product effectively.

One of the common techniques is to assure the reader that he or she is someone special to receive this letter:

> PLEASE—do not pass along this letter. If you are not interested in the exciting opportunity this letter announces, please see that this letter is destroyed.
> It is being sent to a very select group of people, and YOU are one of them.
> —Alan Shawn Feinstein

> We want you so much we've put together this special MR. N. H. MAGER "WE CARE" PACKAGE with a beautiful personal transistor radio, and your choice of up to $81.76 worth of new records for only $2.86.

You're hard to find, Mr. Silver:

Locating individuals who have the income, position and business interests of FORTUNE subscribers—yet are not already FORTUNE subscribers themselves—is like trying to find a Phi Beta Kappa without a key.

And now that I've found you I don't want to lose you. So I'm going to make you a great offer.

—Fortune

Or a special invitation in the format of an invitation:

You are cordially invited to become a Charter Member of Sophisticated Investing, Inc.

Mr. David A. McDermott,
Director of Membership,
on behalf of all its members
cordially invites

to
become a member of the
American Management Association

Or:

Management executives like you are a special breed. They couldn't care less about free gifts just because they're free. But if they see one that can help them be more effective, put more black ink in the company's books, and put more money in their own banks and investment portfolios, their minds are wide open. That attitude is one reason they hold the jobs they do.

—Business Week

I had a hunch about your company—and I was right.

—RYDER TRUCK RENTAL, INC.

Dear Reader:

Several months ago you were one of a select group of Americans who received an invitation to become a National Associate of the Smithsonian Institution.

—SMITHSONIAN INSTITUTION

Some carry the "you are special" idea even further. *U.S. News & World Report* uses the idea effectively in all its advertising:

SPECIAL OFFER
On America's only un-sugar-coated news magazine . . .
. . . I think you can handle it

U.S. News & World Report is the news magazine for the one person in twenty who . . .

After the offer of a free copy:

Dear Friend:

I'm not joking. This is *not* an ordinary letter.

And quite frankly, if you're the kind of person who's pretty much resigned to accept "life as it is," then this letter is *not* for you.

This letter is intended strictly for the man or woman, perhaps like you, who is *not* content to just let life "happen to him" . . . for the man or woman who *knows* they should be doing better . . . who *knows* he has the God-given desire, intelligence and strength of character to *do* more, to *achieve* more, to *enjoy* more of life's rich rewards and satisfactions—if only someone would *show him the way*.

If you're *that* kind of person, I hope you'll read this letter *very* carefully. For it could, literally, *change your life*—forever!

Sometimes the appeal to vanity is in a different vein:

BE THE *FIRST* TO READ THE *FIRST* ISSUES of the *FIRST* daily fashion newspaper in the world . . . FREE!

This 425 plus page invaluable "What, Where, Who and How" reference book you get FREE . . . when you subscribe to Gifts and Decorative Accessories.

—*Buyers Directory*

A free gift holds attention:

Free for your child to develop a love of reading . . .

—Xerox

How to get almost any book you want absolutely free.

—Free Book Secrets

With your "OK," I'll send you a copy of "Business Secrets" and the current issue of BOARDROOM REPORTS, absolutely free.

—*Boardroom Reports*

I would like to send you FREE one of the most helpful charts ever devised. It won't save you time, money or energy. It's far more valuable than that. All it can do is retain your most valuable asset—your good health and fitness.

—Fitness Finders

Here's the better news: You can keep this gift even if you don't buy a sizable bargain we're offering.

—*Business Week*

It took our editors two years to gather the material for this handbook. You get it FREE—by just returning the enclosed card today.

You get over 100 inspiring sales promotion ideas that have paid off brilliantly for industrial advertisers during the past two years.
—Industrial Marketing

Sometimes the gift is self-liquidating; that is, it pays for itself.

Certainly you want to keep fit and healthy—and the National Jogging Association wants to help you! What's more, we offer you a valuable premium now to encourage you to join us. (20 jogging shoes at a 37% discount.)
—NATIONAL JOGGING ASSOCIATION

A free trial is often offered for a publication or for mail-order products:

Discover the real possibility of profits in real estate. Try the next 3 issues of the *Real Estate Investing Letter*—without risk—and receive valuable information like this in every issue. . . .

The opening headline is the key to reader involvement. Decide what will be of greatest interest, then offer to provide answers or solve problems. This may be put in the form of a question. Kiplinger services uses this device very effectively.

Will you be ready for the new Rural PROSPERITY?

Will there be boom and more INFLATION ahead?

Here are some others:

Did the information in your annual report create the interest you desired within the investment community? If not, perhaps we can help.
—Investment Dealers' Digest

IF YOU ARE CONFUSED BY THE CURRENT INVESTMENT SCENE . . . JOIN THE CLUB! Many investors are confused. Where are interest rates and inflation headed? Should you be conservative or aggressive? Should you seek short term trading opportunities or invest for long term in companies with proven earnings records?
—MULLER AND COMPANY

Should you . . .
Buy? Sell? Do nothing?
—Value Line

The question may be even more rhetorical:

> Want to
> GET RICH OVERNIGHT
> through INVESTMENTS?
>
> *—Investor*

The pertinent selective question (direct or implied) makes an excellent headline:

> *DO YOU* own stock of 414 top companies rated by Forbes?

> When you're concerned with improving product performance . . .
> —METCO INC.

An opening with emotional impact is a "grabber":

> WHY
> SONS OF BITCHES
> SUCCEED
> AND NICE GUYS FAIL
> IN A SMALL BUSINESS
> —FINANCIAL MANAGEMENT ASSOC., INC.

Asking a favor sometimes works because it tickles the reader's vanity:

> Will you help me
>   find 975 Gentlemen
> who are seeking
>   a Custom Cigar Maker?
>
> —THOMPSON & COMPANY

> Now I have to bother you with a problem . . .

> We ask a favor!
> Would you mind just giving us your date of birth so that we may furnish you information on a contract which, because of its low cost, is probably one of the most discussed policies in the insurance world today?
> —UNITED STATES LIFE INSURANCE CO.

> Who, me??
> Yes, *you!*
>   It may come as a mild shock to you that I am asking you to make the experiment, for a trial period of your choice, of reading *The Wall Street Journal* under the plan described below.

People are always receptive to ideas with which they already agree, or to discussion of their problems. And they respond to people who express these ideas. Similarly, they respond when you hit a chord that chimes with their experience.

"There's never enough time
  for all the reading I should do!"
You have probably heard that statement often from your staff physicians. As Medical Librarian you will be interested in this tested system to help your doctors in Family and General Practice keep up with the periodicals in your library that they should be reading every month.

— PAUL BRINGE FOR UPDATE, INC.

"You know men don't like girls who are too smart."
"I hope your baby is a boy!"
"We've already hired our woman for this year."
"Sorry, but we don't hire . . .
  . . . single girls; they'll just leave to get married.
  . . . married women; they'll just leave to have kids.
  . . . mothers; they should stay at home with their kids.
  . . . lesbians; they might make advances to other women.
  . . . women whose husbands are working; they don't need the money."
"May I speak to your husband? It's important."
"I'll have my girl call your girl to set up a lunch next week."
"Sorry, I didn't recognize you without your husband/date/boss."
"Just like a woman driver!"
"What's a nice girl like you doing in medical school?"

Dear Friend:

You've probably heard at least half of these witless remarks about women. Remarks that make you want to scream!

— *Ms. Magazine*

I'll bet you get a lot of mail. If you're like me, you probably find it very difficult to decide what offers are valuable and make sense. I despair receiving exaggerated promotions in the mail. So I understand your own hesitation because I often feel the same way.

— THE MINTAGE COIN CLUB

Unexpected changes. You know how they can upset even the most careful business and personal planning. There isn't much you can do to make "bad" news "good"—but you *can* do something to make certain you aren't caught off-guard and unprepared when it strikes:

— *U.S. News Washington Letter*

It can't happen here, you say? But it *is* happening here. Every day. And that's not just opinion. That's indisputable fact.

When one man pays out over two million dollars to presidential and Congressional campaigns (yes, it's a fact!), the United States Government is virtually up for sale.

—COMMON CAUSE

The excitement of a special opportunity stimulates further reading, at least.

Once or twice in a reading lifetime, a book comes along which is so important, so enthusiastically praised by the experts, and so outstandingly successful that no well-informed person would wish to miss the opportunity of reading it.

We take special pleasure in calling your attention to such a book, which we have the honor of publishing.

—SIMON AND SCHUSTER, INC.

URGENT! This is the most important letter you will ever read! Please spare me five minutes right now. It is in your interest!

—CO-OP ADVERTISING PROGRAM

For the financial executive who wants a terrific new life of happiness and achievement—a discovery that's taken the country by storm!

—PRENTICE-HALL

Promises of comfort and easier living are very effective, especially to homemakers:

How to make raising your new baby easier and more rewarding in the first three critical years of life.

A direct appeal to comfort is a basic:

NOW—Stop complaints of tired aching feet and legs and stop that late afternoon production letdown.

—IROQUOIS PRODUCTS

The appeal to profit is one of the prime stimulants to reading. Here the appeal is made directly:

Two significant events occurred in the past week which will interest you as a Smilson stockholder.

How would you like to triple your advertising rate?

—MEMPHIS MEMORIAL

If you are *Profit Oriented* and desire the best quality uniforms and supplies that *money* can buy . . .
                                    —L.I. KARATE SUPPLY CO.

Here's a promise:
SIX MONTHS FROM TODAY
you can have more money in the bank
be on a sounder financial foundation even without an increase in your family income.
                                    —*Changing Times*

Yes, I'll show you how to pick up an extra $1,000, $5,000, $10,000, or even MORE in your spare time!
                                    —PICTURE PROFITS

People want to improve themselves but don't always succeed. An appeal to self-doubt is commonly used:

How confident are you in the investment decisions you make in today's economic environment? Do you feel that the research and other information at your disposal is adequate for forecasting returns over just the coming months . . . let alone into the 1980's? How do you handle equity and total portfolio risk? Is your diversification really adequate?
                                    —WELLS FARGO INVESTMENT ADVISERS

Expertly designed Pension Plans will always benefit Key People, right?
Maybe not!
                                    —THE PHOENIX COMPANIES

The "scare" technique is especially useful for medical products and political causes:

80% of the people who come to me are not metabolizing properly. The people take vitamins by the barrelful, yet they just get sicker and sicker.

I am writing you this special letter because I am worried about the rise of the "radical right" in our nation's political process.
                                    —DEMOCRATIC NATIONAL COMMITTEE

Why do you suppose twelve of the most powerful union bosses in America would get together and launch an all-out attack on our charitable foundation, filing what they call "the largest multi-union legal action ever undertaken"?
I'm sure you know the answer, Mr. Silver.

DOOMSDAY!
Will it be October 15, 1979?
Dear Reader:
    I don't mean to scare you, but after reading this letter, I think
you'll understand why I'm convinced that our economy may be
heading for a breakdown of awesome proportions. What's more, I
think you'll agree that *your own future security may depend on your
taking the same precautions I have.*
                    —NATIONAL RIGHT TO WORK LEGAL
                    DEFENSE FOUNDATION

   The "bandwagon" approach utilizes "Everybody's doing it,
why don't you?"

    More and more people enjoy shopping by mail.

   Don't be left behind in the rush.
   Sometimes adding a story or bit of entertainment and
information enhances the sales package and helps set the
proper receptive climate. Enclosing a relevant history, anecdote, or recipe helps.

    Dear Intelligent Lay Reader:
        There's a story about a little boy, a devotee of *Sesame Street* on TV,
    who woke his parents at an early hour with a triumphant discovery:
        "Mommy, Daddy! My pillow! It's a rectangle!"
        For good reason—the fact that you are an Associate Member of
    the Smithsonian Institution—we think you've shared his kind of
    pillow talk—the joy of learning—all your life: the yen to know, the
    keen pleasure that comes from new insights.
                        —WOODROW WILSON INTERNATIONAL
                        CENTER FOR SCHOLARS.

    You are in a strange town, strolling aimlessly down a street. You
    could—if you don't fully understand your rights—wind up in jail for
    the night.
    Your son is riding back to college with three classmates. Police stop
    and search the car. One boy possesses marijuana . . . but all four are
    arrested.
                        —TIME-LIFE BOOKS

   Some beginnings try to make a chummy, personal approach:

    I had a hunch about your company—and I was right.

I thought a large portion of our customers were small, at least in terms of employment—probably under 25 employees. My research people told me that my hunch was correct.

—RYDER TRUCK RENTAL, INC.

Hello, my name is Norris Strauss . . . and I've got to get something off my chest before I explode!

I work at a regular job which I enjoy. I was born and raised in Brooklyn as were my parents—I have many relatives here. I've only moved once in 28 years. The above is my real address.

—NORRIS M. STRAUSS

"Forget it, Dick," they said. "It sounds so simple and inexpensive nobody will go for it."

I had reason to believe the experts were wrong . . . and proved it when over 120 mail order and display advertisers just like you snapped up our new space buyer's planning guides in the first two weeks!

—DM DATA, INC.

This idea may be extended to a sympathy approach—"I'm on the spot, help me."

If you ever saw a man behind the proverbial 8-ball, you are looking at one now. I have the job of convincing you that the Clipper Creative Art Service with all of its features can be a most profitable tool in your operation. My problem is that I must do this without being able to speak directly with you when there is so much to be said. Therefore, I invite your careful consideration of the enclosed material, for I am certain it will be rewarding.

—DYNAMIC GRAPHICS, INC.

My name is Barbara Andrews and I work for the "big wheel." Someday I figure I'll be vice president of the company—but you're not helping me establish my reputation.

Several months ago, Mr. Nissman (he's the man who wrote you last) asked me to be on the lookout for your request for our free catalog offer. "Yes, sir!" I replied, burning your name into my brain.

A few days ago, he said, "Barbi" (we're very informal here—he calls me Barbi and I call him Mr. Nissman) "could the catalog request have been mislaid?" I told him I'd check and I did. *And it hadn't!*

—H-M . . . THE IDEA COMPANY

A low-keyed approach sometimes gets under the reader's guard:

I would have written to you sooner, only I had nothing to really say. Now I do. Oh, it's nothing earth-shattering, but it's conversation. I mean, the new low-calorie dish we have at the place called the "Skinny Ho," a delicious high protein blend of crab meat and steak, garnished in a bed of assorted Chinese vegetables. It's not on the menu—you simply request it.

—BRUCE HO, FOUR SEAS

Similarly, nostalgia, startling facts, ideas, or quotations can break the ice:

You may never win a prize for knowing—
What President's hat was held by his defeated rival
   while the victor read his Inaugural Address?
What President applied for a patent on a flatboat he invented? (It had air chambers for floating over shoals.)

—*American Heritage*

Twenty years ago, Dwight Eisenhower was President, Casey Stengel managed the Yankees, and Wall Street was a lot more predictable.

—*Barron's*

Do you remember when
. . . you were young and most of the presents under the Christmas tree were for you?
. . . you "came home for Christmas" for the first time?
. . . you and your spouse spent your first Christmas together?
. . . you watched your own youngsters wait breathlessly for the arrival of Santa Claus?

—*Reader's Digest*

More than 1800 years ago T'sai Lun, a Chinese, first manufactured paper in the modern beaten pulp manner.

—EQUITABLE PAPER BAG CO., INC.

An appropriate story has been used effectively:

"I know that I shall never see another sunset. In a sense, I am glad. The burns on my feet are all infected and the pliers used on me have left some nasty gashes. I have been the object of such sadistic display that I am kept constantly awake because of the pain. It is a strange feeling to be a hostage. You are caught, beaten, tortured, but you remain hopeful. It is your strength against theirs. It is your faith in a high cause, namely the defeat of an inhuman enemy who has forgotten all feelings for kindness, understanding and compassion. I must be mad to talk of hope in this hell . . ."

Dear Friend,

He never did see another sunset. My friend died the next day, the victim of Nazi torture. After 45 days of being tortured, too, I managed to escape. While I was recovering in a hospital, a priest brought my friend's last note to me. Its words still burn in my brain.
— AMNESTY INTERNATIONAL USA

Once upon a time . . . there was a little home with blue shutters in the suburbs, really a very, very happy home. Neat and orderly, too. Until one amazing evening. Papa bounced up the walk, hurrying to get as far as the rose bush . . . that was where he always got the first whiff of his dinner cooking. But tonight he stopped there, puzzled.
— *Redbook*

"Fashion passes, style remains," Coco Chanel once commented. Her apartment is a monument to her own unerring style, a style that influenced decoration as much as it did the couture. There are objects from everywhere—Greece, Egypt, China, Africa, Italy, a meteorite from outer space, a statuette from the Flea Market—all put together with matchless flair.
— *Architectural Digest*

Atmosphere alone may entice:

If you think of a Florida of gently rolling hills, moss hung live oak trees, forests and marshes teeming with wildlife . . .
. . . If the Florida you want to *live* in is one of clear, fresh rivers and lakes and warm Gulf waters that are alive with a hundred varieties of fish and other aquatic life . . .
Then you could fall in love with Sugarmill Woods:
— SUGARMILL WOODS

An enclosure (seeds, a pen, an obsolete foreign currency, a calendar, special souvenir stamps) tends to help get attention. The letter should, of course, tie in with the gift.

Plant the seeds of your retirement today.

Inflation made the enclosed cruzerio virtually worthless in Bratislava. Will the same thing happen to your dollar?

Bribery for attention? A bright penny, a postage stamp— anything of value—inhibits the reader from throwing the letter away.

Here's a crisp one-dollar bill for you—for just one minute of your time.

A penny for your thoughts!

> Here is the biggest *something for nothing* you've ever received—and
> we solemnly promise that there are no strings attached.

Although testimonials are usually part of the selling
portion of a letter, a dramatic testimonial statement can
serve to arouse enough interest to hold the reader. If you
wish to quote an opinion or to provide a testimonial, it is best
to use as an authority someone of the group to which the
audience belongs. The image of the testifier in the mind of
the audience has more to do with convincing an audience
than does his knowledge or experience. The voice of a
mother is more convincing to mothers than that of a
professor of pediatrics.

Testimonials have been effective in selling all types of
things, particularly those that involve a new product or a
new idea. They don't even have to be specific:

> "The Best 175 Dollars I Ever Spent"
> That is the response we are receiving from the bankers, bond
> dealers, corporate treasurers, and consultants throughout the coun-
> try who are using the 1978 edition of our state books.
> —SHESHUNOFF

> If someone had told me a month ago that I was going to fall in
> love with a clock, I'd have said he was crazy.
> But here I am today—in love with a grandfather clock!
> —AMERICAN EXPRESS

Remember that although sensational statements have
value as attention grabbers, every degree of a claim beyond
the audience's experience adds to disbelief and lack of
credibility in the source. Extremes in statements, or claims,
or even testimonials, regardless of the truth of the statement
or evidence presented, are resisted. You will be more
convincing if you announce a car which gets 33 miles to the
gallon than you will be announcing a car that gets 50 miles to
a gallon—regardless of the facts.

MIDDLES THAT CONVINCE

The basic part of the letter, the body of it, must sell: it
must create a desire, convince, and stimulate the desire to
buy.

No matter how effective your sales message may be, the heart of it lies in the value and desirability of what is being sold. The product-package and the price speak very loudly in every sales message.

Every decision a logical person makes equates the benefits with the costs. Sales theorists call the end result "value." Increasing the perception of benefits is one aspect of selling; decreasing the perception of costs is another. Either or both may be involved in selling. It is a good idea to test the effectiveness of what you want to say merely by having a chat with some prospective customers, finding out directly the receptiveness and the objections to your product or service, and overcoming them first on a person-to-person basis. If you can't find a prospect, imagine yourself in his or her place. So to begin:

1. Make the offer attractive.
2. Make it believable.
3. Prove it is a good value.
4. Make a response easy.
5. Induce an immediate action.

Arousing desire and convincing the prospect are the functions of the body of the letter. The basic emotional appeals still have to be used. But more than that, you must tell the reader what your product or service will do for him or her—and, if necessary, how.

Mass appeals have been used effectively to meet a physical want (food, water, sleep, sex); to fulfill a desire for profit; to allay fear for personal security (against crime, fire, lawsuit); to stimulate vanity (esteem of friends and neighbors); to create a sense of belonging and acceptance by friends and neighbors; to reinforce hate and anger (in the form of an attack on what is seen as a common enemy); to provide information in which readers have an interest.

Put another way, the appeals can be listed: profit, ease, pleasure (comfort), ego (praise, popularity, individuality), life, health, cleanliness, sexual attraction, protection of property, fairness, loyalty, courtesy, possession, curiosity, appetite, and avoidance of pain, trouble, and criticism.

Translated into more specific terms, sales appeals can promise customers that they will (1) make more money, (2) save money, (3) advance in position, (4) be popular, (5) gain prestige, (6) enjoy themselves, (7) get more leisure time, (8) be more comfortable, (9) be healthy, (10) avoid worry, particularly in old age, and (11) be secure.

From the writer's point of view, to write an effective sales letter, you must first have an understanding of the product or service being sold, and of the reasons customers need those products or services.

No matter how large your mailing, when you write, write to one typical person, not to a "market." Every letter should tell not only what the product will do, but also what it will do for the prospective customer—as specifically as is practical.

Honesty and sincerity are difficult to convey in a cynical world where anyone can write a letter and a promise is only as good as the reputation of the sender. Facts are therefore important to make a convincing presentation. They are effective principally to increase the conviction of those already favorably impressed:

> You're going to relish this one-day seminar on the fine art of direct mail advertising. Although direct mail is too big a field to cover completely in one day, you will pick up at least 50 proven-effective techniques to improve the pulling power of your upcoming mailings.

> I can't promise the *Architect's Digest* will increase your profits overnight, but reading it on a month-in-month-out basis will keep you in touch with all the latest trends in your profession—trends you can put to work at once.

> Every issue of *California Business* is jam-packed with news from all over this booming state of ours. True, you won't find your business in every issue, but you'll find enough business issues—all carefully explored—to give you a keen insight into your economic future.

When the subject to be covered in a letter is complicated, it is often necessary to enclose a circular that tells more about it or shows it pictorially. Adding these details in a letter makes the letter too long and boring. Remember that circulars sent in a letter are often separated from the letter, so make sure that each enclosure contains essential information, including name and address of the sender.

Here are samples of some effective letters.

Comparing a book or service with an employee can be a reasonable selling point:

Gentlemen:

I am herewith applying for employment with your organization.

I am asking for less than one week's salary, and in return I am willing to work all year without any further cost to you. I have had years of experience in office work and have never been absent due to illness. With me in your office I will earn my salary many times over by helping you to:

—Increase sales

—Locate people who have moved

—Collect old accounts

—Improve direct mail results

—Cash personal checks with confidence

—Improve service to customers

—Cut costs and save time in your office

—Increase employee job satisfaction

I am available now. I am full of the most up-to-date information about people in your city and surrounding areas (including all the NEW NAMES AND CHANGES since last year.)

Please give me a trial. (Would sure like to work for your company.)

Sincerely,
Cole's Metropolitan
Householders Directory

The following one presents specific facts backed up by statistics:

APARTMENT LIFE READERS ARE COUNTING ON YOU
TO MAKE THIS A MAIL ORDER MERRY CHRISTMAS!

That's right. Our readers are depending on the ideas you have for shopping by mail. This is a busy time of the year and our readers are the busiest people around. They're on-the-go with careers and socializing and they don't have time to spend in stores that homeowning folks do. They depend on *you* to bring the store to them. This time of year, convenience is especially important to them, so put your goodies in the Apartment Department where they'll really move.

Mail Order professionals have been discovering our hot market of young apartment people. 77.5% of the mail order ads in the first six months of 1978 were repeats. That's an increase of 76.4% in repeat ads over 1977. These advertisers have found that APARTMENT LIFE really produces results for mail order firms. If you haven't tried the Apartment Department, now is the time to do so!

Our audience is young and affluent. They have more discretionary income than their homeowning counterparts because they aren't tied down by mortgages and upkeep. That means they have more money to spend on mail order merchandise . . . and they do.

The November issue of APARTMENT LIFE closes August 20, goes on sale October 20. A ¹⁄₁₂ page (2¼″ by 2½″) is only $600. We're printed offset so don't need metal plates . . . camera-ready art will do. If you have any questions, please don't hesitate to call me collect (212-557-6527), or send me the enclosed form in the postage paid envelope provided. Make this a Merry Christmas for our readers . . . and for yourself.

The letters below all make their sales pitch by appealing to the desire for profit, prestige, convenience, and so on:

Dear Customer:

Having owned your home for some time now—and with values in California soaring—you probably have a great deal of equity. The Wells Fargo Homeowner Loan Program allows you to turn this into cash to use just about any way you wish.

This program has at least three major advantages—advantages that set it apart from any other way you may have considered to meet your needs:

* The Wells Fargo Homeowner Loan Program offers low monthly payments. (You can take up to seven or ten years to repay.)
* The interest rates (as shown in the accompanying folder) are probably a lot lower than you would expect . . . with no points to pay and no prepayment penalty.
* You can use the money for virtually any worthwhile purpose; for example: paying off debts, educational expenses, home improvements, car purchase, starting a business, travel abroad, vacation home, new furniture, swimming pool, you-name-it.

Why does this program offer so many advantages? By utilizing the equity in your home as security you can borrow large sums of money without straining your budget with large payments. This means that—depending on the difference between your mortgage balance and the value of your home—you could borrow any appropriate amount between $5,000 and $20,000 (or more), secured by a Deed of Trust on your property and, you choose payments that are best for you. The accompanying folder gives you a good selection of repayment plans. You'll want to select the one that best fits your budget and future plans.

—Wells Fargo Bank

Dear Customer:

Visa is here now and it's yours for the asking. By simply signing the enclosed Acceptance, you will receive your new Wells Fargo Visa with privileges that will include:

* the most versatile and widely-recognized card in the world for purchasing products and services. (Honored wherever you now see BankAmericard signs.)
* charge privileges at over two million merchants in over 110 countries around the world. (Visa signs will go up wherever you now see BankAmericard.)
* a credit line equal to your present Wells Fargo Master Charge line.
* the ability to obtain cash advances from more than 42,000 bank locations.
* extra features, including emergency fund service.

And—like your Master Charge account—you'll receive a supply of Visa Superchecks. They're every bit as acceptable and easy to use as your personal checks, but they can do even more for you. Whenever you use a Visa Supercheck, it will be charged, not to your personal checking account, but as a Loan Advance to your Visa account . . .

—Wells Fargo Bank

Robert Cunnion of *Grit* magazine sends some of the cleverest of today's sales letters.

GRIT PUBLISHING CO.
Williamsport, Penna. 17701

Our 95th Year

LISTS

What are the ten most beautiful words in the English language? According to *The Book of Lists,* published by Morrow & Co., they are these:

1. Chimes.
2. Dawn.
3. Golden.
4. Hush.
5. Lullaby.
6. Luminous.
7. Melody.
8. Mist.
9. Murmuring.
10. Tranquil.

Well, son of a gun, Here all these years I'd been thinking the ten most beautiful words were

1. Grit—	6. America's
2. economical	7. hard-to-reach
3. big	8. ready-to-buy
4. frog	9. small town
5. in	10. market.

My list may not conjure up stardust and honey, I admit. But it does constitute a phrase that's worth adding to your marketing vocabulary. . . .

Why GRIT, you ask, for our product or service? And I answer back, unhesitatingly, in the most beautiful words in the language:

"Because, thanks to GRIT, in small towns across America, from misty dawn through luminous noon till the hush of dusk, you'll soon be murmuring a melodious and tranquil lullaby to the golden chimes . . . of cash registers!"

Cordially,
Robert J. Cunnion, Jr.
Advertising Director

ENDINGS THAT BRING ACTION

The function of the ending of most sales letters is to induce the action desired. Usually it is the sending of an order, the return of a card or form, the lifting of a telephone to make a call.

The degree of pressure varies with the type of person reading the letter and the weight of the sale you have to push. Obviously a new expensive product being sold to a stranger takes more pressure than a resale for a low-cost well-known product in response to an inquiry from an old customer.

The close may begin with a clincher:

Every Whatzit comes with our 100% guarantee for sixty-seven years.

Only a few of these numbers remain in stock, so act now.

Our future as a great university is dependent upon the number of alumni who accept this challenge.

Did you know that your Associate Membership provides a real bonus for us, as well as for you?

It's true, because your membership dues qualify the Museum to apply for matching funds from the National Endowment for the Humanities Challenge Grant.

There is so much to tell you about the Whatzit that we can't possibly tell you all about them all in a letter. But if you come to our showroom at 4 Chestnut Street, we'll be glad to demonstrate it for you.

Be the first on your block to have the new dramatic Whatzit in your kitchen. Return the enclosed card now.

If Speedy Reader doesn't double your reading speed in 7 days, return the entire package and receive a 100% refund.

. . . and the savings don't stop there. Beginning with this month's SPECIAL, you'll be able to cash in on some real bargains above and beyond our regular values. I hope the extra savings of this month's featured SPECIAL will be an incentive for you to give us a try.

I look forward to being of service to you!

Can you afford to miss this opportunity for a free trial that requires only your dialing 277-7777?

Sometimes the question is followed by further assurance:

The oil is sure to keep your engines running more smoothly for only pennies a day.

The guarantee always helps.

And here's my *personal guarantee:*

If you're not 100% delighted with American Art & Antiques—at any time, for any reason—just let me know. I'll see to it that your subscription is canceled immediately and that you receive a full refund on copies still due you.

If for any reason, after completing the loan and receiving the cash, you are not pleased with the entire transaction, you may return the check within 10 days and no charges will be made. Your satisfaction is guaranteed.

Then there is the instruction:

Why not tell your agency to place the Daily on your current schedule?

Return the enclosed card today to receive a full description of what the Whatzit can do for you.

We're ready for you now. Fill in and return the enclosed card. Or better still, call MO2-2222 and our representative will call to show you what our Whatzit can do for you.

Send your order by December 31st at the special Discount Price shown on the enclosed sheet and you get one extra lamp free with each dozen ordered—a baker's dozen offer that increases your profit by more than 15%.

Use the enclosed form to send your order today. Immediate shipment of all three styles in the color you prefer. Send your order now before you put this letter aside.

To accept my invitation, just return the enclosed order card in the postage-paid reply envelope. No need to send payment now; we'll be happy to bill you later for your dues. Our thanks, in advance.
—AMERICAN MUSEUM OF NATURAL HISTORY

Dig down now. Walk over to the desk right now. Make out a check. Mail it.

If you are at all interested, I urge you to complete and return the enclosed reply card quickly—even if your plans for using the funds are not firm or immediate. In this way, we can establish your qualifications and work with you to structure the best possible plan to meet your needs when they arise.

Take advantage of this remarkable Wells Fargo Homeowner Loan Program. Complete and return the enclosed card today. There's no obligation and it can give you a real freedom of choice.

Please return the completed form to us in the postage prepaid envelope provided and allow a week or so for us to process your request. You will receive your Acceptance, Safe Deposit Certificate (for validation) and a letter of introduction to the branch office of your choice.

The close may be in the form of a question:

Why not check the space below and let us send you a trial order of six cases of Grade A oil?

A postscript is one way to add an extra punch to your letter:

P.S. Send your subscription card by return mail and you will receive the Special Booklet "How to Clean Everything." Only a limited supply remains.

P.S. One added feature is available if you purchase a Whoozit before December 10. The Whoozit Cleaning Kit comes to you at half the regular $10.00 price if your order reaches us by that time.

P.S. You may also wish to order a Whoozit Cleaning Kit at the special price of $12.00 to ensure the maximum efficiency at all times.

P.S. If you already have a Wells Fargo Master Charge card, it will not be necessary to fill out the main portion of the application. Simply complete the gray sections along the left side—then sign along the bottom edge. Please note that joint accounts require both signatures.

P.S. We're attaching a duplicate copy of this letter in case you wish to pass it along to your tax lawyer or accountant.

So your sales letter failed! What can you do to try to salvage the sale? A "second-try" piece may be enclosed: Here's how some letters do it:

DON'T BOTHER TO READ THIS
unless you're not sure about
accepting our proposal.

READ THIS IMPORTANT MESSAGE ONLY IF YOU HAVE
DECIDED NOT TO JOIN NTU

If you're still undecided about sending for this book—I have a proposition for you . . .

See enclosed

PLEASE DO NOT OPEN THIS LETTER UNLESS YOU HAVE
ALREADY DECIDED *NOT* TO SEND FOR MY BOOK!

Please read this only if you've decided *not* to renew your subscription to *Business Week* now.

And an insert:

If you've decided to say "no" to this subscription invitation, please take a minute to reconsider this no risk offer.

—*Quest/78*

In the final paragraph, a number of elements will add to the results. A time limit increases responses. A special price inducement or a premium for acting now increases responses. A guarantee or free trial offer increases responses. Installment payments or thirty days to pay increases response. Return cards, "yes-no" tokens, stamps, sweepstakes entry forms, increase response. A no-postage business reply envelope increases response (and return stamped envelope, much more costly, is even better.)

When you have a mailing completely planned, check these factors before you proceed:

1. Is the letter easy to read?
2. Does the value in the package justify the price?
3. Does the value compare favorably with the competition?
4. Do headline and beginning attract attention and tempt further reading?
5. Does the letter arouse an emotional desire to buy?
6. Have you pointed out the features—particularly the exclusive ones?
7. Have you used the believable testimonial available?
8. Have you satisfied the reader about product satisfaction? With a guarantee perhaps?
9. Have you made it easy for the receiver to respond?
10. Does the overall package give a favorable impression?   .

GETTING LEADS AND THE FOLLOW-UP

Some things just can't be sold effectively in a single letter. The prospects may be relatively few and must be narrowed down. Or the price of the product discourages impulse buying. So you look for prospects.

Letters designed to get inquiries almost invariably contain a return card. Usually they offer some premium for responding: a special report, a booklet of loosely related material, a gift.

In direct mail advertising this is known as the *bait piece technique.* Almost any company can use it. A moving company might offer "a moving checklist—what to do before the van arrives." Those who respond to such an offer probably have a move in mind. So a salesman from the moving company phones and offers to deliver the checklist. If the prospect doesn't warrant a personal call, the salesman mails the helpful list and follows up by mail or merely makes a friend for a future sale.

Usually inquiries are solicited through print media which reach a large audience in a special field. The objective is to find prospects more particularly interested in what you have to sell. Occasionally a mass letter is used to cull a large list.

When the objective is to obtain an inquiry, it is important to give just enough information to select or "qualify" a good prospect, but not so much that curiosity is satisfied. Giving too much information may even be counterproductive. Don't try too hard to sell if your objective is to get leads.

In fact, one effective method is the teaser letter that gives virtually no information at all: not even the name of the product. The aim here is to induce the reader to send for a booklet with more information.

A gift may be offered to anyone to solicit inquiries or to stimulate responses. This technique is particularly useful for those who already know you and your product and require an extra push to respond.

A common objective of the "bait letter" is to create a mailing list of good prospects from a larger list. Suppose you have purchased a list of antique dealers. You want to select from this list those who have stores that would be prospects for selling your furniture polish. You could, of course, solicit all of them, but each mailing would be costly. Instead you narrow down your list by offering a free booklet: "A Guide to Selling and Using Furniture Polishes for Antique Furniture." Those who respond are far better prospects for future mailings. Your letter will sell the usefulness of the booklet. More important, it will select prospects who already feel friendly toward you for your useful gift.

Responding to inquiries

The response to a letter of inquiry bears the burden of doing a selling job. Of course, it includes the premium offered in previous letters. If it is in the form of a letter, it assumes a basic interest in the field.

The letter can sell a single individual's service:

Dear Mr. Silver:
Thanks for asking about my sales letter writing service . . .

I'm going to tell you everything you want to know: How it's done by mail. What it costs. What others say about it. Why you can't lose.

It doesn't matter what you are selling. A service or a product. Simple or complex. Books, magazines, machinery, cosmetics—even ideas. Anything. When you ask me to write a sales letter for you, you'll tap techniques that have sold everything from a $4.95 children's book to a $3,000,000 jet. Techniques that worked for them and can work for you, too!

It's simple. Just jot down a few facts about what you are selling. If you want to send some of your ads, brochures, catalogs or present letters—fine.

In about a week, you'll receive a hard-working sales letter tailor-made for you. A letter crammed with powerful sales arguments from start to finish. The kind that make people *more* money. A letter designed to bring back leads, orders—money!

You want to know more, of course. And you should. When you buy a sales letter, you're not just buying so many words and sentences like a bushel of peas. You *are* buying the knack, knowledge, intuition and interest of another human being. You have a right to *know* that person before you agree to work with him.

That's why I've enclosed a very personal autobiography—brief, but flesh and blood. It may be "better business" to do otherwise. But I believe we should know each other as *people*, if I'm really going to help you.

Sig Rosenblum

Enclosed are some samples of text used by prior users, in order that you may see some typical uses. Also enclosed is a matching envelope, in which the Speed-Dispatch transmission is sent to your customer.

If you will call me further, I will be pleased to personally assist you in preparation of your transmission.

Very truly yours,

. . . *new, helpful information about ways to streamline your mail and paper flow.* Because your time is valuable, I'll be brief in making this offer.

We've just prepared a complete portfolio of solutions to some of the major paperwork problems plaguing government offices today. This timely "ready reference file" will be mailed to you without obligation, after you return the enclosed mailing label . . . as explained below.

The catalogs you'll receive examine mail/paper-handling in terms of *your* particular needs. They'll show you how to increase productivity without having to "staff up," "borrow" extra hands or resort to overtime.

To find out how *you* can achieve greater levels of efficiency and economy, just check the enclosed mailing label for correctness. (Please add your name and title, if not shown, since we *must* have this information for proper handling of your request.) Then return the label to Pitney Bowes in the postage-paid envelope provided. You'll receive this valuable information promptly—without any cost or obligation.

Very truly yours,

P.S. Your local Pitney Bowes office is presenting a special "Government Paper-Flow Systems Show" on April 21st and 22nd. We hope you'll plan to attend.

Thank you for requesting the enclosed information

Benefits, descriptions, specifications, prices, ordering procedures: you'll find just about everything you need to know about streamlining paper-flow.

As you'll see, Pitney Bowes offers you dozens of solutions to Government paperwork problems . . . products and systems designed to give you greater efficiency, economy and productivity.

But you should also know that Pitney Bowes can help you in other ways. Your local PB office can provide a *free*, no-obligation survey of all your mail/paper-handling needs. Pinpoint trouble-spots. And make specific recommendations.

Moreover, the Pitney Bowes service corps enjoys the reputation of being one of the finest in the industry. From hundreds of service points throughout the country, our service people respond to calls promptly . . . and professionally.

Why not call your local PB office, today—or return one of the postage-paid request cards bound into the catalogs—to discuss how much Pitney Bowes can do for *you*.

Very truly yours,

Here's the material you asked us to send you.

We hope you'll find some profitable ideas in it.

If you'd like to know more about using our products in your business, just fill in and mail the handy reply card in the booklet. You'll hear from us soon.

Thanks for your interest in Pitney Bowes.

Very truly yours,
Pitney Bowes

Follow-up letters

Having compiled a list of prospects, how do you proceed to convert them to customers? In fact, you may have other lists of prospects in your files: old customers, present customers, little-active or inactive charge accounts—and especially present customers. The more business a person has done with you, the better prospect he or she is for future business.

Here's the information you recently requested . . .
and thank you for your interest.

With this informative booklet, you can learn all about Response Phone, Western Union's incoming toll-free phone service that *you* can use to take orders . . . answer customer inquiries . . . accept reservations . . . and much more.

Place the special ResponsePhone number in your print, broadcast and direct mail advertising, and you can get *fast response*, 24 hours a day, from coast to coast. *Without* spending a penny for new personnel or equipment.

It's easy, fast, economical. In fact, with ResponsePhone, you'll enjoy *seven* major benefits, as described on Pages 4 and 5 of this booklet.

If you would like more information on ResponsePhone, just dial toll-free—800-325-6400 (in Missouri 800-342-6600) and ask the operator to arrange for a Western Union representative to call. We'll get back to you promptly.

Sincerely,
Western Union

If the list of prospects is small, i.e., if it encompasses a local community or a small industry, it may be wise to plan a campaign of several mailings, each with a different approach. The campaign should be designed completely in advance although you may wish to make changes as inquiries come in with unforeseen requests. By planning the whole campaign, you are able to cover all the arguments sensibly and in some sort of order.

Mailings may be spaced ten days apart or even longer, but if you wish a letter to carry over its impact, two weeks' spacing is about as long as you should go.

Once you have an inquiry, the name of a prospect is a valuable asset and deserves a good and sustained follow-up.

First, make sure the name is properly entered on your prospect list. A mistake in the spelling, address or zip will be very costly because your inquiry list will probably be used time and again.

The response to an inquiry usually includes thanks for responding, a tie-in with the source of interest (letter, advertisement, etc.), the information promised, a tie-in with your product, and an appeal for an order.

Sometimes a questionnaire is more effective in finding leads for follow-up by mail or by salesmen than a direct sales approach. Although some questionnaires are thrown in the basket immediately, a large percentage are returned. One help is to affix a stamp on the return envelope, indicating that you expect a response. This is more efficient than using a business reply envelope.

Follow-up letters are usually prepared in a series and sent to prospects as long as the letters and the lists pay off. Part of the decision of how many letters to send depends on the cost of the mailing, the gross profit margin of each sale, and the opportunities to sell the product or service at less selling cost.

Each follow-up letter must have a different angle or appeal to induce the prospect to read further, because each one may face a reader who is more and more familiar with your sales talk and has probably made an increasingly negative decision at each previous letter. But do remember, some if not most of your previous letters have probably not been read; possibly they have merely been glanced at and tossed into the wastebasket. It is usually best not to refer to previous letters in your follow-up. Remember, too, that the prospect's memory is very short. Whatever you have said or done in the past fades—slowly at first, faster as time goes by.

Here are two of a series of follow-up letters:

To protect your contact, follow up inquiries, orders, and the people you have seen or spoken to. This keeps your image alive. Most sales require several calls, particularly if your proposals have several facets, some of which you cannot stress in one contact. Your prospect may have new problems, new perceptions, new ideas that would make him or her more receptive today than yesterday. Or he or she may just never have gotten around to sending in that order.

So follow up. No matter how effective your sales presentation is, no matter if you have or have not received an order or an inquiry, you have a financial interest in every prospect you have contacted.

Follow up your best prospects first and most frequently. Follow up with a plan—not just one letter following another. (But one letter is better than none.)

SECOND MAILING

Mr. I. M. Tuffsell
Ace Supply Company
99 Yellow Brick Road
Oz, Kansas

Dear Mr. Tuffsell:

Wouldn't it be great if every hundred dollars you sold to customers generated
almost eleven dollars of net profit? That's almost a license to print money.
Well, we know of how you can do it with at least one product line. . .
Rapistan casters.

Casters? Yessir. It may interest you to know that 75% of our present distri-
butors report that Rapistan casters rank among their top ten most profitable
lines. And that's really not too surprising when you also hear about the
average gross margin (25.1%) and average net profit (10.7%) they report.

Then why isn't every distributor carrying the Rapistan line? Quite frankly,
because we don't want every distributor. We want the ones who can offer us
as much as we offer them. And that, Mr. Tuffsell, is exactly why we want you.

Higher profitability is only one way Rapistan puts a lot more clout into your
caster sales. I'll get back to you in a few days with another powerful idea
I'd like to share.

Cordially,

K. P. Denisty

P.S. You might like to have fun with a youngster you know, using the enclosed
      "money machine" to change blank paper into dollar bills. While you do,
      remember Rapistan casters could be generating the real thing for you.
      And almost as fast.

Dealer Products Division   144 Trowbridge N.W., Grand Rapids, Michigan 49502   Phone (616) 451-6200

THIRD MAILING

Mr. I. M. Tuffsell
Ace Supply Company
99 Yellow Brick Road
Oz, Kansas

Dear Mr. Tuffsell:

Please accept this feather duster as a gift from the last distributor who
converted to the Rapistan caster line. He used it on his slow-moving caster
inventory.

He won't be needing it any more, now that he's handling the Rapistan line.
Our average distributor turns his caster inventory 6.2 times a year. (Hardly
enough time for the dust to settle.)

Faster inventory turnover--and therefore better return on investment--is only
one reason why the Rapistan caster line ranks among the top ten most profitable lines in 75% of the distributorships we deal with.

That's not all. Watch your mail for some more good news on how Rapistan puts
muscle in your caster sales.

Cordially,

K. P. Denisty

Dealer Products Division   144 Trowbridge N.W., Grand Rapids, Michigan 49502   Phone (616) 451-6200

Your letter can do several things:

1. Fill in facts slighted or overlooked initially.
2. Give additional problem-solving help.
3. Refresh the initial sales approach with repetition of facts in a different way, with fresh examples.
4. Express an interest in sales—or problems—first discussed.
5. If a sale or part of a sale has not been completed, keep the welcome mat out. Most sales require several calls.
6. Help the prospect.
7. Stimulate the prospect's thinking and move the sale along.
8. Show your people how to be problem solvers, not order takers.

In short, follow-up sales letters can continue the sale or the sales call or the sales letter in another form.

If your proposition is simple and you just want to leave a friendly feeling, a cordial, friendly note is enough. If you have found a clipping, a new idea, a new catalog or sample, a simple letter of transmittal may be enough. Sometimes you may just want to know if your prospect is still around, so you send a list-clearing note:

> We haven't heard from you recently.
> Would you be good enough to let us know if we are addressing you properly.
>
> Please check the enclosed reply card and make any corrections that are necessary.
> Thank you.

Sometimes the follow-up is an excuse for a salesman's call:

> Your request for a personalized leather memo pad and information on (effective estate planning) has been received by my company.
> It will be a pleasure to pass them along to you, so I'll call as soon as the pad arrives.

A basic kind of follow-up is the letter asking for renewal of a subscription to a periodical. This is the acid test of a publication's survival. The renewal letter series may have to offset any faults of the magazine, newspaper, or service itself. It can no longer sell "pie in the sky"; the customer knows and has already appraised the product. It must sell its record as well as its future. The first message is simply:

It's renewal time, Mr. Mager . . .

. . . so take a moment please, and okay the attached.

Cordially,

P.S. Even though you may not be a fund raiser, we're sure you'll be mightily interested in the debate that starts on page 23 of your May Issue. Father Alfred Schmit, who heads the gigantic . . .

Stop us from canceling your subscription. There's still time. Just enclose this card in an envelope with your payment and mail it right away.

Charles Mason
TIME, *The Weekly Newsmagazine*

P.S. There is no need to return this card if you've already sent in your payment.

For those who don't respond to reminders, a longer letter may be effective:

Dear Subscriber:

This is just a reminder that your subscription to the Kiplinger Washington Letter will be due for renewal shortly. And I welcome this opportunity to say a few words to you, in appreciation of your past support.

We've been writing the Washington Letter for more than 50 years. Many of our subscribers have been with us steadily for 20, 30 and even 40 years or more. But no matter how long you have been reading our Letters, I want to tell you it's *you* who makes our job interesting and worthwhile.

For years, our top editor started each weekly Washington Letter by typing out "Dear Mac," then continued as though he were writing to his old boyhood friend in Bellefontaine, Ohio. And this same spirit of writing to you, the individual reader, still governs our staff in every Letter we send you.

We are looking forward to serving you for another year because we feel the country has never faced twelve months of more significance to business. Right now, while you are reading this, far-reaching moves are being planned in Washington . . . moves that will affect all of us profoundly, including you and your business.

It will be our job to keep you informed about all such developments . . . all the various government plans and projects prompted by the rapidly changing picture at home and abroad. And we believe during the eventful months ahead, our reports and forecasts from Washington will be more important to you than ever before.

To make sure our Letters continue to reach you without interruption, I'd appreciate it if you'd approve the enclosed notice and pass it along for payment promptly. Thank you for your cooperation.

Dear Subscriber:

I shall try to take a leaf from the editors of THE U.S. NEWS WASHINGTON LETTER, and say my piece about your renewal quickly, clearly, and with the appropriate information in useful order.

Your subscription has 90 days to go before renewal is due.

You can mail your renewal as late as a few weeks before renewal date, without seriously jeopardizing every-week delivery.

But the earlier, the better.

Mailing it *now* will provide a comfortable margin for once-in-a-while delays and errors—in the mails and, admittedly, in our own offices.

Rates shown on the enclosed form remain in effect for your renewal order. I cannot guarantee those rates, if your subscription lapses.

We want very much for you to continue with us as a subscriber to THE U.S. NEWS WASHINGTON LETTER, and we will appreciate your mailing your renewal instructions now—to give us a little extra time to handle your order.

Thank you.

Sincerely yours,

Dear Subscriber:

You are known to us as a devotee of the Arts. This is why I am concerned to learn that your name has been deleted from our active list of subscribers.

The Connoisseur is edited for a very select audience who truly appreciate art in all its forms . . . paintings and sculpture, architecture, tapestries, old silver, glass and porcelain, arms and armour, furniture produced by old masters—the rare and precious objects of every age. The Connoisseur belongs in your home and should continue to grace your reading table.

The Connoisseur is printed in limited quantities, and is available only at select newsstands. Rather than find it sold out at the newsstand, you can be assured of receiving it regularly and conveniently at home or office, and at a substantial saving by renewing your subscription now. What's more, The Connoisseur is now being rushed by air from London to New York. You can be absolutely up-to-date on the international art and antique market.

The one-year subscription price of $48.00 saves you $12.00 from the single-copy cost; the two-year subscription price of $85.00 saves you $35.00.

You may charge your subscription, and we will bill you later. Or, send us your payment in the enclosed postage-paid envelope.

Please complete the accompanying order card and mail it to us at your earliest convenience. We hope to hear from you soon.

Sincerely,

Dear Former Subscriber:

Do you *really* want us to destroy the plate pictured above, formerly used to address your subscription copies of THE GIFT AND ART BUYER?

You did not renew, but there is a blunt finality in destroying this symbol of what I hoped was a friendly relationship between us.

Each of these little plates represents real people to us, not merely names on a list. You see, we get many letters from readers about their problems and interests; others we see in person. Through these thousands of contacts we have come to think of our subscribers as people we know. I cannot be complacent about the loss of even one subscriber.

—*The Gift and Art Buyer*

Dear Subscriber:

May I introduce myself? My name is Bill Armistead. I'm in charge of Kiplinger's Statistics Department, and I've just noticed that you are about to become the kind of statistic we don't like—an "Ex"-subscriber to CHANGING TIMES.

I don't know how it is at your house, but out in Berwyn Heights, Maryland, where my wife and I and our 4 children live, we depend on CHANGING TIMES to guide us through the really tough job of running our family finances.

We find articles on schools, health, recreation, wise spending, college funding, etc. especially important as our kids grow up and get ready for the big job of making a living and raising families of their own.

Surely you have had similar experiences with CHANGING TIMES—ways it has helped you or someone in your immediate family make or save money, and get more out of living. After all, that's what CHANGING TIMES is all about.

And that's why I couldn't resist taking a moment of your time today to tell you a little of my own experiences with the magazine. Naturally, I hope that this will mean we'll be hearing from you with your renewal instructions.

Since you have already received the last copy on your current subscription, I urge you to mark and mail the enclosed card today. This will make it possible for us to get the next issue to you on time, and instead of becoming a statistic, you will stay in our "Active" file where you belong.

Thanks very much,

GOOD-WILL LETTERS

Not every letter to a customer is necessarily designed to sell a product or service. Some letters create and develop friendliness, reputation, integrity, and impression of good service for a business. They try to create a climate which will induce prospective customers to think more favorably of you than they do of a competitor.

A good-will letter usually requires a concrete reason for being sent, although the reason given may merely be an excuse and a minor factor in the effectiveness of the letter.

Good-will letters may welcome a new customer, extend holiday greetings, note a local event (graduation, convention), advise of a change of address or of the opening of a new store or a new department, or note a customer's birthday or anniversary or an event in which he or she figures. They may thank the customer for an order or note inactivity in an account. The theory is that every contact makes a customer a better customer. Families moving into the neighborhood may receive a gift and/or an invitation to visit.

Good-will letters may also serve "sales" functions, inform of new products or of a new sales promotion or marketing plans, call attention to an improvement, stimulate inventory increases, change loyalty from one of your products to another, more profitable line, stimulate more attention to your product, encourage more display or sales effort, reinforce a salesman's talking points, resell all or part of a line lost to a competitor, reinforce product loyalty, stimulate usage (perhaps by suggesting new uses), refute a test by a competitor, etc. A store may run special events and invite customers or prospects. Here are a few typical letters.

From a salesman

> Thanks a lot, Mr. Danti:
>   I certainly appreciate the fine reception you and Mr. Wetzel gave me yesterday.
>   During the course of the day I make so many calls on "tough" purchasing agents and sales managers that a pleasant reception goes a long way.
>   I certainly hope that I can be of service in keeping your customers sold on Jumbo Whatzits.
>   Again—many thanks!
>   Sincerely,

To a new customer:

WELCOME! We're mighty happy to have you with us!

As a special "guest" of the Around the World Program, we know you are going to enjoy this first "Magic Carpet Tour" of a foreign land—as well as this beautiful, large-sized wall map. Both are yours free of charge, as promised.

This "introductory" gift will start you and your family on a thrilling new adventure. . . .

Dear Mr. Masters,

American Express Publishing Corporation is giving things away!

As a new Cardmember, we want to say "welcome" by presenting you with a *free* copy of TRAVEL & LEISURE—the finest travel magazine published today.

At the same time, we invite you to find out if you already have won the $25,000.00 Grand Prize in our fabulous new WANDER-LUST III Sweepstakes. The winning entry number has been preselected by computer. And it might be the one on your enclosed Sweepstakes Entry Certificate.

The Grand Prize is very special: A trip to anywhere in the world worth $15,000.00. And, upon your return, we'll give you the American car of your choice worth up to $10,000.00! Or, if you like, you can take the alternate Grand Prize: $25,000.00 in American Express Travelers Cheques to spend any way you want.

You can reserve your free copy of TRAVEL & LEISURE— and find out if you've won the Grand Prize or any of 138 other valuable Sweepstakes prizes—by saying "YES" and returning your enclosed Entry Certificate today.

At the same time, we'll reserve in your name a one-year subscription to TRAVEL & LEISURE (12 additional issues) at the special Cardmember price of only $7.

Your free issue will give you the opportunity to fully assess our magazine for yourself. If you don't agree that it will stretch your travel dollars and enrich your leisure time, just say the word and we'll void your subscription reservation. For that matter, you can cancel any time, and receive a pro rata refund for the amount due you. . . .

To an old customer

Dear Mr. Masters,

You were among the first to become an American Express Cardmember in 1958, when the Card was introduced.

This is an uncommon distinction and one that we feel, after twenty years, should not go unnoticed.

To mark this anniversary, we have created a special American Express Card that will be released only to Charter Cardmembers such as yourself who have been associated with Cardmembership since its beginning. You will receive this Card, distinguished by the inscription "Charter Member," on your regular Card renewal date, and on all renewal dates thereafter.

In the meantime, I would like to thank you personally for your two decades of Cardmembership. It is especially gratifying to know that we earned your confidence in that first year and have served you well enough to have kept it for so long.

I look forward to many more years of association with you as a valued American Express Cardmember.

Sincerely,

To a new resident

Dear Mrs. Guthrie:

Establishing your home in Painted Post means new things to do, new places to go, new friendships to be made. Of course, the last is of greatest interest. We want to be one of your first new friends and to become well acquainted with you.

Johnson's has a thirty-two-year-old reputation of the highest degree for serving and satisfying the people in this community. Truly, this is the store that every woman thinks of first when she starts on a shopping tour.

Will you let us have the pleasure of assisting you in your "discovery" of our store and its many features? We have opened an account for you and our credit personnel will enjoy showing you about. Your most convenient time will be our appointment with you.

Sincerely yours,

Holiday greeting:

Dear Mr. Wallace:

I've been wished a Merry Christmas, a Happy New Year, a Happy Birthday, and what have you . . . but this morning one of my customers wished me "A Happy Spring Season."

It's a good thought . . . so I'm stealing his idea by passing it along to you, and wishing you "A Happy Spring Season." But, I'm going to carry it a bit farther, and wish you not only a "Happy Spring Season" but good Spring business, and a pleasant Summer Season as well.

With all of my well-wishing, I almost overlooked thanking you for your trailer order, which has already been shipped. So, once again . . . please consider yourself heartily thanked!

Sincerely,

Dear Mrs. Dworkin,

"A Merry Christmas" . . .

What a wealth of meaning there is in those words! They stand for joy, good feeling, good fellowship. To me, they will never grow old or trite.

Some men have thought of fancier ways of saying it. I've seen some tricky greetings and some beautifully written sentiments. But I believe, if I lived to be a hundred, I'd still stick to the plain, old-fashioned, sincere greeting—"A Merry Christmas."

I want to extend that greeting to you in this letter, since I cannot greet you face to face with a warm handshake. I want you to know that we're all mighty grateful for the privilege we've had of serving you.

I hope the year coming to a close was a good year for you, and that 1980 will be still better. You can count upon our 100 percent cooperation to help make it so.

Cordially yours,

On a personal occasion

Dear Mr. Samuel,

Because we take a personal interest in all the things that are important to Miami, we are taking the liberty of congratulating you on your approaching marriage to Miss Elizabeth Parker.

Many young married people come to Burdine's for advice and help in planning their new homes—in fact, they've been coming for two generations! We have several convenient plans that help them keep their money in the bank and pay out of their incomes.

We hope you will come in and bring the future Mrs. Samuel. If you are interested in joining our family of "pet" customers, you have merely to say so.

Please feel that you are always welcome at Burdine's—whether you've come to buy or to browse around the store and just "look."

Cordially yours,

Welcoming new policyholders:

It's a pleasure to welcome you as a member of our company. As time goes on, I think you'll feel an ever-increasing sense of satisfaction with both your new protection and the company you bought it from. Connecticut Mutual is a strong, liberal company; managed by people with a real sense of obligation to their policyholders.

Also, Bob, I'd like to get together with you once in a while to make sure your life insurance is still accomplishing exactly what you want it to. As a Connecticut Mutual policyholder, you're entitled to this service and I'll do my best to provide it.

I look forward to many years of enjoyable association with you and your family, not only as a life insurance advisor, but also as a friend. Let me assure you, too, that everyone in our office is available and anxious to serve you at any time.

Very cordially,

On an engagement

Congratulations on your engagement:

As a life underwriter, one of my basic aims is to establish good working relationships with young people contemplating marriage. I do so because it's my belief that the financial plans and services I offer can go a long way toward helping you meet your future goals and responsibilities.

It has been said, in fact, that a person's three best friends are his doctor, his lawyer, and his life underwriter. I'd like to apply for that underwriter's job. Like yourself, I'm young and learning more each day—two important reasons why I feel I can give you the competent, lifelong service you'll be looking for.

With this in mind, I'll call soon to ask you for a few minutes of your time . . . at your convenience, of course. I'd certainly appreciate the chance to meet you personally and briefly show you samples of the work I've been doing for other young people in the Hartford area. I also promise to do my best to leave you with a few worthwhile ideas . . . whether or not you decide to act on them, now or ever.

I hope we can get together.

Very cordially,

Congratulations (promotion, election, etc.)

It's always a pleasure to read good news about good friends. That's the way I felt about the notice of your promotion to Vice-President. Certainly, this is richly deserved. I'm delighted.

I thought perhaps you or Mrs. Bronson would like this copy of the newspaper account.

My warmest congratulations!

Very cordially,

Congratulatory (birth)

Congratulations on your brand-new (son) (daughter). I'm delighted for you both!

(As you know) (As a father let me assure you) an even greater experience is in store for you . . . watching and guiding your (son) (daughter) as (he) (she) grows to maturity.

My best wishes to all of you.

Very cordially,

An article of interest

Knowing your interest in (antique furniture), I thought you might enjoy reading the enclosed article I clipped from a recent issue of (*Time*).

No need to return.

Very cordially,

Greetings (birthday)

Happy birthday! I hope the coming year is the best ever for you and your entire family.

Cordially,

New parents

Congratulations on the arrival of your new son!

Your new son and heir, of course, brings along with him many new responsibilities. My company has developed a plan that can go a long way toward helping you meet them—at a price I think you'll find is surprisingly low.

While you live, for instance, this plan builds guaranteed cash reserves, readily available to help meet unexpected medical bills, today's high educational costs, or any other need. And if by chance something should suddenly happen to you, the plan provides your family with a guaranteed monthly income, assuring your child of his mother's full-time care during those critical growing-up years.

I'd like to tell you more. That's why I hope you'll allow me to arrange a brief interview when I call next week. It won't take long and I promise to do my best to make it time well spent.

Very sincerely,

Asking a favor can be a plus

Dear Customer:

Once again we are asking for your help and direction in maintaining the level of high quality service that you deserve. This semi-annual request, which is only one part of our ongoing program to accurately monitor our performance, gives us the means to using our customers' suggestions and responding to their needs in developing plans for future operations.

If you are one of our newer customers, this may be the first time that we have asked for your help in participating in the Quality Survey. Every six months we write to our entire list of customers requesting their evaluation of our services. We would appreciate your completing the enclosed survey form and giving us your candid opinions, suggestions, and any additional comments you care to make.

Please return your reply to me at your earliest convenience using the enclosed envelope. (Should you have other correspondence relating to particular services, billing, payments, etc., please *do not* use the enclosed envelope for that purpose since it may get misdirected.) If you are using more than one ADP service, you will receive a separate form for each service, and I would appreciate your returning each one.

Thank you for your cooperation. I assure you that your comments will receive my prompt attention.

Sincerely,

AUTOMATIC DATA PROCESSING

GIMMICKRY AND SHOWMANSHIP

In the competition for attention endless thought has been lavished on devices that will make a message stand out from the ordinary: size, shape, thickness, smell, material, method of delivery, sequence (interspersed with phone calls), premiums, messages sent on phonograph records (thin disc inserts), magnetic tape, or singing.

Showmanship may be attained through anything out of the ordinary in a letter: paper, type, layout, color, unusual foldings, unseasonable timings, unusual envelopes, unusual stamps, unusual postmarks, (Hell's Half Acre, Wyoming). Effects may be obtained through enclosure of gadgets, clip-ons, souvenirs, even money (sometimes foreign currency) or stamps, or simulated checks or money.

A frame is the simplest device for emphasis:

SMITHSONIAN INSTITUTION
Washington, D.C. 20560
U.S.A.

```
***************************************************
* "What is the use of this new invention?" someone *
* asked Franklin.  "What is the use of a new-born  *
* child?" was his reply.                           *
***************************************************
```

An Invitation -- for Smithsonian Associates only . . . .

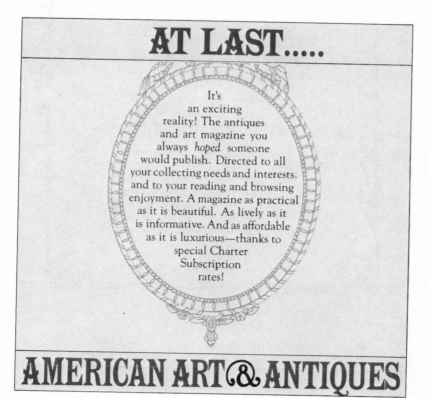

Simulated handwriting gives the effect of a personal letter—
at first glance:

AMERICAN KIDNEY FUND
P.O. Box 3586, Washington, D.C. 20007

Dear Friend:
   ~~This is probably the most unfair letter~~

Dear Friend
   ~~I'm pretty sure this is the meanest letter~~

Dear Friend:
   ~~This may be the most unfair letter you~~

Dear Friend
   As you can see, I have found it difficult to
begin — but I think you can gather enough
from my false starts to get the gist and be warned.
   Probably my inability to write down exactly
what I want to say stems from a certain amount
of rage and frustration.
   It says "Dear Friend" at the top of this —
but of course I don't know who you are — exactly.
I do know that I have mailed a great many
letters to people like you, people much like my
own close and good friends.
   The message in the letters I have mailed is
simple. We are working to bring an end to the
suffering and financial worry caused by kidney
disease. When your kidneys stop working, you

**The Translation Company
of America, Inc.**

A Division of The Traductor Group

500 Fifth Avenue
New York, NY 10036
(212) 594-8720
Telex 640218

July 5, 1978

Office of the
Executive

The other day, we mentioned to you our interpretation services.

Today, we want to emphasize that our major activity is translation from and into English of corporate documentation. Technical literature, legal texts, promotional materials, and commercial correspondence are our bread and butter.

We enclose a brochure for your future reference and invite your inquiries. Please return the business reply card or call us collect.

*Sincerely yours,
Jonathan Gray*

Jonathan Gray
Assistant to the President

Simulated handwriting as marginal notes provides a means
of emphasizing key points for the skimming reader:

Mail
Marketing
Minnesota

ORDER CENTER
P.O. BOX 8123 San Francisco CA 94128
Tel. (800) 227-6900
California Residents call (800) 632-4777

*A calculator that lets
you check your calculations and
gives you a permanent record.*

Dear Friend:

In this age of pocket calculators you might think a printing calculator is obsolete. But consider this.

Successful business practice depends on accuracy and good records. A printing calculator lets you
check your calculations on the paper tape. It also gives you a permanent record for taxes, filing,
records, receipts, etc.

Ask your accountant. Pocket calculators are fine for grocery shopping and quick estimating. But a
successful business needs the accuracy and recording ability of a printing calculator. And the Facit
1190 gives you all that and more.

The Facit 1190 Electronic Printing Calculator gives you every feature that demanding office figuring
requires (see the brochure for full list of features). And at a lower price than most machines with
far fewer capabilities.

In addition, Facit is a well known name in office machines, marketing a full line of printing calculators and typewriters through 1600 dealers nationwide. This means that you will get a quality product
backed by a reliable company.

factory warranty

Service? The Facit 1190 is factory guaranteed for all parts and labor for 6 months. If it doesn't work
properly Facit will repair it free. An annual maintenance agreement is also available, plus you can
always call our toll free number for service information.

free trial

You don't have to take our word for any of this, though. Try the Facit 1190 out in your own office
for 15 days – free. You don't send us a penny. If you don't like it, just send it back.

If you decide to keep it, the total price is only $119.95 plus $4.65 shipping and handling. And you
can even spread that out over 4 months with payments of only $31.15. With no finance charges!

bonus offer

We think you'll agree that this is a very good deal. But we'd like to go one better for you. Take us
up on the free trial offer and we'll send you a Brink's Security Marking System from Sanford Pen
and Swingline Stapler Kit. Free. To Keep. Just for trying out the Facit 1190.

If your Business doesn't have a decent printing calculator, don't pass up this chance. Send in the free
trial card today.

Sincerely,

J.L. Peterson

J. L. Peterson
Merchandising Manager

JLP/aa

*P.S. Now you can order by phone –
call toll free (800) 227-6900.
California residents call (800) 632-4777.*

A photograph or a lively illustration on the letterhead or in the text can be used to establish a more personal relationship:

April, 1976

My name is Rita Malm
and you can think of me
as ... permanent.

I guess when most people hear the name Kelly
Girl, they automatically think of temporary
help ... and that's absolutely great.

But it isn't true exactly.

Because while most of the help we offer is
for a temporary situation, our service is
permanent. We're here in our office every
working day, year in and year out.

We know New York. We know the business situation
here and how it changes. We know the problems and needs
that most companies face. Most of all, we know how to
solve these needs with skills that get the job done ...
quickly, simply and guaranteed to your satisfaction.

As a result, we can make your job easier, your problems smaller, and your work more profitable.

I suggest that when you have a temporary need of any
kind you get in touch with me or any of my permanent
staff at 227-3262.

We may be the lasting answer.

                              Sincerely,

                              Rita Malm
                              Manager, New York

RM/ybc

150 Broadway, Room 2220, New York, New York 10038

HIS REWARD...

...OR HER PUNISHMENT?

It all depends on your point of view.

Sometimes customers and prospects look at your advertising and sales promotion from a different point of view - aren't sold by the message you spend hard-earned dollars to put across.

That's where I can help. Creating advertising from your prospects' point of view.

For over 20 years I've planned and written inquiry-building, sales-producing campaigns for America's most successful direct response advertisers ...

... created hundreds of thousands of live leads, sold millions of dollars worth of portable adding machines, fishing lures, dress forms, notions, chemicals, drugs, wire & cable, scientific instruments , greeting cards, executive gifts, stationery , correspondence courses, books, records, magazines, insurance, financial services, much more.

Awards? Sure, I've got those too. But frankly I'm more interested in the bottom line on your annual report than the picture frame on my wall.

Let me contribute to your profit picture by analyzing your campaigns and making helpful suggestions ... preparing effective new promotions ... writing action-producing copy.

If it will help I can also provide artwork, printing and production by top-notch pros with whom I'm associated, even place advertising space. Any or all this - on a monthly retainer, or per project basis.

Why not look me up in WHO'S WHO IN THE EAST: then to discuss how I can help you increase sales, multiply live leads, build prestige, etc. - phone me at 441-5358.

Best wishes for more $$$ in your mailbox.

Richard Silverman

83-33 Austin Street, Kew Gardens, New York 11415

Dear Subscriber:

We hate to say goodbye ...

... to a subscriber friend and
not be able to share with you
the pleasures of Art in America.

But the issue you have just received is the last one we can
send, and your subscription has now expired.

During the past year, Art in America has strived to serve
your best interests and your finest tastes in bringing
you a better understanding and appreciation of the visual
arts.

You will not want to miss the issues just ahead: exciting
and informative features about the world of art and artists --
and hundreds of works of art reproduced in full color, more
than in any other art magazine.

Fortunately, this need <u>not</u> be goodbye.

You can continue receiving Art in America by simply returning
your enclosed renewal form today. Your subscription will be
renewed immediately and you will not miss the next issue.

If you wish to be billed later, fine -- the important thing
to do is mail your renewal instructions right now while you
are assured of continuous service and the lowest renewal
rates.

Thank you.

                                        Sincerely,

                                        John Hanner

                                        John Hanner
                                        for Art in America

JH:ad

Art in America

SUBSCRIBER SERVICES DIVISION
115 TENTH STREET • DES MOINES, IOWA 50301

◈ Standard Rate & Data Service, inc.

OVER FIFTY YEARS THE NATIONAL AUTHORITY SERVING THE MEDIA-BUYING FUNCTION / 5201 OLD ORCHARD ROAD, SKOKIE, ILLINOIS 60077 / (312) 966-8500

We're extremely pleased . . .

to introduce you to your new SRDS District Manager, Mary Sue Jedele.

She brings to Standard Rate a wealth of list marketing experience.

Mary Sue's work experience at Woodruff/Stevens and Names in the News make her a valuable list marketing consultant.

She is looking forward to putting her knowledge to work for you. You can expect professional, personal service.

Cordially,

Rick Botthof
Publisher

P.S. Mary Sue will be in our New York office. She may be reached at 212-935-7594.

Foreign stamps, United Nations stamps, old postage stamp issues or new ones have attention-getting value. One advertiser shipped his mailings to France for a mailing to carry out his theme.

One special letterhead has a pocket into which a return card is inserted. The address on the card does double duty as the inside address. (These letterheads are offered by Reply-O Products in New York.)

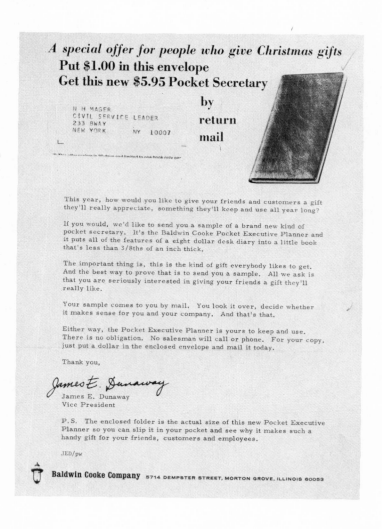

Multicolored letterheads with a variety of headings can be purchased in almost any quantity from Idea Art, New York.

Attachments to a letter in the form of miniatures, a coin, a match, a key, seeds, foreign moneys, stamps—even pennies, dimes (please call me) or dollar bills attract attention:

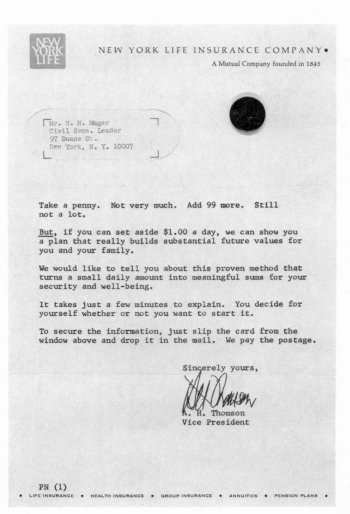

Pseudo telegrams get a high rate of readership:

MAIL THIS
FORM TODAY.
NO STAMP
REQUIRED.

REPLY-O-GRAM

THIS IS ONE OF THE MANY SHAPES REPLY-O TAKES. TO FIND OUT HOW

REPLY-O-LETTERS, GRAMS, MONARCHS AND BARONIALS CAN HELP YOU ACHIEVE

MORE RESPONSE FROM YOUR MAILINGS, JUST RETURN THE POSTPAID CARD

ENCLOSED ABOVE. WE'LL SEE THAT A PORTFOLIO OF SAMPLES AND PERTINENT

INFORMATION REACH YOU WITHOUT DELAY.

CORDIALLY,

NEAL HARRIS, VICE PRESIDENT

Reply-O-Letter Co., Inc., 1860 Broadway, New York, N.Y. 10023 • (212) 245-8118

One copywriter crumpled the letter and won attention with:

THIS LETTER IS PRE-CRUMPLED
IN CASE YOU ARE SICK OF GETTING DUMB LETTERS
But this is not a dumb letter. If we thought so we wouldn't have
printed it and mailed it to you.

A translation company took advantage of a well-reported faux pas:

The Translation Company of America, Inc.

A Division of The Traductor Group

500 Fifth Avenue
New York, NY 10036
(212) 594-8720
Telex 640218

.February 15, 1978

President Carter
The White House
Washington, D.C.

Office of the
Executive

Dear Mr. President:

Ah, the perils of trusting a bad translator to say what you mean!

We have a suggestion. Next time you're speaking in a strange country, have one of your staff give us a call.

We'll be pleased to supply an expert, as a courtesy to you. Someone you can count on.

We've got more than 2,000 of them. Highly-skilled linguists, all listed by language and training, in our computer bank.

And although our regular work is major translation projects for business and the professions, many of our people are fine simultaneous interpreters.

Just give us a call.

Pozdrowienia platoniczne!

(That's "Platonic Greetings!", in Polish.)

Serge Raffet
President

SR/jl

The Translation Company
of America, Inc.

A Division of The Traductor Group

500 Fifth Avenue
New York, NY 10036
(212) 594-8720
Telex 640218

May 5, 1978

Office of the
Executive

Dear Mr. Mager:

Here's a little irreverence we thought you
might enjoy.

It's a letter to the President, Jimmy Carter, offering him one of our translators
free, the next time he goes abroad.

Our point is simple.

We have a lot of very skilled translators.
For political speeches. Conventions. Sales
meetings. You name it.

But ... just in case you thought we only work
in print ... we figured we'd better open our
mouths!

Best wishes,

Serge Raffet,
President

SR/jl
Enc.

An antiques dealer enclosed an 1890 French postcard with the follow-through:

> The naked truth is
> I need money!

A formula that has been used successfully is the "you may already be a winner in our contest" approach:

"A WINNER!!??
ME?!"

Dear Reader,

Hold it, now. You're <u>not</u> about to win the recreational vehicle of your dreams. You're <u>not</u> competing for a two-week, all-expenses-paid trip to Des Moines. You have <u>not</u> been awarded a lifetime subscription to anything.

But you just may be a winner.

Because in the past few years, a totally new kind of man and woman has emerged. The kind who thinks "winning" is more than what football teams do. Or what being boss at the office is all about.

Who instead care about <u>how</u> they win, and <u>what</u> they're competing for. Men, for example, who think "winning" includes the freedom to cry, or women for whom it means running a great hundred-yard-dash. Or people who think a group working together can be more exciting than one individual beating another...

<u>That's</u> what the new "winning" is all about -- and that's why <u>you</u> may already be a winner. Because if <u>you</u> want that kind of richness, growth, change -- and are ready to get off the treadmill -- we want you to meet MOTHER JONES.

That's right, MOTHER JONES -- a magazine for men and women who still want to win, but don't want to do it at the cost of their souls. Who want to try out some of the new rules that have grown up in the tumult of the last decade, and who are wise enough to want some help and companionship along the way.

This is <u>your personal invitation</u> to try MOTHER JONES, a very special magazine, at our risk. And to find out what winning a new life for yourself is all about.

That's right, MOTHER JONES. Named after a woman, an unsung heroine of American history, who won more than a few struggles herself. A woman who lived a full century, from 1830 to 1930, challenging, pushing, prodding for change, winning in the process battles that helped institute the first child labor laws in America, helped alleviate some of the worst working conditions in human history, helped win for women and men a new respect and power in the world.

We borrowed her name and we borrowed her spirit too. At a college commencement, when she was already into her late 90s, she was introduced to the audience as "a great humanitarian." "No," Mother Jones rose and roared, "I'm a hell-raiser..."

Mother Jones
607 Market Street, San Francisco, Ca. 94105

PUTTING THE TELEPHONE TO WORK FOR YOU

Almost every general approach that applies to the emotional content of a letter applies to other media: printed advertising, television, radio, direct sales approach, etc. The medium that is most widely used, perhaps even more than the letter, is the telephone.

Telephone communication is a part of America's way of life. It has multiple advantages, not the least of which is the ability to exchange information, receive an answer, and provide a counterresponse in a single encounter. Speed, lower cost, and convenience are additional factors that favor the telephone.

The telephone gets you to your destination quickly, sometimes even letting you bypass people who have been ⊛waiting outside an office for hours. It gives you a chance to be specific, to respond to questions, to use your personal charm—inflection, language, slang. It permits you to make a deal in minutes.

Incidentally, a person who answers your phone should be specifically instructed on how to respond if you are away from your desk. Phrases to be avoided particularly are: "He's not in yet." "He's not back from lunch yet." "He's gone out for the day." Tact suggests: "I'm sorry, he's away from his desk. I expect him about three o'clock. May I have him return your call?"

If you use telephones extensively for selling, collections, or any other purpose, it is important to know about all the facilities available. Some areas have toll-free calls to certain exchanges, other areas are billed by message units over the number allowed without charge. One telephone service, the Foreign Exchange (FX) line, gives you the advantage of calling a certain area at local rates for that area. A WATS line permits you to call an entire area, a state, or the whole country for a flat fee per hour with additional calls at a proportional rate. (The relative costs of these have to be measured carefully.)

Similarly an inward WATS "800" line permits you to take toll-free calls from the area you contract for, even from the whole continental United States. These are widely used by hotels for receiving reservations, by insurance companies as "claims centers," and by national advertisers. Toll-free 800 lines to receive calls can be arranged nationally through National Communications Center, (800) 824-5120.

There is another way to buy out-of-town calls to a big city at a lower price. Several companies offer a system, for calls to the metropolitan areas of most of the large cities of the nation, through a non-AT&T set of lines. There is an access charge of about $80 per month and a minimum usage charge of about $75 a month. Other companies offer microwave telephone service to avoid long-distance charges.

Nowadays talking to one person is only one facet of telephone communications. You can talk to many people at the same time through a conference call (most switchboards can arrange it, or your phone company will). You can communicate pictures, drawings, or typed material by tele-copier. A telephone blackboard is available in some areas. With this, a visual display is created on a four-foot by six-foot panel. The chalkboard has a pressure-sensitive surface that senses the location and direction of lines. This is relayed to remote TV monitors which reconstruct the image. A "marriage" of mail and toll-free phone centers and a large computer system is often effective.

The telephone is particularly effective in responding to complaints or inquiries, qualifying prospects, reminding old customers, reviving old accounts, collecting bills, and even in direct selling.

For almost every purpose where a letter can serve—except the formal invitation, the recitation of complicated informa-tion, and the provision of a written record (especially necessary where money or the law is involved)—the tele-phone is at least an alternate to the letter.

Inasmuch as a business letter costs an average office $4.47, it is usually much more expensive than a telephone call. In addition to being less costly, the telephone call can do many things more effectively than a letter; but remember, some things it can't do nearly so well.

When to call

If you wish to reach a person high up in a company, you will invariably be screened by a secretary or some other intermediary. Chances are you will end up talking to someone far down in the hierarchy. To reach a high official you must have a good reason for him or her to get on the phone. Timing of telephone calls is particularly important. People with a day's work to be done are more relaxed and receptive at some times of the day than at others. Best time for housewives is 10 to 11:30 in the morning. These are the best phone times for various professions:

Builders and contractors, 8–9 A.M., 4:30–5 P.M.
Chemists, 4–5 P.M.
Dentists, 8:30–9:30 A.M.
Doctors, 9–11 A.M., 1–3 P.M.
Druggists, 1–3 P.M.
Executives, 10:30 A.M., noon, 4–4:30 P.M.
Grocers, 1–3 P.M.
Insurance brokers, 9–10 A.M., 4–4:30 P.M.
Lawyers, 11 A.M., 2 P.M., 4–5 P.M.
Salaried workers, 8–9 A.M.
Stockbrokers, 9–10 A.M., 3–4 P.M.
Teachers, 4–5 P.M., 6–7 P.M.

It is not always easy to get through. Leon Henry, Jr., says his approach has been effective:

"Good morning, Mr. James. This is Leon Henry, Jr., of Leon Henry, Incorporated. I have a service that will provide your company with an increase in net profits at little outlay of expense. May I have an appointment to discuss it with you?"

Sometimes calling during lunch hour, when an executive may be without screening, gets you through.

Selling by telephone

As a sales device the telephone has some major advantages. It reaches people quickly, easily, inexpensively, and impressively. In most offices a telephone will reach people and places where a salesperson might never get. One computation notes that ten part-time phone salespeople can contact 12,000 homebodies in a month—anywhere in the nation, in all weather.

In modern business, the telephone is now a powerful marketing medium. A recent survey found that 7 million people will listen to a sales talk each day, and 460,000 will buy something for an estimated total of $28 million.

Telephone selling is now made practical by automated sequential dialing systems. These dial in turn each of the numbers placed into the system, they give a greeting, wait for the response, and then go into a prerecorded selling pitch. Although some people resent this, a few do not know that it is a machine talking. In many cases, with the saving in manpower, the device is cost-effective in bringing sales or carrying a message. In some cases, a live human voice interferes after the greeting. (This automatic sequential dialing system is banned in twelve states.)

Telephone solicitation is used effectively in direct selling, for producing leads, in collecting moneys, in gaining support for a candidate or an issue, and in many similar types of campaigns. Some sales organizations train housewives so that they can call directly from their homes.

Producing leads for a call by a salesman is a major use of the telephone in business. Often it involves presentation of a gift: free Pepsis by Kirby Sweepers; a snapshot camera by Technicolor; a free yacht cruise by a Florida land company; a free lesson by a school. Usually the gift is valued at less than 2 percent of the anticipated unit sale.

A sales presentation by telephone must be limited to what can be said convincingly in about two minutes. It is usually made up of five or six paragraphs totaling fewer than five hundred words in all. The "conversation" proceeds:

1. To introduce the speaker and his or her company
2. To explain the purpose of the call
3. To tell the basic offer
4. To recite the benefits
5 (and, if necessary, 6). To close a sale.

By telephone, the salesperson comes unannounced, usually unknown, without the visual support or preceding warm-up and face-to-face confrontation of a visiting sales-person. He or she therefore must have a fast and convincing introduction, a simple logical talk, and a series of alternate closings which will meet any resistance offered by the customer. Professional telephone salespeople use two addi-tional devices: test questions and a pinch of negativism.

Language has to be simple (not more than three hundred syllables in a two-hundred-word "pitch"). There must be a rigid elimination of distracting or confusing statements. Interruptions by questions—a desirable element, showing interest—should be answered simply and directly, with an immediate return to the sales talk.

Closing a sale is the key to every successful presentation. One way is to offer alternatives and ask for a choice of colors, model, etc., assuming consent. One never ends with "Are you interested? Would you consider making a pur-chase?" etc.

Another help in closing is the insertion of test questions after certain points are made in the conversation. These usually "involve" the prospect. They allow you to learn how he or she feels (although they do not usually close the sale).

> I know you won't want to miss the chance of earning an extra hundred dollars a week, would you?

> If the gizmo will save you an hour of cleaning a day, it's certainly worth seven dollars, isn't it?

A direct sale by telephone usually involves the right to return the product without obligation. On-approval or invoice sales are another important element in telephone selling. The most effective programs make it very easy to receive a product and relatively difficult to return it. The salesperson must be discriminating in whom he or she accepts as a customer and a supervisor must be careful that the sale is not made carelessly.

In making publication subscription sales by telephone, the first copy may involve a "keep-it-without-obligation" offer, and "cancel your subscription merely by returning the invoice within thirty days." Human nature being what it is, relatively few people bother to cancel within the allotted time.

Always be cheerful on the phone. Your voice and its emotion are the only contact the other party "sees." Your cheer, your enthusiasm, your excitement is contagious.

Obviously, the better you can qualify your prospects for the item you are selling, the better are your chances of making a sale. For some products, everyone is a prospect; for others you need to have specialists, just as you would for a mailing. Often the prospect is a special member of the family: it is a waste of time trying to sell the husband for a product the wife usually buys and vice versa. Try to select customers who can afford your product, or else you may end up with uncollectable bills.

In some areas, and for some products, where prospects include most telephone users, it is profitable to use telephone directories where numbers are listed by streets (criss-cross directories). From this the names can be selected from high- or medium-income areas, even by types of residences. Sometimes certain zip codes identify an area as high-income, middle-income, etc.

Speak to each prospect as if he or she were the only one you will speak to in the day. Establish a mood in yourself. It usually carries over to the listener.

Professional phone sales managers find these the basic objections or resistance factors:

> No money: can't afford it.
> No hurry: maybe later.
> No desire: I can do without it.
> No need: I have no use for it.
> No authority: I have to ask my husband.

An answer for each of these should be prepared in advance. Some sample responses:

> "As a matter of fact you really can't afford to be without it. And the cost can be spread over 16 months with only $1.00 down. The cost is less than a . . ."

> "The price on gizmos will never be so low again. This is a special introductory offer being made to a selected few . . ."

> "You will enjoy the convenience and time saving that each gizmo brings you, time you can use for relaxation, reading . . ."

The start on the telephone goes about this way:

> "Good morning, this is NDC Industries. May I speak to Mr. Murdoch?"
>
> "This is Mr. Murdoch."

Often a talk begins with a question.

> "Mrs. Jones, do you know about the new clean-on-sight gizmo?"

The talk which follows bears no relationship to whether the response is yes or no.

> "You will be surprised how many times in a week you will find this device useful. Moreover, you can have this on a ten-day trial basis and see for yourself how much pleasure . . ."

Here is a typical sales talk from a text on the subject, *Profitable Telephone Sales Operations* by Robert C. Steckel.* It is prepared for a company that sells stereo records and stereo record players through fine retail outlets. The company adopted a telephone campaign to stimulate sales by offering a stereo player with a contract to buy 48 to 215 stereo albums. This was the telephone presentation. It allows for two alternative offers, each made in about three hundred words.

	Comments:
"Mrs. Smith? I am Mary White and I am a customer representative with National Record Club. I have a very special reason for calling. Are you acquainted with our stores? (Yes or No) Actually, we are the largest stereo record album store in the area."	The source of the call is established. The opening avoids "Have you ever heard of our company?" which inevitably kills the effort.
"Mrs. Smith, I called because you may qualify for a very nice gift and I would like to ask a question or two. Do you have a stereo player in your home?"	The answer to the question is a plug either way. Reason for call. Guarantees customer interest.
(If no, present offer #1) "Well, maybe we can do	Yes or no will still hear a presentation.

*—Arco Publishing Co., copyright © 1976 by Robert C. Steckel.

something about that. After all, you can't very well buy albums from our stores unless you have a stereo to play them on! My company has decided to offer several hundred beautiful stereo sets to people like yourself who do not have one, but I'm sure you can understand we want to give them to people who will use them, and enjoy playing their favorite songs whenever they want to."

The offer.
Holds prospect's attention.
Mild qualification.
First benefit.

"Of course, the size of the stereo record player we give you would depend on how often you might use it. If you had a beautiful new stereo at home, would you be likely to add two or four new records to your collection each month?"

Presents "visual" image and stimulates desire.

First closing attempt.
Alternate close.

(If "I don't know")
"Well, to help you enjoy your favorite music, we deliver six albums with your set. After that we feel you will like it well enough to buy just two albums each month from our store. Do you think six is enough or would you prefer more?"

Benefit.
Benefit.
Close II. Alternate.

(If yes, set appointment)
"Well, that is all we ask and there is nothing more to buy or pay for. All we have to do now is have our assistant manager stop and show you the models we are giving. You can even choose between Motorola, RCA, or GE. Will you be home this evening or would tomorrow evening be better? What time is best for

Number with set is not important.

Always recap.

Every salesman is an assistant manager.
Benefit.

Pleasant sign off.

you? Fine, Mrs. Smith. Congratulations and I hope your new stereo will give you many pleasant hours of enjoyment."

(End of offer #1)

(If they do have a stereo, present offer #2)

"The reason I called is to announce a new discount plan through our record club program. Usually there is a membership fee to receive this discount, but we are offering a limited number of memberships absolutely free. Our members receive a list of over three hundred stereo albums each month and they can select any they wish to have for just $2.98 after the first album at the regular price. In many cases, this is less than half the usual cost.	Reason for call established. The offer. Benefit. Benefit. Benefit.
"There is no limit on your purchases, and you are not obligated to buy any at all if you don't want to."	Benefit. Benefit.
"I am authorized to reserve a free membership card for you, Mrs. Smith, with no strings attached, and one for another member of the family. Would you rather have just one for yourself, or is there another member of the family who might also like one?"	Benefit. Alternate close.
(Wrap-up) "Thank you, Mrs. Smith. I'll see that your free membership cards are mailed to you in the next few days."	Pleasant sign-off.

Sometimes the question is best put negatively; but not too

negatively: A "no" answer is obviously something to be avoided.

> "Not everyone is eligible for this service, Mrs. Jones, and it is possible it will not be a good thing for someone in your particular situation. You may be in an income bracket where five thousand dollars a year has no meaning for you."

A "yes, but" answer is most common and it indicates the direction which must be taken by the salesperson.

> "When our representative drops off a machine at your house, it involves no obligation on your part. You may not find it as useful as most people do. Then, all you need to do is to pick up your telephone and let us know. We will have the machine picked up and give you full credit. Isn't that fair, Mrs. Jones?"

> "Most people think our product is the best news for the housekeeper since the vacuum cleaner, but we want you to decide for yourself."

Where a sale is made before the whole talk is finished, it is a good idea to repeat the offer so as to avoid a misunderstanding or the use of a "misunderstanding" to create a cancellation.

After a telephone conversation, a confirming letter is often advisable. This pins down a record of the conversation, any facts or figures involved, and any conclusions reached. If there is a misunderstanding, a correction can be made quickly. And if the conclusion was equivocal, you can swing it a bit one way or the other.

Some hints given to telephone salespersons

1. Make your voice smile.
2. Don't read your message. Radiate it! Be alive.
3. Isolate each call. Forget the previous one.
4. Pause after each sentence. Don't rush. Let the message sink in.
5. Lower the volume of your voice at the end of each sentence. Avoid scaling down toward the end.
6. Provide variety in tone and pitch. Don't chant in monotone.
7. When you are interrupted, answer the question, then continue where you left off.

8. Know what you are selling.
9. Confirm the address. (Telephone directories may be out of date.)

An average telephone salesperson will dial 28 calls in an hour, 13 will not answer, 2 will say call back, 7 will say no immediately, and 6 will listen to a presentation. In twenty-five working days of eight hours each, a salesperson will run up a local call bill of $250.

Sometimes phone calls are used as a sort of market research. Norman Cousins used this technique when he took back management of *Saturday Review,* following with this letter:

> *Dear Mr. Mager:*
>
> My colleagues and I deeply appreciate your vote of confidence. You are among our very first charter subscribers.
>
> The response to our exploratory telephone project was successful beyond our most extravagant hopes. When I learned, on December 24, that these tests were highly favorable, enabling us to proceed with the new magazine, I can assure you that this was the finest Christmas present I have ever received.
>
> What makes this experience so gratifying is that this is the first time a magazine has been launched, not by investors, but by its future readers. For your part in making this possible, I thank you most warmly. We'll do everything we can to justify your hopes.
>
> What about the magazine itself?
>
> We believe that a magazine is essentially a reading, rather than a viewing, experience. In this sense, we shall publish for a readership rather than a flippership.
>
> Your new magazine will be concerned with the ideas and the arts. Our arena, however, will be the world. We will do more than report on books, plays, movies, music and the arts in just the United States alone. We will attempt to review and report on cultural events on a world scale.
>
> We will write about the human condition at a time when the ability of a human intelligence to meet its problems is being tested as never before. Our hope is to see the world as the astronauts saw it— a beautiful wet blue ball with millions of factors in the delicate combination that makes life possible. Our dominant editorial concern, then, will be the proper care of the human habitat—whether with respect to world peace and everything that is required to bring it about, or world environmental deterioration, or overcrowding, or any of the things that indignify and humiliate human beings.
>
> We are enclosing an invoice for your subscription to the new magazine. (The first issue will reach you in late April or early May.)

We are also enclosing a form for ordering gift subscriptions in the hope that the excitement of our new publishing venture may be something you will want to share with your friends.

Again, my heartfelt thanks for your confidence.

Faithfully,

Follow-up with a thank-you letter

Thank you, Mrs. Ackerman . . .

. . . for the comments and courtesy extended when you were called by telephone recently.

I was doing a little inquiring to be sure that the old friendly relationship still exists. You know, it is almost impossible for me to keep personally in touch with each of our customers, so I decided to use the telephone as a good medium of contact with you.

The idea behind this letter, as well as the telephone call we made recently, was just to see if Parker's can be of any additional service or help to you.

We assure you we have appreciated your patronage in the past and will deem it a pleasure to number you again among those we serve frequently.

Sincerely yours,

Chapter 3

Handling Sales Problems

CLAIMS AND ADJUSTMENTS

If something is wrong with a purchase or you have any grievance with a company, you will undoubtedly end up by writing a letter. However, you may wish to phone first to determine who is the person in authority who can provide a remedy. Complaining to the wrong person, especially to the person responsible for an error, can be a frustrating exercise in futility.

So, having determined the person most likely to be helpful, you write. Make sure you provide the essential details: where and when the purchase was made, the sales number, model number, who purchased, who sold, what is wrong, what inconvenience it is causing, remedies you have tried, and what you want (refund, replacement, repair). If a purchase is involved, don't wait: large stores file their sales on microfiche or microfilm in a system that requires endless search to retrieve. So your delayed complaint letter waits till someone gets to it—which may be never.

If after more than a reasonable time you get no satisfaction, jump to the top. A letter to the president of a large corporation, even General Motors, gets attention immediately. Even a curt note from "upstairs"—"What's this about?"—goes to the top of a pile of letters, and a great deal of "get-rid-of-this" attention. A letter to a higher official might stress the threat of bad publicity or legal action.

Complaints
Always be as specific as you can be.

Blumberger's
Gainsborough, Mass.

Gentlemen:

It is now six months since I ordered a set of 246 dishes in Spode pattern 67890 in maroon. When I made the purchase last December, you advised me that the set was part of a shipment already on its way to you and that I might expect the dishes by March 31. It is now three months since delivery was promised to me.

I can understand some delay caused by the dock strike in New York, but three months is an inordinate time to be late.

Please look into this and let me know within the week when I may expect delivery. Thank you.

Very truly yours,

A complaint should focus on who did what.

Gentlemen:

Your records will show that I have been a charge customer at Blumberger's for more than eight years. During that time I have never had cause for complaint of your service or courtesy.

However, last Saturday, during the first few hours of your Summer Sale, I had a most distressing incident due to the discourtesy of a young lady in the negligee department. (She was a short blond girl wearing a blue dress.)

When I asked for your new camisoles, she brusquely informed me that these were not in the sale, and then turned away with an expletive that was not very complimentary. It was more than half an hour before I could get another saleslady to wait on me. Then she learned that my size was out of stock.

There was absolutely no reason for the first young lady not to show me what I wanted to see. If she knew that my size was not in stock, she should have told me so simply and courteously. I resent being treated so cavalierly and I will certainly think twice before I do my shopping in Blumberger's again.

Very truly yours,

Gentlemen:

Please cancel my order for the set of dishes I ordered last December for delivery before March 1st.

The set was made up of 246 pieces of Spode dinnerware pattern 67890 in maroon.

It is now three months past the delivery date, and I find I will have no further use for the set for at least some time.

If and when the dishes arrive, if you will let me know, I may reconsider the purchase. But in the meanwhile, consider this a cancellation of my order.

Very truly yours,

Gentlemen:

Three months ago, on January 25, I placed an order for

Swansdowne Wallpaper style 3762 in blue to be delivered on February 10 when my paperhanger was scheduled to work.

In spite of your assurances that the paper would be available on time, it was not delivered to me until February 18 and I was forced to reschedule the workmen. When the paper finally arrived, the paperhanger discovered that it was printed in two different shades, entirely incompatible with each other. I understand that this does happen occasionally, but obviously the paper is useless to me.

I have now had to delay completing the work in my house for two months and have greatly inconvenienced the workmen who have come twice on fool's errands.

Please arrange to provide a new shipment of paper in uniform color and to deliver it as quickly as possible to replace the bolts I now hold. Let me know immediately when I may expect these so that I can reschedule the work.

Thank you.

Very truly yours,

Blumberger's Department Store
Gainsborough, Mass.

Gentlemen:

Yesterday I received a delivery from you of Spode dinnerware pattern 67890 in maroon including 246 pieces.

Three of the dinnerplates and two of the cups arrived chipped.

If you can replace these within the next sixty days, please pick up the broken dishes and send me a notice to the effect that they will be replaced.

If this pattern and color cannot be replaced within the period, please arrange to pick up the entire set and credit my account accordingly.

As you know, I have been waiting for more than six months for your shipment to arrive and would be very disappointed if I were forced to return this set.

Very truly yours,

Gentlemen:

The enclosed bill No. 6789 for 276 widgets at 79¢ each is returned herewith for correction.

I wish to call your attention to page 69 of your January 1 catalog, which quotes these at 72¢. The order was placed on the basis of this price. I assume the pricing is in error.

Please note also that 6 widgets were returned as damaged and unsuitable for our use.

We would prefer a corrected bill to a credit on this to facilitate our own record keeping.

Thank you.

Very truly yours,

Incidentally, a complaint record is one means of checking the quality of your product and service. Tabulate these—and your responses to complaints—to pinpoint failings and also to be consistent in your responses.

Response to a complaint

If you are on the other side, handling complaints made to you, the objectives are to retain the good will of the customer, to protect your employer against fraud, and to rectify any errors or omissions. Always accept a complaint as if you welcomed it. Don't show resentment. Empathize with the complainant: "I would feel the same way you do." Take some action quickly to show you have a genuine interest in the complainant. Examine, investigate, phone to check on the situation.

Remember, the complainant believes he or she is right. Begin by understanding what is bothering the writer. Acknowledge a complaint promptly. If an answer will take more than three days, merely acknowledge receipt and let the complainant know you are looking into the matter. Even if the complaint is not justified, provide, at the very least, an explanation.

Before you respond, collect all the facts, then organize them. In your first sentence acknowledge the complaint. If information is missing, ask for it, then go on to the problem. Admit the error if one has been made. Don't shift the blame. Try to solve the problem in a single letter: correspondence is costly. Show concern for any inconvenience. Be warm, concerned, simple, concise. Avoid technical language unless it is essential. Where required, enclose printed material.

Writing a complaint is principally a matter of detail. Writing a response poses two problems: how much of an adjustment to make, and how to make the adjustment so as to keep the customer happy.

When a complaint will require several days to study or investigate, an interim letter is essential even if it is only an acknowledgment. The complainer is irate. A delay in receiving an answer usually makes the situation more difficult, may cause the customer to bad-mouth the company, and sometimes leads a complainant to take some action which magnifies the problem.

If the complaint is valid, there is only a small problem:

> *Dear Mr. Manning,*
>
> You are absolutely right about the overcharge for the widgets.
>
> A new price schedule went into effect on February 1st when the price of steel was increased, but we failed to advise you of this and it is obviously unfair to pass this additional charge along to you without the usual notice.
>
> We are therefore sending a corrected invoice at the lower price and changing the quantity to reflect the return of the damaged widgets.
>
> The widgets were apparently damaged in transit, but we will pursue the adjustment on this through our shipping department.
>
> Rest assured of our policy of fairness in all of our transactions. We consider you one of our old friends and we would not under any circumstances take advantage of you.
>
> > Very truly yours,

That was easy, but:

> *Dear Mr. Manning,*
>
> You certainly have a right to be upset about the damaged widgets and the rise in the price of No. 68 widgets which you ordered. I wish I could say right off that we would credit you with the difference in price.
>
> Your request for credit for the broken widgets is easier to adjust. We have filed a claim with Brown Insurance Company which protects all our shipments and will adjust your bill accordingly.
>
> However, Mr. Manning, we have a problem on the pricing which is inherent in our whole operation. On January 2, United States Steel, our chief supplier, announced a 6 percent increase in the price of rolled steel, from which the widgets are made. They in turn were forced to agree to a wage settlement retroactive to October 1 that increases their labor cost by $6.00 a ton. This increase they immediately passed on to us, a step they had the right to do as specified in all trade agreements: "All orders are subject to price adjustment at the time of delivery." A similar clause is written into all of our schedules. This is a protection we find necessary because of the uncertainties of the marketplace. Otherwise we might be shipping widgets in March at January prices, possibly below the cost of our raw materials.
>
> I know you will understand our position. Although the price adjustment does not involve a substantial sum in your case, our total shipments in January were substantial. If we were to credit all of our customers for all price increases which reflected the increased cost of steel, it would certainly be an unfair burden on us.

Under the circumstances, I hope you will accept the shipment at the current price. However, if you feel that this is impractical for you or for any reason you do not wish to pay the new price, we will accept the return of the widgets for a full credit.

Rest assured of our continued respect for you as a customer and our desire to cooperate with you in any way possible.

Very cordially,

Dear Mr. Johnson,

Your reluctance to pay a higher than catalog price for No. 6789 widgets is understandable.

However, I do want to call your attention to the paragraph on page three of the catalog, that notes: "All prices subject to change to current prices at the time of shipment." That paragraph is standard in the trade. It is made necessary by the rapid changes in the cost of raw materials in these times. When United States Steel raised its price on rolled steel on January 2, it understandably made necessary an across-the-board price change in all our products which are made from rolled steel.

The three-week strike which precipitated the new labor agreement and the consequent price increase had left us with no inventory of rolled steel on hand. Thus all widgets in production had to be made with material purchased at the new price. This additional cost just had to be passed along to all of our customers.

I know you can understand the necessity for the price change and will accept it under the same necessity with which we were forced to accept our increased cost. If you find this unacceptable we will accept return of the widgets for full credit.

With regard to the broken widgets, there is of course no problem. A credit has been issued to you for the full amount including proportionate shipping costs.

John Brown, who covers your area, had asked me to send along his regards. He will be in Peoria next week and will stop in to talk to you.

Very cordially,

An old adage tells us, "Every challenge is an opportunity." Every complaint should be viewed as a way to solidify your relationship with a customer. If the fault is obviously yours, admit it and make the best explanation and amends you can. Never admit the complaint is widespread or even not unusual. Give graciously, not reluctantly. Then describe what procedure you plan to follow, explaining about when an answer or adjustment will be made. Do whatever you can to compensate: replace, refund, provide an extra service or courtesy.

Don't just forget about the problem. Follow up for the complainant. And follow up for the boss: find out what went wrong and tell someone who can see that it doesn't happen again.

When you have to say no you can make these points:

1. You regret it.
2. How the error occurred or why the cause of complaint arose.
3. The policy is fair.
4. The damage of a different policy would be great.
5. You respect your customer and want to keep him or her.
6. Any substitute compensation you can suggest.

Don't:

1. Dwell on the complaint. But do identify it.
2. Discuss your company's failings (or those of employees) or negligence.
3. Express anger or disappointment or surprise that the complaint was made.
4. Minimize the error on your company's part by using such expressions as "Some errors must occur in view of the volume of shipments" or by blaming inefficient workers.
5. Deny the complaint on the ground that it never happened before or it was unavoidable or that the error happened because the customer requested special service.
6. Indicate that you did or are doing a special favor or are making an adjustment grudgingly.

Dear Mr. Johnson:

As soon as your letter about the price of widgets and the damages to four of them arrived at my desk, I marched down to the billing department to see what went wrong.

I had a long conference with John Brown, who covers your territory. I'm sure you know John. He replaced Timothy Smith two years ago.

Our problem arises from the fact that steel prices jumped 6 percent on January 7 and the prices of our entire line had to be raised from 2 percent to 4 percent to absorb this increase. Otherwise our whole line would have been selling at less than cost and you can see what would have happened to the Wacky Widget Company in a short time if this continued.

Frankly the rise in steel prices was totally unexpected by us when we made up the January catalog three months ago. All the steel companies had given assurances that the price line would be held.

Apparently the cost of their labor settlement after the strike made this impossible. They raised their prices and we were forced to raise ours.

Although we always like to give adequate notice of price changes, and almost always do, we have to protect ourselves. For this reason we note at the beginning of our catalog, "All prices subject to change at time of delivery." This was one of the rare occasions in our history when we had to invoke this clause without longer notice to our customers. Believe me, Mr. Manning, we just had to. I know, that as a businessman, you will understand why.

However under the circumstances, if you feel you cannot accept the widgets at this price, we will accept them for full credit including shipping costs both ways.

Regarding the broken widgets, of course we will give you full credit. Just return them. We will also credit you for any shipping charges involved.

Sorry I can't be more helpful in this situation. But you can count on my help in anything we can do in expediting service in the future.

                                                        Very cordially,

It is relatively easy to say yes.

Dear Mr. Johnson,

Thank you for calling our attention to the error in the spelling of Namibia in the last issue of *World Geography*.

The correction has been noted in our files and a note about it will appear in the next issue.

                                                        Very sincerely,

In answering a complaint, acknowledge what is right in the complaint:

You are correct in saying . . .

Our branch manager at . . . will be glad to help you.

As in all good letters, response to a complaint should establish an empathy with the one who is complaining, but the approach should not be too obvious.

Set your mind in gear by putting yourself in the place of the "injured" party—whether you think that person is right or wrong. The complainer (usually) thinks he or she is right;

respond with the "you" attitude—from the reader's point of interest. Of course, don't overdo it. A too-much-you letter can sound hypocritical or corny.

It is sometimes even possible to go a long way in being nice:

Dear Mr. Sanders:

Thank you for bringing to our attention the loose screw in our widget. It is only because of the practical experience of people like you that we can find out about any failings in the Master Widget in actual use.

We certainly want to find the root of the problem, so if you will return the Widget we will be happy to replace the screw with a double-bolted screw. In the meantime we can check whether the failing is in your individual Widget or is a fault in the design that can be corrected in our 1981 model . . .

Very truly yours,

Dear Mr. Stone:

Our apologies for dunning you for the payment of your September bill.

Your check arrived here on October 20 and apparently crossed our bill in the mail or reached us while our letter to you was being processed.

Inasmuch as our reminder letters are keyed to a computer system, they are sent out automatically on certain dates unless the operators are advised of the payments as soon as they are entered. This is usually done within 24 hours but Friday the 13th was Good Friday so our staff was left short and many of the usual steps were not taken. This is apparently what occurred in this case.

Your check has been properly applied to your account and it is now charged only with a balance of $1,975 for October purchases.

Very truly yours,

Dear Mr. Madd:

Within the next day or so you should receive a fresh copy of the deluxe edition of *Art of the Orient* to replace the copy which had soiled pages. The enclosed $1.07 in stamps is to reimburse you for the postage in returning the original copy.

Please accept our apologies for sending you a soiled copy. Apparently some ink was spilled in the printing process and the spots escaped our inspection process.

As you probably know, *Art of the Orient* has become a best seller since you first ordered it. I know you will enjoy every page in reading it and treasure this first edition for many years.

Very sincerely,

Dear Mrs. Busby:

You were completely right in informing us of the rudeness of our salesgirl at the lingerie counter last Thursday. Beeps Department store prides itself on the courtesy and efficiency of its staff and we certainly want to know of any incident which violates our rules or hurts our reputation.

Our personnel department is making a thorough investigation and I assure you that steps will be taken to avoid a similar incident by any of our staff to any customer. Any employee who violates our standards of courtesy will be properly disciplined for the incident itself and to ensure that such discourtesies do not occur again.

Very sincerely,

Dear Mrs. Cortlandt,

I want to thank you for making light of a most difficult situation yesterday and helping us pin down a difficulty which might have been a source of much embarrassment to us.

All of us at Beeps regret the loss of your purse at the perfume counter. Whenever we have a big sale here, unscrupulous petty thieves take advantage of the bustle to filch whatever they can, expecting to escape notice in the crowd. Your alertness in noticing the loss of your pocketbook made it possible to identify the thieves and have two of them arrested.

The police feel certain they will recover the wallet that was removed from the pocketbook, but we urge you to advise companies that issued credit cards to you.

Very sincerely,

In every business there are some cranks that cannot be pacified. A really kooky letter is often best not answered. In responding to a crank letter—from someone who is continually complaining or whose complaint is entirely without foundation—it is best to be brief and firm. Remember that your response in such a situation may be the basis for a lawsuit or a complaint to a consumer or government agency at a later time.

CREDIT AND COLLECTIONS

The process of investigating, granting and maintaining credit is an integral and essential element of our system of doing business. But it does not always work smoothly. Recent regulations protect personal privacy and laws restrict the giving of personal credit information, even restrain the diligence of collectors of past due accounts. These laws complicate what you can say and how you can say it.

Collection letters should accent friendliness, fairness, and firmness. They require great persistence. Even the toughest collection letter, the end of a series, should express sorrow rather than anger.

The application for credit should provide the information you would want to have directly from the prospective debtor if you were to extend credit: principally, where he or she can be reached, what he or she earns and has in assets, and if possible, a credit experience record.

Sometimes you promote sales by soliciting credit accounts:

> *Dear Mrs. Sample:*
>
> A Sanger Harris charge account should be especially useful now, since our newest store will open soon, near you.
>
> In fact, for a limited period of time, I have tentatively reserved a Sanger Harris charge account in your name.
>
> Simply complete the attached Acceptance and return it today. I'll do the rest.
>
> As soon as your account is approved, your personal charge card will be issued in advance of our Opening . . . so you may enjoy all that's new and nice . . . at our Richland Hills location. It's near the intersection of Interstate 820 and State Highway 121-A.
>
> At Richland Hills, you will find that "if it's new, it's at Sanger Harris first." In other words, our new store will be a very special experience, for very special people . . . such as you. Assortments will be unequaled in the Sanger Harris tradition . . . and everything will be dedicated to the life-style of you, your family, and your home.
>
> A Sanger Harris charge account is so practical. It makes check cashing a breeze. When you don't want to leave home, mail and phone orders can be handled easily. And our charge customers often receive special "first choice" notice of new arrivals.
>
> Opening Day will be exciting. Now is the time to get ready. Take a few moments, please, to complete your Acceptance and return it to us today.
>
> Sincerely,

Sometimes a stray order is received for which no account has been opened. Here is how two companies handled the situation. Typically:

> We do not question your credit; we simply are not equipped to open an account for a single or only an occasional purchase. We shall be pleased to ship upon receipt of your remittance. Thank you.

Gentlemen:

Thank you for your Order 5609 for 50,000 tags. We are glad to have it.

Now, however, we find the information that is available through the regular trade channels is not complete enough to establish your company's credit. We realize a thorough credit investigation would probably indicate that your company is in good shape financially, but investigations of that kind cost quite a bit and consume considerable time.

Since you want the tags as soon as possible, I thought you might like to send us a check for $100.00 to avoid the delay that would be caused by our making a credit investigation. Or, if more convenient, send $50.00 and we will ship them "Balance due—C.O.D."

We will enter your order as soon as we receive your check; or, if you prefer, send ten or twelve credit references and your latest financial statement, if you have one.

Very cordially,

To apply for credit

Gentlemen:

Please be good enough to open a charge account in my name at Blumberger's Department Store.

I have been a resident of Gainsborough for twenty-five years and have a Master Charge card from Gainsborough National Bank, where I have both savings and checking accounts. I also have charge accounts at Blue Bell Market and Saks Fifth Avenue.

If you require references, I am known to John C. Hayes, attorney, at 6 Main Street in Gainsborough.

Very truly yours,

Collecting accounts

As long as business is run on credit, there will be some debtors who are slower in paying their bills than others, and some debtors who are so slow that special collection procedures are necessary.

The approach to collecting past due monies varies with the nature of the business and the status of the debtor. An account with a poor record must be pushed more aggressively than an account that is delinquent for the first time or one which is normally behind in payments at certain seasons.

In general a collection series begins with a simple bill with a note attached:

Please remit!

We know this bill must have been overlooked . . .

Is something wrong?

You know it isn't fair to hold back payment on our credit terms.

Most of the costs involved in filling your orders involve payrolls which must be paid each week.

We need your prompt payments to meet our payrolls.
When you delay payments past the due date, you know you jeopardize your credit.

A collection letter—in fact, the whole series of letters—must be designed to collect debts without losing customers. The letters require not only an understanding of the debtor's situation but also both tact and pressure. This is usually attained by a series of reminders with increasing emphasis and a variety of appeals ranging from "it must be an oversight" to an appeal to fairness, the creditor's needs, maintenance of credit position with the company, and, in the trade, threat of a cut-off of credit, threat of a lawsuit, and ultimately a letter from an attorney. In general, it is a good idea in each of the collection letters to indicate the amount of the debt, when the money was due, and a deadline. This may appear as a preword or in the text.

$468.50 due January 10, 1979
Payment required February 10, 1979

Inasmuch as collection letters are generally sorted with bookkeeping mail and quickly get filed with current bills, special attention-getting devices are important. These may start with a simple handwritten addendum:

"Please" or "Past due"

If these receive no attention, stock stickers with a more imperative message, a telephone call, a mailgram, even a telegram gets more attention.

First collection letters should include an itemized statement. A debtor, looking for reason to delay, will usually ask for this. Sending it immediately eliminates this excuse for delay.

These are samples from several typical series:

Please

Please note: This bill is overdue.

Is there any reason why the enclosed bill was overlooked for payment?

The enclosed duplicate bill for $198.60 was due for payment on December 30. Undoubtedly this bill has escaped your attention.
Please see that a check is sent out this week. Thank you.

                                                    Sincerely,

Reminder: Your account with us is past due. May we have a check by return mail?
Thank you.

. . . A Friendly Message
In sending you the enclosed Maturity Notice, may we also take this opportunity to suggest that, if unforeseen conditions now make it difficult for you to meet this payment, you get in touch with us before the due date, as it is possible that we may be of assistance.

Gentlemen:

As you know, our operation here is highly competitive. Our prices are based on a small margin with a quick turnover. Maintenance of this price structure assumes prompt payment of bills.

Your invoice of $81.40 has been outstanding for more than sixty days. Undoubtedly it has been overlooked.

Won't you please look into this and try to get a check out to us within the next few days.

Thank you.

                                            Very sincerely,

Dear Mr. Wilder,

We like to consider all our customers good friends. And occasionally being a good friend is embarrassing.

Have you overlooked our September statement?

We have always counted on your prompt payment. So we are taking the liberty of sending this reminder in case you have forgotten.

If there is some other reason your check is being held up, please do let us know.

Of the $327.50 on your current statement, $127.50 is now more than thirty days past due. We would appreciate it if at least this amount can be sent to us within the next few days.

                                            Very sincerely,

Dear Mr. Wilder,

Have you forgotten us?

We know there are many problems in the week's work and the less pressing papers sometimes get put at the bottom of an endless pile.

Somewhere in the pile of letters on your desk is a note from us about the $250 bill which is past due.

If your check is already being processed, forgive our bothering you. But if it is not, please dig it out and pass it along for payment.

Very sincerely,

Dear Mr. Wilder,

Please help us.

We cherish good relationships with our customers and try not to give them unnecessary pressure.

However, your account with us is now more than thirty days past due and we cannot continue to extend further credit until your account is up-to-date.

So do have your office process a check now, before you forget.

Thank you.

Very cordially,

Dear Mr. Wilder,

All of us cherish our credit rating, so it is only under the most trying circumstances that we report delinquent accounts to the Credit Bureau.

However, your unpaid balance of $3,000, is more than ninety days past due and we have had no response to our several letters.

Please help us avoid the unpleasantness of turning over the account of a good customer for collection—which we must do after 110 days unless we hear from you.

Thanks for understanding—and for your check.

Very sincerely,

At this point, if not sooner, a telephone call to the person who placed the order or to the bookkeeping department may be effective. Then more follow-ups.

Unless payment is received by ——— we will be forced to report your delinquency to the Apparel Credit Rating Agency.

Payment must be received by us not later than February 10 to avoid our placing your account in the hands of our attorneys. To avoid the expense of legal action your check must be in our hands by that date.

Regrettably we have been forced to refer your account to our attorneys for legal action.

The attorneys usually follow with one or two requests for payment. If this is not effective a summons is served.

Here are some other letters which have been effective at various stages:

Dear Mr. Wilder:

In our office every once in a while a bill manages to get hidden in the day's mail and we neglect to send a check in time.

I'm sure this happens in most offices and I assume that is what happened to our September statement.

The amount isn't large, but it is important to us to keep our accounts receivable up to date.

So won't you please do me the favor of tracing down the statement and having your bookkeeping department get out a check?

If your check is already on its way, just toss this reminder into the wastebasket and accept our apology for the unnecessary bother.

Very cordially,

To assure remitting future installments in the correct amount, please refer to your coupon book.

THANK YOU FOR YOUR RECENT PAYMENT.

In checking our records we find that you owe late charges in the amount shown because of delayed payment.

Your contract provides for a late charge when an installment is paid after the due date. We are reminding you of the amount still owing to avoid any misunderstanding later.

Please remit promptly the late charges due and ENCLOSE THIS REMINDER to assure proper credit to your account.

Dear Mr. Wilder,

It's a great feeling to be up to date!

Why not send us a check for $98.76 and see for yourself.

Cordially,

Dear Mr. Wilder:

Your July statement, with a detailed tape showing the dates and the amounts of your purchases, is enclosed.

All of the amount shown on this statement is past due. No further charges will be allowed on this account until this sum is paid.

As you know, in spite of all our bills and reminders during the past four months, your account has not been paid. We must, therefore, request that your check in full for this amount be paid without delay.

Very sincerely,

Dear Mr. Wilder,

It's a privilege to have you as a customer. Credit is the privilege we willingly extend to you as good business policy.

Both these privileges depend on both of us doing our parts: we, providing the service you require; you, making payments when they are due. The obligations for a good relationship go both ways.

Please don't jeopardize that relationship by delaying further the overdue payment of $25.00, due last month according to your credit terms.

Very sincerely,

Dear Mr. Wilder,

As a businessman I am sure you understand that we are pleased and proud to have you on our books as a customer.

You know, too, that we must collect our accounts at the agreed time if we are to continue to operate and to give the kind of service on which we pride ourselves. For this to be practical, we need your cooperation too.

Our records show that $27.50 of your account is now thirty days past due.

Won't you please see that a check goes out for at least this amount so that we too can take care of our accounts.

Thank you.

Very cordially,

Have you ever faced the problem yourself Mr. Wilder:

of asking for payment of a past due account from an old customer?

saying enough to get the check for the amount that's past due? and not offending?

Then you understand why I must write to ask you for your check to cover the $327.50 balance of your account.

If it is not already on the way, I hope you will be good enough to send it within the next few days.

Thanks.

Very sincerely,

Account_____
Date Due_____
Amount Due__
Late Charge__
Total Due_____

A few days ago we sent you a letter requesting payment of the first installment past due on your contract, but apparently it was overlooked.

The purpose of this letter is to direct your attention to the terms of your obligation to effect immediate payment of the past-due item and to pave the way for a mutually satisfactory relationship.

Please detach the first coupon from your payment booklet and mail it, or this letter, at once with your remittance for the total amount due.

Very truly yours,

Account_____
Date Due_____
Amount Due__

Recently you requested an extension on your account which we were pleased to arrange for your convenience. Naturally we understood that future payments would be met promptly when due and, consequently, the delay in payment of the above installment is disappointing.

Your contract includes a provision for late charges, which may be avoided by prompt payment.

Please send your remittance by return mail in order to avoid the need for our representative to call.

Very truly yours,

Account_____
Date & Amt.
Due_____
Late Charges__
TOTAL
PAST DUE__

Although we have written you a number of letters, neither payment nor word from you has been received. Your contract clearly provides that installments be met when due. If we are to continue to carry your account, these payments must be paid now and future payments made promptly in accordance with the terms of your agreement.

Unless you pay the amount past due immediately, our representative will take whatever steps are necessary.

Very truly yours,

Sometimes a face-to-face confrontation seems necessary. An appointment is made by telephone and confirmed:

Dear Mr. Wilder,

This is a personal appeal from one person to another.

You may remember me. It was I who interviewed you when you applied for credit at Sponsor's Department Store two years ago.

At that time your ability and willingness to pay, and the references you provided, showed that you deserved a credit account, and I was proud to approve it. I still believe in your willingness to pay your just debts and I am at a loss to understand what has happened to cause you to leave such a sum delinquent for so many months.

Was my judgment in error or is there something I should know that puts you in a different position? Perhaps if you cannot pay the balance in full, I could arrange for a series of small part payments over a period of time. If you care to call me at (212) 222-2222 I would be glad to see if there was some way in which I could help.

Certainly you must be aware that a bad credit rating would be a difficulty for you for a long time. That is why I am so reluctant to turn your name in for the routine collection procedure. This will add attorney's fees to your debt and help no one except the lawyers.

Give me a ring. I'll be glad to do whatever I can.

Very sincerely,

Gentlemen:

Registered mail is being used for this letter because something has gone wrong; somehow you must have missed our previous communications.

Now I learn that your name is to be marked "uncollected" on our credit records. You ordered a subscription some months ago but it was never paid, and is about to be canceled for nonpayment with the next issue.

Of course, your name does not belong on any list of uncollected accounts—but auditors will be auditors. And they point out that our various letters have already cost us almost the amount of the bill.

I'm writing this special letter because it is unthinkable that you intentionally ignored our bill and subsequent letters. There must be a misunderstanding; perhaps you have been away, or the letters were not called to your attention.

That being so, I hope you will accept this special letter as the sincere effort to be of service which prompted me to send it. And now that you have the facts I'll be looking for your payment by return mail in the enclosed envelope; the file is on my desk.

Cordially yours,

Dear Mr. Wilder,

It is now ten days since your payment of $125.00 was due according to the arrangement we both agreed upon to settle your account.

As you know, failure to pay any installment makes the full amount due immediately and would force us to send your account to Commercial Collection Agency for more drastic action.

Obviously we do not want to do this, for it adds to our costs. And we are certain you would not want us to do this because it would affect your credit.

We will wait until next Monday, September 27, before we take this action. So won't you try to get your check to us before that time?

Thanks—for both of us.

Very truly yours,

Sometimes installment payments help.

Dear Mr. Wilder,

Can we be of any help?

As you know, your September bill remains unpaid for ninety days, and we are concerned about it and you as an old friend.

You have been a customer of ours for a long time and we certainly don't want to lose your business if you are having temporary cash difficulties.

If you are having a cash-flow problem, may I suggest a practical way in which we may be of help.

Suppose we divide your balance of $750.00 into four parts and arrange a series of monthly payments that will take care of this over the next three months. You may prefer to give us postdated checks or notes for this or just leave our arrangement a personal understanding.

You see, we are trying to be helpful in the way we can.

If this suggestion meets the needs of your situation, just say okay on the bottom of this letter, and send us a check for one third the amount, $250.00. We'll put your account back in good standing.

Or if you have an alternate suggestion, note it and we will try to work out a suitable plan for you.

Very sincerely,

Dear Mr. Wilder,

Sorry, but this is the last letter we can send you as a debtor.

You understand, I am sure, that no business can exist if it does not collect its accounts. For the past four months we have been reminding you that your account is past due and your credit is in jeopardy.

At this time we must advise you that unless your account is brought up to date, we will place it in the hands of a collection agency with the consequent loss of your credit credibility in the trade.

So why don't you do the right thing and forward a check to us today. If you are not in a position to pay the whole amount, pay as much as you can and let us know when we may expect the balance.

Very truly yours,

P.S. If your check is not received by October 10, we will be forced, reluctantly, to put your account on a C.O.D. basis.

Dear Mr. Wilder,

Regretfully we must advise you that your line of credit with this company has been terminated.

You know, I am sure, that high costs do not permit us to extend credit much beyond the term specified on our invoices. On several occasions we have pointed out to you that a termination of your credit would result unless your account was placed in a satisfactory position.

If you will send us a check before November 1, we will reevaluate your credit rating and arrange for a line of credit for you. If we do not receive a check, we will be forced to take such legal steps as are available to us.

Very truly yours,

Dear Mr. Wilder,

Inasmuch as we have not received any payment on your account for more than sixty days, we must (reluctantly) revoke your credit privilege.

Please return to us the credit identification card issued to you. Further use of it will be without our permission.

Very truly yours,

Dear Mr. Wilder,

As you know your credit line at Norman's has been terminated. We must ask that you return your credit card immediately.

We urge you, too, to send us a check to clear up this card and reinstate your credit standing with us.

Very sincerely yours,

Sorry, Mrs. Johnson.

We have had to resort to legal action to obtain payment of the $2,500 outstanding on your account. Your failure to send us a check during the last few months in spite of all the reminders leaves us no choice.

If we receive a check from you by return mail we may still be able to avoid the addition of legal costs to your bill. So take out the checkbook now and send your payment along.

Very sincerely,

Dear Mr. Wilder,

How are you getting along? You will remember that six weeks ago we marked your records "Hold for a month," hoping that by that time you would be in a better position (in better health).

How are you doing? Please drop us a line.

Very sincerely,

After a payment plan is accepted

Dear Mr. Wilder,

The payment plan you suggested in your letter of $125.00 has been submitted to our credit manager and has been approved.

The dates on which payments are now due are listed on the attached schedule. It is important that your checks reach us on the dates indicated so that your credit standing may be maintained.

Needless to say, we are pleased that a workable arrangement could be made and we look forward to working with you in the years ahead.

Very sincerely,

Branch_____
Account No.__
Date Due_____
Amount Due_
Late Charges_
Total Due_____

Although several reminders have been sent you, we have not received payment of this past-due installment and another installment will become due in a few days.

It is most important that you fulfill the terms of your contract which call for prompt payment of all installments. Therefore, we urge that you pay two installments without delay.

Your failure to do so will necessitate a personal call by our representatives. This can be avoided if you forward your remittance at once.

Very truly yours,

Dear Mr. Wilder,

This letter calls for a check from you.

The check we'd like most to see is one for $376.48 which will clear up the past due balance on your account.

But if, for some reason, you can't send a check, please check one of the boxes below so that we will know what we may expect.

☐ A check will be sent to you
☐ Next week
☐ Next month
☐ A check is on its way
☐ A check for part payment will go out today. Will send additional payments next week.
☐ There is an error in this account. Please have your bookkeeper call me.
☐ I am enclosing a postdated check.

Dear Mr. Wilder,

Thank you for returning the credit card issued to you.

As you know, a balance of $125.00 remains on your account for purchases made as long as six months ago.

Would you care to make an arrangement to pay this sum in equal installments over a six-month period beginning October 1? This will avoid our taking legal action which would be a nuisance to both of us.

Very truly yours,

When payment is received

Dear Mr. Wilder,

The mail this morning brought the good news of your payment on account.

It always gives me good feelings to know I have saved a customer for the company and hopefully a good friend.

All of us at Stanhope's look forward to the clearing up of your account and the expectation of renewed credit for you.

Very sincerely,

Dear Mr. Wilder,

It is a pleasure to tell you that your credit status has been reinstated in accordance with the arrangement for payment of your past due accounts. We hope that this signals a return of your permanent good credit standing and our continuing business relationship.

Very sincerely,

In "can't pay" situations

Dear Mr. Wilder:

We are sorry indeed to learn from your letter of your unemployment (illness, misfortune). Hopefully this situation will be only temporary and you will soon be at work (well, in a better position) again.

Under the circumstances, we are pleased to postpone the payments on your account (car, furniture, purchases) for thirty days. If, at that time, your situation has not improved, we will try to work out another arrangement for payment.

Your records have been marked to indicate this so that there will be no reflection on your credit rating.

We extend our best wishes for your efforts (good health, good luck). In any case, please let us hear from you in four weeks.

Very cordially,

Response to collection letters

When you are on the receiving end of a collection letter, you will usually (1) want more time to pay or (2) want to pay less than the amount billed.

Usually it is best to respond in a friendly manner. A partial payment is an indication of good intentions and usually helps stave off drastic action.

Dear Mr. Collector,

Enclosed is a check for $100 to be applied to my account.

As you probably know, we have had serious production problems in our area and cash has been rather short.

The situation should right itself within the next few months and I will continue to make payments as frequently as I can.

Very sincerely,

Dear Mr. Collector:

You probably know that I have been a customer at Goodbys for many years and during all this time I have paid my bills regularly on time.

Unfortunately our industry has been in a recession during the last six months due to the strike in the steel industry. With the strike over, I am sure business will pick up again.

However, the situation has left us short of cash at this time.

Will you please bear with us for several weeks (months) until the cash flow returns to normal?

Rest assured that we will make every effort to send payments on account as the situation improves.

Thank you for your patience.

Very truly yours,

If the situation has deteriorated you might start with an apology:

Please excuse my delay in responding to your bills and letters. Our situation here has been so uncertain that I really did not know what kind of commitment I could make.

When you are disputing the bill:

I am returning herewith your January 17 bill for 24 dozen Whatzits and the February 1 statement.

The bill is in error on two scores: the price agreed upon was $6 per dozen, not the $8 charged. And only 20 dozen Whatzits were delivered of which ten were delivered broken.

Please be good enough to send us a corrected bill and statement so that these may be processed for payment.

Thank you.

Very truly yours,

Chapter 4

About Your Job

GETTING A JOB

Letters to help sell yourself

On the average, a worker under thirty-five goes job hunting once every year and a half. For the worker over thirty-five, it's once every three years. And experts estimate that the average worker today will change careers—not just jobs—three to five times in his or her lifetime.

Many of us find that the most difficult letters to write are those which deal with selling ourselves. We are brought up with the inhibition of modesty and there is some element of shyness in all of us.

So the first thing you should do when you have to write about yourself is to get out of your skin, view yourself objectively. Better still, view yourself in terms of the buyer.

You are after a job. Pin it down: you are after a certain job.

You have compiled a package: letter, résumé, references, perhaps exhibits. Now evaluate. Put yourself in the prospective employer's place. Read the package and imagine what the competition is like. Perhaps this will give you an idea of how to be more competitive, more effective. Ask yourself: What is the employer looking for? What do I have that satisfies his or her needs? How can I sell what I have to meet those needs?

The employer is looking for someone who can (1) help him make more money; (2) do well a job that is part of his normal operation, without causing problems; (3) provide new ideas that will help sales, cut costs, or improve the product; or (4) smooth out one or more operational problems.

When you want a job, you usually want it now. Your time is very perishable; when time has passed, the income is lost but your living expenses continue. So act quickly. Don't wait for the notice on your present job to expire or for the long delayed vacation, or for a time to get the feel of things. Send the applications into channels quickly so that time, to some extent, will be working for you.

Get off letters—typewritten or well-processed, filled-in letters—to those you think can use your services. (A filled-in letter is processed except for the typewritten name, address, and salutation.)

Get off letters to your friends who are in a position to use your services or who know others who can use your services—but don't count on them.

Approaches

There are five basic approaches to getting a job:

1. Seek prospects by placing situation-wanted advertisements, then write to those who respond.
2. Register with employment agencies or "headhunters."
3. Respond to advertisements in the newspapers.
4. Write unsolicited letters to prospective employers.
5. Write (also call) friends, acquaintances, and friends of friends.

To find a prospective employer

Place ads in the situations wanted columns of trade papers and the large help-wanted advertising media:

> Creative designer with experience in ad, magazine, and newspaper production available September 1. Box 47.

> Marketing and market research graduate, MBA, with proved creativity seeks challenge with new or nonmoving product or service.

Agencies and headhunters

Find out who the headhunters are in your field. Headhunters are specialists who find talent for large employers. A list of them is published by Consultant News, Templetown Road, Fitzwilliam, N.H. 03447. Ask at trade associations, among those who work in the field, for the best in your trade.

Some employment agencies also specialize. Find the ones that specialize in the type of talent and experience you have to offer. Some agencies are associated with technical or professional groups. Some are connected with universities. Register wherever you can.

In almost every case you will be called upon for a résumé of your education and experience. This should always be accompanied by a letter that adds a more personal touch to your résumé. (See below.)

Answering help-wanted ads

Responding to an ad puts you in direct competition with others seeking the same job, perhaps one or two, perhaps 200.

So your response has to attract the attention of the prospective employer, who will probably only scan the responses on first reading. Typing the letter helps. Using good stationery, good layout, also helps. But an attention-getting beginning is very important:

> If I told you I was the best typist in town, you would probably think I was boasting. And perhaps there are better typists. But I have ranked at the top of typing classes at Brandeis High School for the past four years and I have won three school contests.

> For ten years I have been solving problems in accounting academically—with some fine grades for my answers. Now I would like very much to solve some real problems for you, Mr. Sidney.

> Results . . .
> That is what you have to expect from your salesmen.
> That is what I produced for ———— and I think I can produce for you.

Follow-up telephone call

If you have not received a response, where you know the prospective employer, it is good practice to phone ten days to two weeks after the letter was sent and ask whether the letter was received, if any additional information would be helpful, or if any action was probable on it. At that time, it is important to be pleasant, casual, helpful, and sincere. If your voice is pleasant, your diction correct, and you know what you are going to say, you may be able to get some extra attention for your application, to move it from the bottom of the pile—or at the very least to learn that there is no chance of a job in that direction.

Occasionally you may find that your letter did not mention a key experience the employer is seeking.

> "I'm sorry. We were really looking for someone who has a knowledge of music."
>
> "But I played the trumpet in the school band for five years."

The probability is that you will not get to speak to the employer himself, only to a secretary. Don't drag out the conversation. Try to find out what you called to find out and bring your conversation to a close.

It is a good idea, before you call, to summarize in writing what you want to find out, what you are going to say, and how you will respond to some obvious questions: for what job, when you wrote, to whom, etc.

Experience

The first job presents the greatest difficulty when you are asked about your work experience. Everyone has some experience. It may come from school activities, especially extracurricular activities. It may come from summer jobs or after-school work. It may come from hobbies, special courses, or special interests. Here is how a new graduate can handle the problem:

> Experience? Inasmuch as I was graduated from Gainsborough High School only last month, my experience has been limited to school activities.
>
> As treasurer of the Gainsborough Dramatic Society, I kept a full set of records which were periodically audited by a member of the faculty. I arranged for the dramatic group to travel to Boston for the annual festival, reserving bus and hotel facilities and providing for feeding the group while in Boston.

Here's another approach:

> I DON'T HAVE MUCH EXPERIENCE BUT MY POTENTIAL RANKS 25 PERCENT ABOVE AVERAGE.

Everybody has to start somewhere.

Frankly I haven't had much experience beyond mowing lawns for neighbors and running errands for the town drugstore.

But my records at school are outstanding and last time my school had a testing program, I rated in the top 10 percent, with a score 25 percent above the national average.

All that goes to prove is that I can learn quickly and do a job that's required of me better than most people of my age.

I will be graduating next June 25 and I do want to start work in a job where I can be useful, learn, improve, and progress.

Everyone tells me that your company is the one that offers the best opportunity for this and that some openings occasionally occur during this season.

If you would like to have an intelligent, ambitious young career man in your organization, will you be good enough to consider me for the job?

Very sincerely,

Don't mention salary in your first letter—or really until you have to. A demand for too high a salary will cut you out; too low will lessen your apparent worth.

Don't appeal for sympathy.

But *do* be concise, use an upbeat tone, give your qualifications, but not in detail (leave that for the résumé), tell what you think you can contribute to the prospective employer's company. Here are some sample letters responding to help-wanted ads.

JJ 1000
New York Times

Gentlemen:

My last boss, J. J. Gonzalez, who was the leading merchant on Livonia Street, thought I was a crackerjack comptroller and says so in his reference.

However, Mr. Gonzalez has retired so I am responding to your advertisement in Sunday's *Times*.

I offer six years of challenging experience in a medium-sized department store with all the accounting problems of a big one. I was the person everyone turned to for dealing with costs, pricing, government regulations, credit, collections, and a host of other areas—a larger organization might have three or four experts. [Etc.]

Gentlemen:

Some secretaries are "gal Fridays" capable of handling all the miscellaneous details that come into an office. Some are just secretaries and sometimes even just stenographers.

I've been "gal Friday" at ABC Corporation for four years, serving under first, the comptroller, then the president of the Corporation. If you knew Joseph J. Johnson, the president of ABC, you would know that no slouch could be his executive secretary unless she was a pretty good "gal Friday" five days a week, and not a few evenings too. [Etc.]

J 100
New York Times

Gentlemen:
    Will Rogers once said, "I never met a man I didn't like." May I misquote him and say, "I never met a man who didn't like me."
    I'm a genial salesman of anything for the consumer market, with eight years of sales experience behind a counter, door to door, and on the road.
    For the past three years I have been selling white washing widgets for the Black Star Widget Co., covering the southeastern United States. During that time I opened 427 retail outlets for Black. My earnings have been averaging $17,000 a year.
    Now I'd like to take on a new line. [Etc.]

Unsolicited letters

Unsolicited job-seeking letters may be sent to any one or all of the companies you would like to work for. When you write to a large company, write to a top official. The personnel manager will eventually get your letter, but coming from "upstairs" may get it some special attention. At any rate, you will have a chance to make a point with an important official. But, of course, don't write to the president of a company if you are looking for his job.

Make up your list of prospects carefully from trade directories, trade papers, the *Wall Street Journal,* and the general newspapers. Watch particularly for personnel changes and companies that are not doing as well as last year, where changes are likely to occur, or companies doing well that may be expanding.

Almost every field has a directory with information that indicates the officers and the size of the company. In addition there are general national directories of manufacturers, retailers, etc. (Thomas Register), credit directories (Dun & Bradstreet), advertisers' directories (Standard Register), and financial directories (Standard & Poor's) which can provide leads.

Mail your letters on Monday so that they are not received on the difficult mail days (Mondays and Fridays).

Your approach should be different if your letter is unsolicited from what it is if it is in response to an advertisement.

When you respond to a help-wanted ad the probability that there is a job open is great. But it faces competition with many other job seekers. Here the attention-getting device has to be close to the point, designed not merely to get attention but to pull your letter out from the many that are seeking the same interview. It must not only call favorable attention to itself, it must also do part of the selling job.

On the other hand, an unsolicited letter is fighting for attention against the day's mail and other calls on the manager's time. A strong headline or attention getter in a personal letter will be read. The big odds against it are the slim probability of a job being open just when the letter arrives.

In an answer to a want ad, you might, thus, emphasize what you have done and how you are better than other applicants:

> I cut the traffic costs for Irving Smith Company 25 percent in two years.
>
> I think I can save money for your company too. That is why I decided to respond to your ad in the morning's *New York Times* as soon as I saw it.
>
> Like everyone else I get satisfaction in doing a job well, and this is one job I think I can do better than just 'well.' [Etc.]

For an unsolicited letter, you might put the emphasis on what you can do specifically for the company, something they perhaps didn't think needed doing:

> I think I can save the John Brown Company 25 percent on its traffic costs.

Here are some other samples of unsolicited letters.

> *Dear Mr. Bossinger:*
> There are some people who can sell anything to anybody, I'm told.
>
> Right now I wish I were one of them because I want very much to sell you on the fact that I can sell your widgets. I'm sure I can.
>
> Up to this time my selling experience has been limited to selling

subscriptions door to door, which I must tell you is about as challenging and instructive experience in selling as anyone can get.

I didn't make a fortune at this, but I was able to earn two hundred dollars a week in commissions while I traveled with a crew from town to town.

I like selling.

I like your product and the reputation of your company.

May I talk to you about merging my two likes into a career for myself and additional profits for your company.

Thank you.

Very sincerely,

Dear Mr. Jones,

It was only yesterday as I was passing the J.J. Store that the thought occurred to me that one element in my experience would be particularly useful to your company. I would appreciate it if you would bear it in mind in selecting your new personnel manager.

Last year, when I was in charge of personnel for the Season Transport Company, we found that some personnel-selection tests were excellent for forecasting the performance of road men. However, we found that it was not those who did best in the test that were best for us, but those who ranked around the middle. The high rankers generally left us within three months because they found routine selling too boring.

As a result I worked out a few formulas which I think can be applied to locating and selecting your road men. I would like very much to share this information with you. [Etc.]

ADMINISTRATIVE ASSISTANT
Experienced in advertising, publicity, particularly in the field of hardware and appliances. Good writer. Willing to assume responsibility, travel if necessary. Salary commensurate with ability to produce for your company.

Mr. James Jaslyn
President
Whatsis Company
222 Mark Street
New York, N.Y. 10000

Dear Mr. Jaslyn:

This letter is in response to the ad you didn't run. But I am reasonably sure you would be interested in finding a suitable candidate for such a job.

If you had run the ad you would have had the enclosed résumé as a response. I would have written because I believe I have the ability to more than carry my weight on such a job in your firm—to produce good public relations and to relieve you of many details and save you much valuable time.

When you have a personal contact:

Mr. Sidney Dover
77 Warren Street
New York, N.Y. 11007

Dear Mr. Dover:

Your cousin, Sandy Delaney, suggested that I write to you because she felt we could be mutually useful.

I am writing to suggest a meeting with you to discuss what I think I can accomplish for your company as chief financial officer or controller.

As chief financial officer of an undercapitalized, growing company, I developed a cash-management program that so increased our average cash balances that we were able to repay a large bank loan prior to maturity.

With the three companies with which I have worked, I have:

Developed a financial reporting system for a multidivisional company with sales in excess of $105,000 that projected the implications for the future of variances from budgets.

Negotiated lines of credit and bank loans and represented my company during the preparation of a listed convertible debenture issue.

Directed the conversion to a large-scale computer operation within costs budgeted and time scheduled.

Investigated potential acquisition candidates, recommended action, negotiated to consummation, and assisted the new entity in conforming with corporate policies and procedures.

Created a comprehensive accounting manual for a growing, diversified company.

My education includes a B.S. in accounting from New York University and tax studies at Columbia University.

I would be pleased to meet with you to expand on how my experience can have a positive impact on your organization.

Sincerely yours,

What if you have no experience? Unable to get employment because he lacked experience, a young man placed this notice in a New York newspaper. (As reported by *Moneysworth*.)

Inexperience is the most valuable thing a man can bring to a new job. A man of inexperience, you see, is forced to rely upon imagination and verve, instead of timeworn routine and formula. If you're in the kind of business which is penalized by routine and formula thinking, then I'd like to work for you. Inexperience is my forte. I'm 25 years old and have the ability to become enthusiastic and emotionally involved in my work. My grandfather bets me I'll lose my disregard for experience after ten years on a challenging job. Need a man to fill a challenging job?

The résumé

The résumé is the heart of your application. Unless you are seeking a job in a broad-spectrum field where you may wish to adapt your résumé or have several résumés accentuating different facets of your experience, it is usual to have the résumé made (offset or printed) in quantity, handsomely laid out in substantial (but not overwhelming) detail, beautifully typed with headlines and with material that emphasizes your accomplishments. (Your basic pitch, however, is for a personal interview and it is best presented in a special letter, personally addressed, adapted, and signed.)

The résumé is your dossier. It will have to carry the weight of your argument but only after your letter has won a reading for it. It should answer all the basic questions about yourself, especially address, phone number, experience, education, and skills.

Start with a chart, then make a rough draft. Try to indicate what you accomplished, or at least what kind of work you did, not merely what jobs you held. Titles are not important because different enterprises title their employees differently. (Some employers will make you a vice-president in lieu of a ten-dollar raise.)

If you have a stock résumé and it seems suitable, use it. But often there is something in your background which is particularly relevant to the job you are seeking. Don't hesitate to (1) rewrite the résumé even if it's a typing chore; or (2) make mention of it in your letter; or (3) type it in, even if the résumé is not as neat as it otherwise might be.

References: With the use of copying machines there is a temptation to put a lot of material—including references—into your letters.

Don't! A letter and a résumé are all that is necessary until you get an interview—unless, of course, you have a letter of introduction or something very dramatic.

The problem with references is basically that they seldom carry weight unless the reader knows the writer. Most references are given by request. They never say anything bad. (You would not show them if they did.) Everyone knows people give them casually.

However, references are good to have, especially if you can write them yourself (you often can if the giver is a friend). And they sound sincere. They should be specific and unequivocal. They should give an instance of your good work if they are making a point. If possible, have them addressed to a target employer, preferably one high in a company where you are seeking a job.

Remember, if you are responding to an ad for a position that has many applicants your résumé will, at first reading, get a ten-second scanning. It has to be among those pulled out for a second glance.

The word "experience" on the standard résumé tends to induce an applicant to write:

> 1974–1978: Worked for ABC Corporation as superintendent of sales records.

What an employer really wants to know is what you did, particularly what you did that was beyond routine duty.

> 1974–1978: As superintendent of sales records for ABC Corporation I recorded the results of each reported interview by 82 salesmen, analyzed the prospects of a sale for follow-up by mail for each of our products, and developed a direct-mail approach to supplement salesmen's efforts for renewal of sales and initial sales of a line of nine products.

A résumé is usually best presented on white twenty-four-pound bond paper, typewritten (or reproduced to appear typewritten) on one or two pages, organized with headings for personal status, accomplishments, experience, education, references, any other factors you may wish to include. Basically it must show your name, address, phone number, or other most convenient means of reaching you, age and background for the job you want. In many situations it should include a place of birth, marital status, appearance, military status, career objectives. Thus, applicants for a security position should indicate height and weight. Applicants for a position dealing with black, Hispanic, or other minorities might feel their origins give them added advantages. Sometimes being single or married indicates availability for travel or residence abroad.

The key paragraphs, of course, have to do with your accomplishments, education, and experience. Select one, two, or three of those that appear to have most relevance to the job and expand on these factually.

Here are a few typical résumés.

John J. Manor
50 Doe Street
Teaneck, N.J. 07666
(201) 666-6666

PERSONAL
   Date of birth: October 6, 1949
   Height: 5'8"
   Marital status: Single
   Weight: 172
   Health: Excellent

EDUCATION
   Rutgers University, New Brunswick, New Jersey, 1 year Liberal Arts
   Columbia University, New York, B.A. (Economics) Top quarter class
   Fairleigh Dickinson College, Teaneck, New Jersey
   Courses: Marketing, securities analysis
   Earned 50 percent total school expenses

MILITARY
   Enlisted January 1962—USAF Res.—honorable discharge, February 1968

BUSINESS EXPERIENCE
1975–present—Sandy Clothes, Inc., 380 Connolly Ave., Cleveland, Ohio. Annual sales $500,000. Department and specialty stores of apparel in Washington, D.C., area. Created marketing programs for entire East Coast, including creations of advertising programs and fashion shows.
1973–1975—Ideal Toy Corp., 200 Fifth Avenue, New York, N.Y. Created point-of-purchase promotion, handled customer relations for major N.Y.C. and suburban market, R. H. Macy, Gimbels, E. J. Korvettes, Bambergers.
1971–1973—Williams & Hoan, Inc., Grand Avenue, Englewood, N.J. Sales for large Buick, used-car, auto-lease agency while attending college.

1969–1971—U.S. Post Office, Bogota, N.J.—full- and part-time clerk-carrier while attending college.

SUPPLEMENTARY DATA

Active in extracurricular activities in high school and college. Student council, varsity football, baseball, student publications. Addressed groups up to 3,000 associates and students in marketing conferences and promotional activities.

Won four prizes and achievement awards in marketing conferences sponsored by General Motors, American Motors, and Sandy Clothes, Inc.

John H. Nathan
444 Prospect Street
Denver, Colorado 10000

Phone: 123-4567
210-7654

Education: B.A. Political Science, Pueblo University, 1976, Overall average: 3.8, major average: 3.65

Academic Honors: Dean's List; Honors Study (one semester Labor Relations, one semester Political Publicity); Pi Gamma Mu (National Social Science Honor Society); Who's Who Among Students at American Universities and Colleges.

College Activities: Elected Student Government Association Executive Vice-President ('76–'77) and Executive President ('75–'76). Activities included: Participation in planning the Denver Center's $14 million budget; participation in interview and selection of President for the Colorado Center; University committee work on: Curriculum, financial aid, space allocation, counsel evaluation. Assisted in administration of student government programs including: freshman orientation, concerts, drama festival, campus bookstore, student recruitment project, and other projects involving student-faculty cooperation. Newspaper clippings are available for these projects on which I worked.

Other Experiences: Director of Public Relations for the 1975 Pueblo Democratic campaign for mayor. Duties included: Writing press releases, arranging preparation of some campaign literature, arranging press luncheons for reporters from local weeklies, arranging major press conferences.

Conceived and prepared material for direct-

> mail campaign for Colorado University, in-
> cluding copywriting, layout and paste-up, edi-
> ting, dealing with typesetters and printers,
> and mailing.
>
> Conceived and prepared successful direct-
> mail campaign for Colorado Skiing Society
> promotion.
>
> Delegate to Colorado Civic Council for Cit-
> izens for a Better Pueblo. Represented pro-
> jects in various civic groups.
>
> References will be furnished upon request.

The résumé is valuable not only to your prospective employer, but also to you. It helps you to organize your own thoughts about who you are, what you have to offer, and where you want to go. That is essentially what a prospective employer wants to know. So first figure them out for yourself.

Some résumés start with "Vocational Goal." This is essentially a "me" attitude approach, but inasmuch as your prospective employer may well want to know more about how you think, this has its place.

> Vocational Goal: I enjoy helping people and I think I have special
> talents in making myself liked. That is why I think I will be most
> successful in social work with adults.
>
> Vocational Goal: I look forward to being an effective salesman and
> eventually a sales manager because I feel my talents lie in finding
> the right approach to people and finding the right uses of a product
> for each situation. I am particularly interested in the field of
> machine manufacture.
>
> Vocational Goal: With my training and experience in accounting,
> writing, public relations both in college and summer work, I believe
> I have the qualifications for a helpful administrative assistant, with
> particular emphasis on customer and stockholder relations, par-
> ticularly in the field of retailing.

The **functional résumé** is a more direct approach to the prospective employee in terms of what he or she is looking for than the **accomplishment résumé.** It emphasizes even more than the accomplishment approach your qualifications rather than your background.

John Hayward Brown
2222 Winthrop Avenue
Tenafly, N.J. 07668

Telephone: (201) 777-7818

Vocational Goal

Financial officer or administrative assistant with duties in finance, accounting, controls, and/or management where I may utilize studies and experiences in investments, auditing, accounting, and public relations.

Background

Graduate of New York University School of Commerce with one year of graduate courses at the School of Business Administration, specializing in accounting with a view to taking the CPA examinations next March. Undergraduate activities as a member of the Student Council, with extensive work publicizing student activities. Part-time work in accounting for small-business operations in the fields of general retailing, dress manufacturing, and toy jobbing, including preparation of all employer tax returns and income tax returns for proprietors. In some instances, I was responsible for handling customer complaints and purchase negotiations.

Capabilities

Accounting: Capable of setting up, supervising and auditing a complete accounting system with proper controls for a moderately complicated business operation, and understanding where accounting problems exist that may require more expert opinion.

Public Relations: Capable of handling customer and employee problems, both in person and by correspondence.

Purchasing: Knowledgeable in most trade procedures and customs, particularly in retailing and in the toy industry.

Administrative Skills: As a student leader I believe I gained competence in dealing with and influencing people, organizing activities, and gaining the confidence of those with whom I dealt.

Education

B.S. in accounting; one year of graduate work in banking and finance. Graduate of New York City High School of Science (for selected students). Member of Alpha Lambda Phi honorary scholarship fraternity. Editor senior yearbook. Public relations chairman, Debating Society. Delegate to National Student Conference in Dallas, 1974. Appointed to draft resolution regarding student cooperation with faculty in university administration.

Personal Data

Born June 8, 1956, in New York City. Single, 5′6″, weight 150 pounds.

After you have finished a résumé, edit it several times on different days. Then have someone who has experience in hiring people go over it for an employer's viewpoint. Don't be ashamed to make changes.

When you are satisfied with the result, make up a hundred copies and send them, with a note, to a hundred people you'd like to work for and see how they respond. You may get some hints from the questions some ask or the comments they make. If the responses indicate that changes are advisable, make them. Then shoot the works to every prospective employer.

The accompanying letter

The covering letter should be correct in spelling, form of address, and form. Make sure you have referred to an enclosed or attached résumé. Make sure you conclude asking for something:

44 Edgewood Avenue
Painted Post, N.Y.
March 5, 1979

Mr. Joseph Employer
President
Automatic Widget Company
6666 Now Street
Cincinnati, Ohio 77777

Dear Mr. Employer:

The trade grapevine carries the message that you have a fine line for the fall season and an opportunity to promote it successfully in several new territories in which I have worked.

As you can see from the enclosed résumé, I know the Eastern Seaboard area well and I have had extensive experience promoting new products to hardware jobbers. By any reckoning I have produced an outstanding record in opening new accounts.

I think I can do the same kind of job for you.

May I drop in to talk to you personally when I pass through Cincinnati on my route about March 14? I think an association will be pleasant and profitable for both of us.

Thanks.

Very cordially,

225 West 86th Street
New York, N.Y. 10024
(212) 744-6766
March 5, 1979

X 4777
New York Times
239 West 43rd Street
New York, N.Y. 10036

Gentlemen:

Speed. Accuracy. Reliability.

These are three aspects of my record that previous employers will vouch for and which I can offer to you as an employer.

This letter, for example, will take me six minutes to type at my speed of 120 words a minute, and my stenography is on an equal level.

As you can see from the enclosed résumé, I have had four years of heavy clerical experience in firms that have high standards in hiring and production. I think I can meet your standards as well.

May I see you and show you just what I can do?

Thank you.

Very sincerely,

The follow-up letter

So you wrote asking for a job—and there's no answer. Do you just forget about it? Not if you really want the job. You send a follow-up letter.

Assuming your letter is somewhere in pile C on the employer's desk, and you haven't heard in ten to twenty days (even six weeks is not unusual) you might try a follow-up—assuming you know who the prospective employer is. Don't hesitate to write even if you know others have been called for an interview. All you have to lose is a bit of time.

Dear Mr. Sandown:

If your desk is at all like that of most businessmen I have met, it has a large stack of memoranda and letters that have to be taken care of today—or sooner.

I know that the letter I sent to you last month offering my services to help out in your shipping department is not among the most important, but it may be that it has been filed away or passed on to someone else who may have misplaced it.

May I impose on you for a minute to remind you about myself? And if you do not have my last letter handy, to refresh your memory with the enclosed copy.

I sincerely feel that I can be helpful to your organization and I think you will find my services of real value.

Yours truly,

The interview

After you have survived the screening process—meeting specifications, perhaps a preliminary interview, perusal of your application blank, aptitude tests, checking of references—the crux of your opportunity lies in the evaluation interview. This may be one of three types: a direct interview, an indirect interview, or an evaluation interview.

During a direct interview, the interviewer fires direct questions at the candidate. He seeks basic facts about experience, attitudes, background.

An indirect interview is a free exchange and aims to get the candidate to talk spontaneously about anything, to find out more about the character of the candidate.

The evaluation interview is an exploration of a candidate's background. The questions follow no pattern. The candidate tells his own story in his own words. The interviewer does only 15 percent to 20 percent of the talking.

If you get any interview, you have increased your chances of getting the job substantially. You are now in direct competition—on a face-to-face basis—with perhaps half a dozen others.

Often the interview is over a lunch table to promote a relaxed atmosphere. Stay calm. (It helps if you are well prepared and confident.) Try to figure out what questions you will be asked and write out the answers. This will be particularly helpful if you are nervous. Dig up samples of your work. Check out the clothes you plan to wear and make sure you are well groomed. And don't be late or rushed when you have the date. If you are going to be late phone ahead.

Most interviews start with easy questions so that you can get your bearings:

Have you worked before? When? Did you like the job? Why? Did you enjoy school? What subjects did you like best? What do you plan to do as a career?

or just:

> Tell me about yourself. If you were in my place, why would you hire you?
>
> What things do you like to do? What do you think is your greatest strength? Or weakness?
>
> Think of a teacher in school you liked. How do you think he would describe you?
>
> What was the greatest problem you ever faced in life? What did you do about it?
>
> If you were hired for this job, what would you think you would like about it? Dislike about it?
>
> What qualities do you think your boss should have?

Know when to ask questions. It's not your place to start the conversation, so let the interviewer take the lead. Don't be too aggressive about selling yourself; respond to the leads given you by the interviewer. It's quite all right to say, "I'd have to think that over before answering it, Mr. Jones." An interviewer may ask an odd question for many reasons—to test your poise, to see whether you think about questions or just babble an answer, and just to liven up a dull morning. If you suspect a question was asked in fun, smile in your have-to-think-that-over answer.

At a large concern, your chances may hinge on something that seems very impersonal to you: a questionnaire, a checklist, or some other printed evaluation form sent out by a supervisor and then up to another executive who makes the decisions. Don't be surprised at this impersonal approach. Many interviewers believe they will be in a better position to avoid conflict with equal-opportunity laws if they justify personnel decisions by creating uniform appraisal standards from tests or interviews.

Remember, many managers feel threatened by their more creative employees. Because managers don't know how to cope with people who are different, they tend to surround themselves with people who are compatible and immediately dub someone they don't communicate well with a maverick.

Interviews are a means of communication useful for many purposes in addition to selection for a job. They are involved in college selection and placement, work appraisal, discipline hearings, as part of an examination. In fact, interviews are involved each time you meet someone. Essentially the same principles apply in each case.

Sometime during an interview the job seeker will have an opportunity to ask questions. Before you go into the meeting make a list of the things you want to know. If it is a job, what are the salary, promotion opportunities, learning opportunities? Will you get out to meet people? Where will you work? What medical insurance is provided? pension plan? other fringe benefits?

If these are not indicated during the interview, you will want to have them in mind when you are called on to ask them. But try to be tactful. Remember your questions, too, will influence the interviewer. If you are asking about fringe benefits, put the question tactfully:

> I know it is not of prime importance but . . .
> My present employer provides . . . which can be important. Does your company have medical insurance coverage?

Of course, if the job is on a level where previous experience is required, the questioning would tend to revolve around the experience.

Remember that the interviewer has read your letter and résumé and may even have other information about you. Don't lie. Refer to your résumé if you find it advantageous. Don't get angry or indignant.

Assure yourself before you go that you can handle this job. Don't wander in your answers unless you think the interviewer is really interested in what you are saying. (But an anecdote to make a point is fine.) Don't feel rushed.

An application blank may be handed to you sometime during the interview. Make sure you have your own pen. Read each question carefully before filling it in so that your application will look neat. Read it over to make sure you have completed all the answers and sign the form if it says to. The interviewer will judge a great deal about you by the way you fill out this business form.

Taking some tests may be part of the interview. Interviewers allow for nervousness and lack of experience. You may be given some psychological tests with questions that may sound silly to you. Answer them as sensibly and accurately as you can; don't spend too much time over one question; the tests are often timed section by section.

If a job is offered to you, you don't have to make a decision on the spot.

> Thank you very much. Can I sleep on this?
> If it's all right with you, I would like to let you know in a few days. Would Wednesday be all right?

Always end with thanks to the interviewer—even if you think he has been very nasty and you have no chance of getting the position you seek. This is especially important if you have been recommended by someone.

HIRING

The interviewer

The interviewer in all instances has to be a "salesperson," able to ask the right questions, and more important, to interpret the responses correctly. This usually requires considerable training, both in evaluating candidates and in understanding the qualities needed for the job. He or she should understand how to listen and ask questions at the right time to bring out the details that must be known for an evaluation.

Avoid being patronizing or getting too personal in a business situation. Ask the interviewee to face you. Soften your questions with words like "might," "perhaps," "a bit of."

Then bridge over to the subject at hand: "Let me tell you what we are doing at Whatzit Whatzits."

The interviewer should try to put the interviewee at ease from the beginning and keep him or her at ease. The first questions should be routine, followed by questions that allow the interviewee to talk freely.

> Which teacher, job, hobby do you like most?

Then the interviewee should be kept talking.

> That seems interesting. Tell me more about that.
> That was good. Very good.
> I see what you mean.
> That's quite important.

A nod of the head or a smile is also effective.

If a candidate finds an area difficult to discuss, the interviewer produces a "laundry list question"—suggesting some answers from which to choose:

> Tell me about the things you like to do, your favorite courses, the books you read, the plays you have seen.
>
> Another type of question is the "double-edge":

> Do you think you are good at selling ideas or do you prefer administrative work in selling?

Small talk is an important element in communication, not for what is communicated, but for its effect in breaking the ice, getting through the tension of a first meeting. As an icebreaker it should last two to five minutes.

The standard approach is a question:

> What do you think about this weather?
> How do you like living in New York?
> Did you go for what President Carter said yesterday about ———?

The questions should be phrased so that they do not lend themselves to a yes or no answer. If you are in control of an interview, discuss each point fully before you go on to the next area.

In an interview it is a good idea to make a calculated pause to allow the other person to continue the thought you have opened up. But not for too long. Keeping the other party talking is a plus.

An interviewer—particularly one interviewing for job placement or admission to an institution—should be aware of the federal and state laws and executive orders concerning discrimination because of race, color, religion, sex, age, or national origin, both on interviewing and on testing.

Departing employees

You are not required by law or any union regulation to provide a recommendation for a departing employee. But if your company customarily does give such letters, you must also give one to an employee who had previously filed charges for violation of the Equal Employment Opportunity Act or of an unfair labor practice, nor can you refuse to give or provide such a recommendation to a minority person.

When a conversation must be closed, indicate that you are

on a major project and "Let's talk more about this sometime." Direct the conversation to something *you* are interested in. Start doing another job while you listen. Have your secretary call you to remind you about an urgent meeting. Stand up. If necessary indicate you have to leave.

An employer sometimes must say no

When refusing an applicant a job, try to be as diplomatic as possible, and if you feel the turned-down applicant is really qualified for some job you just don't have available, be encouraging:

> *Dear Mr. Johnson,*
>
> Thank you for calling us yesterday about employment. It was nice of you to think of our company as a place where you would like to work.
>
> At the present time I am sorry to tell you we cannot offer you any encouragement. This is not a reflection on your qualifications, however. It is just that we do not have a suitable opening now that fits your abilities.
>
> There are, as you know, several companies which are expanding their staffs at this time and I feel sure you will find, among them, one where your special experience and training will be used effectively.
>
> Sincerely,

RAISES

Getting a raise

When you feel you are entitled to a salary raise, the most effective appeal is made by demonstrating the increased value of your services. But there are other factors which may also be included:

> *Dear Mr. Johnson,*
>
> I understand that every boss is reluctant to add to his overhead by giving raises. But I am sure, you at least, like to be fair and motivating to your employees.
>
> That is why I am taking the liberty of writing to you to ask for a reappraisal of my duties and my work and an adjustment of my salary to my present performance.
>
> During the past year I have added to my duties in the subscription department by assuming most of the work of the stencil cutter who resigned last March. The volume of subscriptions—and the consequent amount of detail—has increased 18 percent without any

increase in personnel. In fact, there has been a reduction in staff because of Miss Jones's departure.

All of us in the department have taken on the additional volume, but most of Miss Jones's work has fallen on me. Although I am able to handle this easily with extra effort and only a few hours' overtime (for which I am not paid), I feel that I should be earning considerably more than the $9,200 I am now receiving. In addition, we are all aware that the cost-of-living increases have diminished the size of each dollar by 6 percent during the past year and thus my real salary has been cut by this amount.

I trust that you will give this note some consideration as soon as it is practical.

Very sincerely,

Refusing to give a raise

Of course, an employer may refuse to grant a raise. It is always a good idea to give clear reasons for this decision.

Dear John,

Your letter makes a very good case for you, and, of course, I am happy that you have progressed so well in your work.

However, I must tell you that it is not possible to raise your salary at this time.

First, I should remind you that reevaluations of all employees' work are made annually in September and salaries for everyone are adjusted at that time.

Second, you will remember that when you began working as an apprentice last January, you were entirely unproductive for us; in fact, your training was a costly process for us. Yet we paid you a salary regularly. It is only a month since you have been adding to our production, hardly enough time for us to recoup the cost of four months' training.

Company policy is based on sound experience and it is designed to be fair to all our employees. When the evaluations are being made in two months, your letter will be given due consideration. I am sure you will get a fair deal in the new salary schedule.

Very sincerely,

When you must refuse to give a raise, do it in a positive way: "You should try to make yourself more valuable to the company and so earn a raise for yourself. Perhaps you can . . ."

LEAVING A JOB

Firing an employee

How do you fire someone from a job if you have to? Your objective is primarily to make the parting with the least injury to the company, to induce the departing employee to feel friendly toward the company. This necessitates sparing his feelings.

When you must fire someone make a clean break. The interview should be short (five to seven minutes), direct, effective immediately or as soon as practical. Don't get sidetracked.

In the interview stress the employee's future, his special talents, the kind of job in which he would succeed.

Try to hold the interview at the beginning of the day so that he can start cleaning up his possessions and start looking for a new job immediately. Offer a recommendation. Provide severance pay.

Letting an employee go, particularly a superannuated employee, is a delicate matter. Sometimes union agreements are a factor. Sometimes there are legal restrictions—age, sex, color. But always financial and psychological hardships are involved.

Some companies approach the parting by trying to induce an employee to leave voluntarily. Sometimes they require him to be at meetings so that his work is not done; sometimes they exclude him from meetings he has always attended. His office may be made less attractive or he may be assigned to a smaller office. His responsibilities may be lessened or he may be assigned to a higher but less responsible position (kicked upstairs). He may be deprived of the key to the executive washroom or lose his parking spot. Suggestions about other job opportunities may be offered.

When you are firing someone on short notice and might expect sabotage or vindictiveness, of course, do the firing at the end of the day. Even in situations where the firing is for cause, try to be tactful. Emphasize the "Sorry" even if you must add, "but you brought it on yourself." Make sure that records, keys, credit cards, and notations on pending matters are retrieved. And prepare to offset any bad-mouthing which may follow dismissal.

On many occasions, the firing is not for fault. Then it behooves the executive to go out of his or her way to be helpful.

It is never a pleasant task to upset the life of a person you have worked with or have had working for you for a long time. You know how it upsets that person's life. But sometimes it is necessary. Try to make the firee understand the necessity of what you are doing.

> You know, Tom, that the situation makes this essential. You've been around long enough to understand that an organization has to make changes from time to time. It's nobody's fault, Tom.

The positive factors you have to work with are references, referrals, and future prospects. Sometimes it is possible to offer help in getting a new job: letters, ads, phone calls, use of the office and a secretary, etc. Severance pay is the kindest way out of all.

Some employers go even further to help employees being "let go." They write to other companies, friends, even competitors:

> *Dear Sam:*
> As you may know, BCB is undergoing a major reorganization this year because of its merger with PDG Company. As a result, several departments are being consolidated and some very experienced and productive talent is going on the market.
> Jim Jones, our advertising production manager, has been with us for seven years and is a real find as a worker. In addition to a vast knowledge of resources and techniques, he has a subtle creativity that has helped BCB sales grow substantially through the years.
> Jim is a real find for any organization that does in-house copy preparation—as I think yours does. He'll be here at BCB for the next three weeks if you wish to talk to him, or at (212) 786-4208 afterward if he doesn't find another place immediately.
> You'll be doing your company—and Jim—a good turn if you can place him in your organization. And I'll appreciate it personally because I hate to see his talents wasted.
> Very cordially,

Losing a job

Every jobholder should have a sixth-sense alert to the chances of losing the job: declining sales or profits, talk of

retrenchment, declining functions, lack of promotions and/
or raises, failure to be invited to crucial meetings, etc.

That is the time to prepare in two ways: (1) consolidate
your background by making notes of your contacts, your
record on the job, essential information that you could use
on a new job; and (2) find out the needs of companies with
which you have contact, and of your competitors.

> *Dear Mr. Supplier:*
>
> You will remember me as the young man who keeps calling you
> for No. 2 What-nots every Monday.
>
> In the course of my experience here as person-in-charge of What-
> not Sales, I have accumulated a good deal of experience from the
> point of view of your customers and their use of What-nots. I think
> some of that experience could be of real value to you.
>
> Inasmuch as I am considering making a change in my position
> and I have a deep interest in all phases of office operations, the
> thought occurred to me that I could be an effective cog in your
> expansion plans.
>
> Could I drop by to chat with you during a lunch hour next week
> or after 5:30 any evening?
>
> Thanks.
>
> Very cordially,

Most people who work, work for an institution, not an
individual. Watch for signs in the institution rather than
depending on your relationship with the person for whom
you are working. And remember that an institution is
nonemotional, that friendships can be wiped out in a single
shake-up.

One way to protect yourself is to make a self-evaluation
from time to time, viewing yourself as an institution would
in terms of value, replacement possibilities, alternatives for
yourself, where you can go and are going. Try to make
yourself essential in at least some phase of the operation.

If you leave or are fired

If you have been working at the same place for a long
time, prepare yourself for a bit of a shock when you leave. It
doesn't hit you right away, but if you do not have a substitute
job immediately, you will find that there are many adjust-
ments to be made in your routine, friendships, habits,
attitudes from and toward friends and neighbors. A working
person usually has his or her image and personality inte-

grated with the work and title. An ex-official suddenly finds that opinions have less weight than yesterday when he or she was chief clerk. Solid friendships may fade quickly. The change in status may affect your marriage, where and how you live, and how clearly you can think and plan. You will be facing new problems of economic survival, of finding a job, of adjusting to "asking" instead of "giving," of feeling guilty and unimportant. They can affect your capacity to find and readjust to a new job.

For this reason—and for others—the time to seek a new job is while you have one. The facilities, status, contacts—phone, letterheads, address, etc., are still available to you. And you are still yourself. In fact, if you feel that your job is in jeopardy or is declining, take the initiative at the first—and best—opportunity. It is substantially easier to get a new job while you are still firm in the old one.

If you are out of work, adjust your thinking to realize that it is not your fault, that you may be out of work for some time, that your family is under some of the same tension you are under, that you may have to ask favors from people you would rather have died than ask yesterday. Keep sociable. Remake your budget priorities. Try to view the change as an opportunity, a challenge.

Then make your finding-a-job plan. Begin by cataloging (a) where you want to work, (b) who can help you, and (c) how you are going about it.

Resigning

When you leave, you may want to urge some of the people you dealt with to send a few recommendations to your ex-employer, for the record. In your letter of resignation, state your reasons clearly and, if you sincerely feel it, express your regret at leaving. Also specify the date you are leaving.

Mr. John Dorman
Editor
Castletown Newspaper
10 Double Street
New York, N.Y. 10000

Dear Mr. Dorman,
    Samuel Doe informed me last week that he is severing formal ties with the editorial staff of the *Record.*

Just a few words to express J.D.B.'s appreciation for the kind of first-rate professionalism Mr. Doe displayed in covering labor relations developments in our city and particularly those related to our activities. In my judgment, his expertise and objectivity in this very sticky field did credit to your newspaper and to Doe himself.

We, of course, wish him well in his new endeavors.

Sincerely,

And to the boss:

Dear Mr. Johnson,

It is with regret that I must tell you I plan to leave Sanders Whatzit Company on June 30.

On the recommendation of my family doctor, who has suggested that my wife move to the Sunbelt, we are planning to move to Arizona as soon as possible.

I have enjoyed working with you at Sanders and I consider the experience I have gained here most valuable. Under other circumstances I would have liked to make my career with your organization.

As quickly as I can, I will advise the people in my department of the details of my work so that no continuity is lost. And if any questions do arise, I will be available to answer them at a telephone number I will leave.

Accept my thanks for the opportunity you gave me to join your company.

Very cordially,

REFERENCES

References are really a form of introduction, but for the specific purpose of recommending someone for a job. They can be general and all-purpose, or aimed specifically at one individual. They should testify not only to the good character of the individual but to his abilities and accomplishments. Remember, though, that most strangers look at references with a jaundiced eye: they realize that you would not present a bad reference and that many references are obtained casually and with no serious opinion on the part of the person writing it. Under these circumstances it is probably best that you write your own references and ask someone with the appearance of authority to put them on a company letterhead and sign them.

To whom it may concern:

Sally Shadow is a highly skilled and competent secretary who has been employed by me for six years. Her work is meticulous, accurate, and effective in every way.

Miss Shadow would now like a change of pace—a shorter work week.

It is with regret that we lose the services of an employee I can heartily recommend.

Very sincerely yours,

Mr. John Brown
President
Brown Shoes Inc.
200 Shady
St. Louis, Missouri

Dear Mr. Brown,

You will remember, I am sure, our mutual association with the Air Cadet Training Program a few years ago. We worked on the annual banquet together.

An old friend, Mr. Jay Sommers, will be visiting your city in June to investigate the possibility of opening a factory there. He is seeking some frank appraisals of the labor situation, the attitudes of the community toward industry, and the political climate.

Will you be good enough to spend a little time with him and give him the benefit of your long experience in the community? I will consider it a great personal favor.

Thank you.

Very cordially,

Dear John,

When Tom Dinkers told me he was visiting Painted Post, I told him immediately you've got to meet John Holland.

So when Tom knocks on your door, extend the same welcome you would offer me. He's a wonderful guy, full of ginger, and a fellow follower of the soccer circuit.

I know you'll enjoy his company and I hope you can introduce him to a few others who deserve to know a good fellow like him.

Cordially,

Sometimes a little ambiguity may be needed:

To whom it may concern:

This will introduce Sandy Smith, who has been an accountant with John Smith Foundries for the past twenty years.

I cannot tell you how diligently Mr. Smith worked for us during all these years. His work has always been considered satisfactory. When we took over the company in 1972 he was already ranked as senior accountant and we have had no reason to question his ability during our control.

Sandy leaves us because he feels there is no avenue for advancement with us. We wish him well.

Very truly yours,

On the other hand you may wax enthusiastic:

TO SOME LUCKY EDITOR:

It's a sad thing to write a letter of recommendation for someone whom you will truly miss. Stella Dorre brings a combination of sunshine and skill that will quickly ingratiate her with you, as she has with us.

She was hired by *The News* because she showed initiative in going from door to door seeking a job, at a time when we had an opening and were swamped with written applications. She has continued to show that "something extra" during the time she has worked here.

If she is not familiar with some aspect of a job, she is fast to learn. Once she has learned, I know I no longer have to be concerned about whether or not someone will follow through on that portion of the job. While I am still articulating my thoughts, Stella will anticipate the need and do what has to be done, even those little nitty-gritty tasks that everyone else shirks.

In addition to her obvious skills in reporting, writing, photography and proofreading, she has a natural flair for administration, being a well-organized person—both on her desk and in her mind.

As a reporter, she is the kind of person whom others open up to. Some of the thank-you letters from her interviewees attest to this. This same objectively friendly quality also enables her to function well as a photographer, while her serious side is reflected in her exceptional ability as a proofreader, a most important skill when you have a limited staff.

If she had been able to stay with *The News*, Stella would have received a substantial raise more in line with the job she has performed with us. But our loss is someone else's good fortune.

Sincerely,

Asking for references

Dear Nat:

I am participating in a career guidance survey which is designed to have others describe how they see me. Results are to be evaluated by Personnel Predictions and Research, Inc., of Denver, Colorado.

You are one of the five references I am asking to cooperate in this survey. I am confident you will be fair and candid in your responses to the descriptive checklist contained in the sealed envelope accompanying this letter. Your responses will be held in complete confidence and only consensus results will be made available by

Personnel Predictions and Research after the evaluation is completed.

Please open the enclosed envelope and fill out the Reference Survey Checklist. It takes only about ten minutes to complete. A self-addressed, stamped envelope is provided for you to send the completed checklist to Denver. It would be most helpful if you could mail it at your earliest possible convenience.

If you have any questions, please call me. Your cooperation will be most appreciated.

Sincerely,

Regulations concerning privacy of records make it advisable to obtain a release from anyone you wish to investigate. This will not only protect you from an accusation of invasion of privacy but will avoid the reluctance of some sources in providing information.

RELEASE

Having made application as above and desiring Showmanship Company, Inc., to be informed as to my previous record, I hereby authorize them to investigate my past record and to ascertain any and all information which may concern my record, whether same is of record or not; and I release my employers and all persons whomsoever of any damage on account of furnishing said information.

_____ Signed_____
Witness to Signature

_____   _____
Date   Date

Chapter 5

Making More of Your Meetings

MEMORANDA AND REPORTS

Internal business communications—memoranda and reports—require a more straightforward approach than do communications to outsiders. That is not to say that internal communications do not attempt to achieve an objective, nor that they do not utilize tact, psychology, or emotional appeal. However, the emphasis here is on factuality, organization, and clarity.

Memos may be casual, but a report is formal. A report assembles, analyzes, and presents information, sometimes drawing a conclusion. The presentation is particularly important, because most reports are scanned before they are read, and many are not read at all in their entirety. Thus they must contain a summary—often at the beginning—headings for basic points, and a conclusion, which is usually read immediately after the summary, even if it is at the end.

A report should be limited to a single subject, but that subject may have many facets. One way to check your thinking is to prepare a complete outline before you prepare your report or after you have collected your thoughts in a rough draft.

Stick to the point. If something extra turns up, e.g., waste or pilferage uncovered while you are investigating a price policy, refer to it and make a special report on the subject.

Ask yourself the purpose of the report, who will see it, what effect it will have on others. Consider the timing—when the facts will be needed, when they will implement a decision, and when the decision will be put into effect. Will all your statements apply at each of these times?

Although a logical sequence following a sensible, parallel outline is advisable, there may be points that should be emphasized to create more impact, or because they are more important. This can be accomplished by underlining, adding an asterisk and a footnote, or devoting more space to this aspect. This facet may also be stressed in the summary at the beginning or in the conclusion at the end.

Selection of contents

The flexible elements in writing a report come from selection of information and which facts to emphasize. At every stage consideration must be given to who will read the report and for what purpose, and to who will object to it. A report to the public or to stockholders will emphasize the positive aspects of a company's operations, but it will be subject to legal requirements on what information must be included. A report on the market for a new product or the cost effectiveness of a project will tend to be conservative and rational, with specific comparisons. It may have to be defended as to methodology and its accuracy will be tested by later experience. A salesman reporting on calls may tend to justify a failure or be optimistic about the long-term results if a survey is conducted. Even a subtle wording will affect the result. The sample group to which a questionnaire is sent can bring a distorted response, advertently or inadvertently.

Memos

Memos are everyday matters. They require only that you be specific as to who gets them, when, and what you say. Misunderstandings can be costly.

Because it is necessarily brief and to the point, the memo need not be stiff and stuffy. Sometimes an informal note will do:

June 1, 1979

To: JBS
From: Sally Saucy

Reports coming in from salesmen in the territory north of Westchester and from Suffolk County indicate that we will end the season with sales down 20 percent from last year. The men have been hustling so I don't think they have been letting us down.

Brown Buttering Company has a new package of Whatzits which is more attractive than ours and their Whatzit is available in stainless steel. They offer a year guarantee and an attractive booklet showing what can be done with the Whatzit. Several of our customers suggest that we lower our price at least 10 percent to counter the Brown product. Johnson of Canandaigua tested the lower price and found a good reception, doubling sales of our product during a ten-day trial period.

As an alternative to price cutting we could offer a copy of our book *How to Make the Most of Your Whatzit* free with each purchase. A point-of-sale poster and new packaging would also be helpful. I think advertising tie-ins, possibly with a cooperative advertising campaign, will be necessary if changes are made in the offer.

Whatever steps are taken, this should be completed before September 1 to reestablish our place in the fall market.

Most memos are essentially shortened in-house business letters. (When they become long, they verge on reports which involve other considerations.) A basic requirement is that they carry the date (sometimes the time of day), the name of the sender, the one or ones to receive it, and sometimes (especially if they are more than two paragraphs) the subject.

If a memorandum is to be longer, a subject heading and even a summary may be placed at the top of the page. It is a good idea to determine what result you want—even if it is only to inform—and to outline your memo to reach your point.

July 17, 1978

Memo to CJ
From Sid Lorb
Re: Sales in upstate New York

1. Sales are 20 percent less than last year.
2. New competition has entered the field.
3. Our customers are seeking lower prices to offset higher quality of competing lines now selling at the same price as we are.
4. Alternate options suggested involving premium, packaging, and promotion.
5. Timing of decision limited by need to produce by September 5.

July 17, 1978

To: Sid Lorb
From: Sally Saucy
Re: Holiday mail

1. Inasmuch as there will be no mail pick up on Monday, all outgoing mail will be delivered to the post office at 3 P.M. by mail-room messenger.
2. By special arrangement, first-class mail will be picked up at the post office at 8:30 A.M. If mail other than first class is expected, instruct senders to mark it special delivery.
cc: JCR
 BDL
 RPC

Reports

A memo that runs more than two or three pages should be considered a report. It may be designed to point out, report on, analyze, or resolve a problem. It may be requested or offered unsolicited or it may be a routine requirement. In each case, the first step is to determine the purpose (and thus the scope) and to define the basic terms, especially the true problem if the report deals with a problem.

The report should first be thought out in outline: the topics to be discussed, the alternatives, the evaluation, and so on. Then determine the methods of assembling the facts.

Some elements in a report may include:

Title and subject
Authorization or origin
Copyright or note on restricted circulation
Letter of transmittal
Contents
List of documentation
List of illustrations
Synopsis
Summary of the problem or purpose
Limitations
Historical background
Definitions or glossary of terms used
Who worked on the report
Other sources of information

Methods of collecting the information
The information
Documentation
Summary
Conclusion
Recommendations
Appendix
Bibliography or sources of information
Index

A major report may have a title sheet:

Survey of Consumer
Attitudes Regarding
Widget # 1

Prepared By
John Brown
Sales Department I
for
Sidney Smith
Sales Manager

National Widget Co.
January 27, 1979

or the same information may be placed at the head of a shorter (two- or three-page) report.

Long reports

Long reports should contain an outline or table of contents, subject headings that follow the outline, and a sumary at the beginning. On typed reports these may be in capitals or underlined. Material, particularly complicated statistical material, should be presented additionally in short form: by graphs, bars, pie charts, etc. Comments involving locations should be accompanied by maps. Samplings should indicate the way in which the list was compiled and why. Surveys should contain the original questionnaire and details on how it was distributed. In all cases, the sources of information should be given. Computer read-outs should be summarized and held in reserve.

Numbers

Most reports involve some presentation of numbers. Here three factors are involved: (1) making the figures readable, (2) making them understandable, and (3) making the point you wish to make with them.

Figures in a text are useful but are difficult to compare with others. Tabular or graphic presentation is usually easier to read and more emphatic and more significant and therefore should be used where feasible. There are many ways of presenting these.

Where large numbers are involved, except for legal documents and tax reports (where, however, including cents is optional) the figures may be simplified by eliminating thousands, sometimes even millions. Thus:

$27,764,468	29,852,758
21,426,972	31,472,840

may be presented without the last three places:

(in thousands)

$27,764	29,852
21,426	31,472

In making comparisons, particularly where the point is to show division of a whole, percentages are often more significant than the figures themselves.

Energy Sources Used in
Area A

	1978	1979
Coal	47%	67%
Oil	24%	18%
Gas	7%	9%
Other	22%	6%

Where many of the figures involve fractions of a percent, it is simpler to raise the denominator to, say, 1,000. Thus, in this table, 2.17 = 2,170.

| | Births Per 100,000 in the Population (rate in thousands) | |
	1978	1979
Area A	2.17	2.19
Area B	2.78	2.80
Area C	4.31	4.27

For many readers even tabular material presents a reading hazard. Scores of different graphic devices can be used to aid understanding and to make the conclusion to be drawn more dramatic. There are also ways to present figures to overemphasize or to dull a conclusion. (See below.) Among the widely used devices are the graph, the bar chart, the pie chart, and pictorial units.

Some continuing ratios are not presented as percentage changes but as changes in terms of an index number set at a "base period." Thus the Dow-Jones Index reflects changes in stock prices based on a composite price of stocks early in the century (adjusted for stock splits and replacement of out-of-business companies). Because the index is now on an 800-to-1,000 range, an 18-point change would be about only 2 percent. The cost-of-living index is based on 100, which equals 1967 figures. A 4 percent change at this time would be about 6 points.

Where percentages are used, one of the first reactions of some readers is to add up the percentage points and see if they come out to 100. Very often they don't. Sometimes not all the answers are available; sometimes (as in a survey) two answers are given by some of those interviewed. Often it is wise to omit the 100 percent at the bottom of a column and to explain why the total does not equal 100 percent.

Where the emphasis is intended to be placed on the comparative number, ratios may be used:

Ratio of Fire Officers to Firemen
(a) Firemen per captain	62
(b) Firemen per lieutenant	15
(c) Firemen per officer	13

Where numbers and percents are in the same table, different colors or type faces may be used to differentiate them.

In arranging tables, the columns can be arranged from cause to effect, in climactic order where the point is to show growth or losses, or in order of size where there is no emphasis to be made:

Causes of Death Among 10-Year-Olds

Accidents	48%
Pneumonia	12%
Neoplasms	7%
Kidney diseases	2%
Diabetes	1%
(etc.)	

Uses of Pain Relievers Among Nurses

Competitor 1	11%
Competitor 2	14%
Competitor 3	10%
Our product	37%
Others	28%

Of course, where the base has a logical order, the logical order should be followed:

Age Group	Cases
1–10	7
11–20	19
21–30	2

Not every set of figures is easily arrived at or simply reported. In cases where three or more factors are to be analyzed, where there are many "undecided" or "don't know" answers to a question, where the factors involved are innumerable, where questions like "why" are involved, where subjective standards are set, more complicated presentation may be necessary:

Vote for Sheriff, Blooming County, 1976

	Lower Area			Upper Area			Total		
Candidate	Dem.	Rep.	Unaff.	Dem.	Rep.	Unaff.	Dem.	Rep.	Unaff.
A	72	47	96	18	19	6	90	66	102
B	18	21	27	64	24	11	82	45	38
C	67	42	2	21	28	21	88	70	23
Total	157	110	125	103	71	38	260	181	163

Questionnaires

A questionnaire used to gather information should be expressed simply, concisely, and in a way so that the information required is easily understood by everyone in the same way. Questions should not tilt the answers:

> How many complaints have you had about PDQ?
> *Not:* Have there been many complaints about PDQ?

Test the questionnaire by asking one or two parties to fill it out and then finding out their comments and questions about it.

Answers may be encouraged by offering choices:

Yes——   No——

Select the most appropriate response:
Good____
Fair____
Bad____

Color choice:
Red____
Pink____
Maroon____
Scarlet____
Another color____

On a scale of 1 to 10 (1 is lowest), give your estimate of the interest in the Company Bulletin:————

Personal interviews in reports

Another method of gathering information is through personal interviews. These should follow a standard format made in the form of a questionnaire. Be careful to avoid bias in asking questions or selecting those you speak to. Avoid particularly questions that indicate a disadvantage to the interviewee from responses (Do you use drugs?), a threat to status or ego (How do you rank in your class?), or unpleasantness (How do you get along with your colleagues?). Prepare the person you are interviewing so that the approach goes through proper channels, or the questioning does not come at an inconvenient time. Give the interviewee time to gather material, especially about dates or figures.

What to include and how much

A report should include supporting documents if any recommendation is being made or any decision depends on it. If there are rejected alternatives they too should be summarized.

In selecting language—technical terms, unfamiliar processes, statistics, etc.—bear in mind who will read your report. Sometimes a glossary may be necessary.

Avoid nonobjective terms. Present facts rationally and objectively, not emotionally.

When comparative figures are given, tabulate them rather than describe them in text:

	Last Year	This Year
Sales	$12,000	$28,000
Profit	$ 4,000	$ 7,000

If a report is to be followed by others—either occasionally or on a regular basis—it should follow the same general outline so that comparisons can be made easily.

Test your report by reading it after a night's sleep. Ask yourself if your sources are accurate, if your conclusions are rational, if you answer the questions first asked, what additional questions will be asked by those to whom you submit the report.

An executive with much to read wants to get the gist of a memorandum or report fast to see whether it is to be passed along to someone else, put aside for more careful reading, or placed on top of a pile for immediate action. Perhaps it is material for a morning conference, or perhaps it can be discussed at a 3 P.M. meeting. There is always a tendency for a long piece of writing to be put aside for later study. But a well-outlined, summaried memorandum will provide a distillation in a minute or less.

If the subject suggests it, write at greater length about proposals, the market and marketing requirements (for a new product), timing, the costs, difficulties, and potential results (profit, savings).

When you have finished a first draft, it is a good idea to write a list of questions that should have been answered—

whether they fit into the required outline or not. Then proceed to find a place for the answers.

After you have finished, ask yourself, too, if you have followed through on the points you raised or merely raised more questions that will come back to delay action. If the conclusion to point C is provided later in the memorandum, mention this at point C.

Now that all the points are covered, check to see that all the details given are necessary and to the point. A digression can cause the train of thought to be broken and the whole memo set aside for later study. A common failing in recommendations is losing sight of the main objective, because a minor detail requires much discussion. These are then overemphasized. This problem can be handled by putting subsidiary items into attached memoranda, referring to them in the basic report.

Although specifying a conclusion is usually more effective, in some cases it is wise not to draw a conclusion. If you have weighed the arguments sufficiently, the conclusion may be self-evident.

Remember, it is helpful in getting your ideas across if you can provide evidence in the form of facts (incidents, reports, surveys, and figures, significant and relevant testimony) and exhibits (charts, drawings, photographs) to support your points, since these make a report more interesting to read.

Reports to the public

Reports that are to be made public—those for stockholders particularly—involve special considerations. Material must be presented in a special "public-relations" way to avoid criticism of management (or whoever else is issuing the report). Certain elements, for example, must be mentioned to meet requirements of the Securities and Exchange Commission or other agencies. Financial statements will have to be included, and anything in the report must be consistent with these statements or the inconsistency must be explained.

Annual reports may be simple offsets of material typed in the office or elaborate booklets in color, with many pages, highly illustrated and detailed by division, products, etc. For public companies they should contain balance sheets and profit-and-loss statements for at least two years and often much more. Usually they also contain a letter from the president, a report on operations explaining changes in the statements, the names of officers, directors, and auditors, and a list of products sold.

THE SMALL MEETING

In business or personal life most meetings involve perhaps six to twelve persons convened to discuss a subject or a problem. These are not usually adversary meetings, but many of us approach them as a means of advancing our image or protecting our positions. These may have the function of idea input (brainstorming), group interaction, feedback, or control. They may meet to solve a problem, to create a task force or leadership, or for any of many other reasons.

Meetings are usually called by an "initiator." The members of the group may include those invited to encourage the project, those who contribute information, those who can set goals, those who can help harmonize a situation, and someone who can summarize and conclude the meeting.

On the other hand, meetings often have members who refuse to take the matter and/or the initiator seriously, those who monopolize the time (usually the initiator or chairman), those who just sit and listen (or daydream), those who object to everything, and those who go off on a tangent.

If progress is to be made, you must learn to cope with these personalities. Of course, if you are in charge, you may be able to select a group whose members are compatible. Remember, however, that leaving out a logical member can be considered a putdown and thus be resented.

For such a meeting, an objective and a tentative agenda, a time suitable for everyone (when pressure to get away is not too keen), and a comfortable, convenient setting are very important. In an emergency, meetings may be held by conference telephone calls, bringing together participants from distant places.

Sometimes such meetings can be called for five to ten minutes (buzz groups, they are called). These may be to pass along information or to present the problem or to get an opinion on a particular happening.

Brainstorming sessions are a valuable form of longer, more relaxed meeting. These depend on interactions in a group to provide ideas and solutions to problems.

Another form of small meeting may be a symposium where various members address a group and solicit questions. A variation is the presentation of two solutions by two members or teams so that the elements of a decision may be clarified. If the meeting is to prepare for a negotiation, one side may assume the position of the opponents. Or one member may play devil's advocate.

In setting up a group, wherever practical select (1) those who have a sense of belonging; (2) people who get along together; (3) people who are the leaders of any group in which a change is to be made; (4) people who know the situation in the area to be discussed. Realize that any radical change in working procedures will be resisted and that members of the group should all be aware of a problem and the need for change. The effect of a change in one group upon other groups should be considered.

In any group certain tensions exist that may deter accomplishment. Some of these are carried into the meeting as a result of previous personality conflicts. Among those in a group meeting for the first time, there is the kind of tension that always exists among those who are not acquainted with each other. And when a group has discussed anything for a time, tensions develop as differences of opinion become evident. The leader of a group must meet the challenge of these tensions to create a successful meeting.

Release from overly tense situations is accomplished with a digression, a joke, a recess, a change of area being discussed, a call for an opinion on some facet from each member of the group.

Speakers at a small meeting should be brief and to the point, dealing in concrete terms (generalizations can be interpreted differently by each member as they apply to his or her area). Contribute your ideas without being prompted (a leader may be forced to ask each member of the group to talk if the flow is not spontaneous). Listen to what others say and comment freely.

If the material is complicated, the leader of the group should distribute an agenda in advance and stop to summarize from time to time, nailing down those points which have been agreed upon.

When a group decision is made, it should be accepted unanimously with full promise of cooperation. Foot-dragging on a policy with which one member disagrees can destroy the success of a project.

If you are the leader of a group discussion, try to keep the group acting as a unit. Establish procedures for arriving at a consensus decision. Try to discourage conflict and hard feelings within the group. If some of this is directed at you, share the leadership.

Make sure you are fully cognizant of the problem discussed. Listen to each person and avoid criticizing any comment on a personal basis. Be impartial in allowing comments. Keep the group moving toward the objective.

Preparing for a meeting

Before a meeting, be certain to find out what is on the agenda, what information will be required, and what problems will be presented so that you can do some preparatory thinking, understand, and contribute more. If you are assembling the meeting, suggest that those being called do this.

If you are arranging the meeting, make certain a comfortable environment is prepared and that pencils, pads, and necessary reference material are available to each participant.

Brainstorming

Brainstorming usually involves three phases: (1) an idea-generating session (tell everyone to come up with thoughts, no matter how ridiculous); (2) an analysis of the ideas session; (3) an adoption session. The key to the success of such a session is uninhibited suggestion—even if the ideas seem ridiculous.

Here it is particularly important not to allow criticisms to be made personal. Don't allow attacks on judgment or intelligence.

Try to stimulate many ideas, especially at the first session. Leave the concentration on a few for the second session.

Try to hitch two or more ideas together, or start with one idea and build on it.

If you are in a brainstorming session, hold your best ideas for the middle of the meeting. First ideas get badly hit because it is easier to talk as critic than as idea giver. But don't wait too long. Someone else may come up with a similar thought. Make your presentation modestly, not as if it were the greatest idea of all time. This reduces hostility. At the same time extend courteous attention to the other ideas. Don't count on personal loyalties to defend an idea. Don't be too slick or sophisticated in your presentation. Keep it simple to avoid criticism of unessential details.

Another type of reaction that can destroy a meeting is a stubborn attitude on an issue. "It just won't work," or "Ridiculous," or "It can't be done" tends to close a discussion that might otherwise be productive. Insist that everyone go into a meeting with an open mind.

Creative thinking and critical thinking are each counterproductive to the other.

If a conference is to make a wise decision, avoid the quick ones made before all the facts are made known. One purpose of a discussion is to seek out problems rather than to minimize them. In such a situation, a majority vote is not always the best method of reaching a decision, if only because not all the elements involved are present with relative weight. The overall consequences rather than personal feelings must be considered. Nor should an expert's opinion be so dominating as to determine the decision. Expertise may be limited to one area or only technical aspects of a problem. It is usually best for the leader of a group to make, announce, and take responsibility for decisions, with any dissent noted for the record.

Whatever the meeting decides, it should not be left to be announced without a "next-step" proposal. Much of what is discussed remains fruitless because no one is assigned to follow up with more thought or action. If no decision is reached, another meeting should be scheduled or the matter specifically closed. Discussion without implementation can be a great waste of time.

When saying no to a consensus is difficult

To sidestep a proposal you can drag, you can listen and reserve judgment, say yes and forget about it, find some other department that objects, forget to follow up on a detail, call many meetings, boost the cost estimate, appoint someone to look into the matter.

Face to face

If you have something important to say to a business associate, arrange for a face-to-face meeting explaining what you want to discuss and what material will be needed. Before the meeting suggest how long you have to talk, set up an agenda for the discussions, and explain the parameters so you don't go off on a tangential point. Try to make a visitor comfortable and at ease. (Perhaps get up from behind the desk.)

Speak slowly. Don't be threatening. Do not interrupt except to get a better understanding of what is being said.

If a plan is being worked out, write out the steps so both of you understand them.

Be on the lookout for signs of reluctance even when an associate is going along with what you say. Don't take silence for a yes answer.

Discipline problems

If a complaint has been made, make sure you identify the problem from the company's point of view. Listen to the employee's point of view fully and privately in a way that will allow him or her to speak frankly and release any pent-up emotions. Make sure the difficulty lies with the employee accused, and not with another employee or with the system. Make sure you have the whole story.

When the interview is completed, reserve judgment. Compare all versions of the situation and evaluate them some time after you have heard the last participant. (The last person you saw leaves the strongest impression.) Make and keep a written record of facts and opinions and read it before you make a decision.

If the employee is to be disciplined, make sure the policy and the penalty match precedent. Consider the long-term record and the morale of the employee and his or her fellows.

If the decision is difficult because of personal relationships, let someone else make it. But don't pass the buck because enforcement is unpleasant.

Make your decision complete, authoritative within your authority, specific, and unarguable. Present the decision with the reasoning behind it. If possible allow the employee to avoid embarrassment with his fellows and at home.

If there is an appeal procedure make sure the employee knows about it.

Bad news
When to spring bad news is always a problem. The consensus is that it should come early in a meeting.

In passing it on to an employee, it should not come (1) before a problem has to be solved or a difficult job done; (2) just before lunch; (3) at the end of the day if there is nothing the employee can do about it, but this is a good time if alternatives are not available.

HOW TO NEGOTIATE

Negotiations and confrontations
A huge amount of our communications involves what might be called "adversary relationships." Negotiations are usually thought of as between labor and management. However, negotiation occurs in all phases of living where there is a difference of opinion: between nations and between husbands and wives; in Congress and in sports; within a business between buyers and sellers; in a school or a club; in the management of a business or even in an individual who has to review two or more alternatives to make a decision.

In a sense, almost everything you do in business is a negotiation—a sale, collecting a debt, hiring an employee, making a purchase, settling a lawsuit, making a union contract, etc. The negotiation may be for price only or may involve a host of details: for status, for a raise, for quantity and delivery, quality, working conditions, ad infinitum. Negotiation is designed to provide the best deal you can get for yourself or for your company. It may relate only to asking the boss for a day off or for a raise, setting the price of a radio or a new car, complaining about something delivered in an unsatisfactory condition, discussing what the mayor should have done, or such important matters as a labor contract or a business deal. Negotiations involve two aspects: the confrontation or negotiation, and the presentation of argument—the real debate on the issues. We deal here with the basic technique of negotiating. The matter of argument is discussed in the following section.

The methods and pitfalls for all negotiations are similar. Some basics: don't talk too much, keep cool (emotion can have devastating results). Keep your mind on the objective.

A veteran of many negotiations once classified the parties to a negotiation as aggressors, victims, and instigators. The aggressors start the ball rolling and carry the action. The victims are those of whom the demands are being made. The instigators are the ones who are always finding objections.

Negotiation is usually a type of eyeball-to-eyeball debate with high stakes and with a strong reason for coming to a specific decision at a fixed time. Negotiation intimates compromise, bargaining, the use of all types of pressures, not always excluding outside opinion.

The goal of negotiation is not always to get (or keep) the most money. You do not want a dead company or supplier or a dissatisfied employee. All parties to a satisfactory negotiation should come out with some needs satisfied. Negotiation seeks out common interests. In a good negotiation everyone gets something, no one gets everything.

Before you start, make sure the negotiation is not merely a fishing expedition to get information about you or your company.

Procedures

Ordinarily a negotiation goes through several phases: an opening session where demands are presented; an exploratory session in which each side tries to find out what is really wanted and what is possible; a bargaining session when the weight of each of the demands is determined; a deadline session when everyone gets down to brass tacks; and a closing session, when a conclusion is reached.

When

Select a time and place that will prevent interruptions. A call-out will often come just at the wrong time—while you are making a crucial point. It could deflate a whole argument. When an issue is first raised or when it is under heated debate is not the best time to negotiate. Wait for issues to cool off or schedule a meeting at a future time and find an excuse for postponing it if the heat is still on.

Where

Try to have negotiations, even preliminary ones, on your home ground. If they are on your premises, see that nothing is in the meeting room that gives a bad impression to your adversary.

If the site is not on your premises, select a light, pleasant, colorful room. Provide for facilities: phones, coffee or drinks, caucus areas, ashtrays, pencil and paper, etc.

Watch out for the opposition's use of a premise to make a point.

Even the seating arrangements can be an important factor. If it is not an issue, set yourself at the head of the table. (Back to the window, facing the door, is best. This puts the disconcerting sun in the face of the opposition and allows you to note who is coming in or out.)

How

Prepare for a negotiation carefully and completely. Know what the issues will be, how they were handled previously, and the positions taken by each party. Learn what you can about the people involved, their education, background, viewpoints.

In a negotiation you will have to become an expert in all the facts of the situation: the costs involved on each side; the history of the issues; the comparative policies among others similarly situated; the personalities of those involved on your own side as well as the other; the public image and how it can affect your future; but basically, how far you want to go, and how far you can afford to go.

In each instance the negotiator must use the basic "you" technique: What will it cost the other party if we pursue each course? Will he have to go to court and undergo the costs of a lawsuit and can he afford it? Will he have to be away from work and can he afford it? Will he have to go elsewhere and will he be better off there? And so forth. Against this weigh your own costs and the risks involved.

Try to take the position of leader. Make the introductions, suggest starting and finishing time, lunch plans, finally suggest getting down to business.

Keep up the initiative so that you are carrying the ball as much as possible. Be the first to set the trivial aside and get to the major problem. Coming early allows you to do this. It also permits some reconnaissance. Being late can discomfit you.

Who

Don't underestimate those with whom you are negotiating. Assume they know as much as you do and are as capable as you are—if not more. Have the most knowledgeable and the most interested people do the negotiating for you. Underling negotiations have a handicap both in presentation and in acceptance.

Person-of-authority-to-person-of-authority negotiations are the most effective. Select negotiators noted for their friendliness rather than for their antagonisms. Avoid using in negotiations those whose record, personality, or manner would be obnoxious to the other side.

Where possible, let an agent bargain for you. This provides an opportunity to refuse the settlement and renegotiate for a better one. The agent may also get a concession and offer to propose it to his client without making a commitment. On the other hand, you try always to negotiate with a principal directly.

If the negotiation is to be difficult or unpleasant, or with a friend or relative, a bonded agent may be in a better position to argue effectively. Bonding is sometimes necessary to protect yourself against sweetheart contracts, extortion, etc.

Try to keep the negotiating teams small. More negotiators mean more objections, more people who have to justify themselves after the meeting, more speeches, and more hours spent arguing. Select your team carefully. Coach it fully. Know what each person will say, which arguments he or she can answer best. Do your homework: bring proof, charts, exhibits. Delegate authority with limitations, to keep control.

Appraising the opposition

As early as possible in the negotiations, find out what the other side must have—and what would happen if they did not get each of their demands. Essentials may be buried in a list of trivia. Sometimes it is possible to find out the opposition's "bottom line," but even this may be negotiable.

Try to understand the pressures on each negotiator—who he is responsible to, what his personal background is, what timetable he has personally.

If it is not apparent, determine who is the leader in the opposition—the most influential on the team—and concentrate on that person. If one person is a chronic objector, realize that his team, too, may find him a handicap.

Learn what you can from the opposition's office decor: plaques, pictures, diplomas. You may find some common ground for softening relationships (So you went to L.G.U. Too!).

Try to appraise how much the opposition really knows about the needs, the background, the process of negotiation—and change your game plan accordingly.

Judge the opposition team by the people who are their friends. If a negotiator's friends lean in a direction, he probably will too.

Watch the opposition for the amount of reluctance they

show for some points. Analyze this. Watch for the amount of attention they are giving, for their reactions, drowsiness, etc.

Preparation
Before you begin an argumentative discussion:

1. Know exactly what you are trying to accomplish— to make a sale, win an argument, establish a principle, or win a friend. Sometimes winning the argument is counterproductive.
2. Try to establish exactly the areas you disagree about and the areas where you are already in agreement.
3. Know exactly what you are talking about; i.e., define your terms. (Many arguments end in finding the parties were talking about different things.)
4. Find an objective that is common to both parties on the subject. (We both want peace, more business for the company, a decrease in crime, etc.)
5. Find the areas of trade-off—if you concede this, we will concede that.
6. Learn to listen. Psychologically, listening lets the other party lose some steam. Often misunderstandings can be laid bare. Sometimes a concession is being offered. Sometimes a weak area or an error in fact is disclosed. Sometimes a motivation is made evident that can be satisfied in another way.
7. However, stop the talking if it is hardening the position of the opposition.
8. Try to close the gap. In many arguments, there are forces which have been trying to widen the gap (e.g., unions in organizing an action). Dwell on shared goals.
9. Look beyond principles (which tend to harden positions) to practical results (which lead to more flexible discussions).
10. Study the adversary—background, history, interests, achievements, hang-ups. These disclose attitudes you will have to overcome, weaknesses you will be able to take advantage of.

11. Once you have an acknowledgment of a point—by a nod of the head, an inflection, or a verbal yes— drop the subject. That is the time to close—and go on to the next point.

12. Be prepared with some humorous stories if the session gets too tense.

Most people enter a discussion with a set of assumptions that may or may not be correct. Try to get the facts straight and to determine the issues to be resolved and the previous positions of each party, as well as everyone's experience with this factor.

It is a good idea to put these elements into an agenda—a general one for the meeting and a more detailed one for your own use. The agenda should not reveal your own position unless this is essential.

The meeting should begin in a way to relieve tension, perhaps with some humor. Then perhaps explain why you are gathered, the advantage of negotiations with you rather than with someone else.

Marshal the arguments

Position set, marshal your arguments on paper. Many ideas seem less logical, even inconsistent, when you put them down substantively than when they are wandering about unorganized in your mind. In this way you will find that one thought leads to another, examples pop up, and a logical order of presentation develops.

The science of logical presentation is complex, but essentially it is a commonsense arrangement of facts and conclusions that leads to the answer you are suggesting. Make sure, however, that the premise you are starting with is sound.

When you have put down all the arguments that you can think of, place yourself in the position of the opposition, assume its point of view, and determine what response you would give. You might even prepare their agenda. Then adapt your own presentation and prepare a rebuttal.

Here is one suggested working outline:

1. Define the problem.

2. Describe the correlative problems.
3. Determine the sources or causes of each problem.
4. Detail the alternative solutions. Analyze them.
5. Suggest your solution. Explain how and why.
6. Listen to counterproposals.
7. Take each disagreement or each group of disagreements and solve them individually, the easiest ones first.

Of course, the functions may be multiplied or telescoped, depending on the extent of the discussion and the strategy as each party sees it.

Sometimes it is advisable to rehearse the negotiations during a brainstorming session with your own team. In such a session one knowledgeable party plays devil's advocate, arguing the other side as strongly as possible.

Beginnings

Begin by presenting basic information and clarifying the issues. Get acceptance on the issues and the facts first, if you can. Start with a fact-finding session where everyone is present and the ground rules are laid down.

Try to get a meeting onto a personal level. Use first names when you can.

Set a policy that everything said in the room is confidential, that outsiders (the press, the other employees, etc.) will not be told what is said in the meeting. Many agreements are foreclosed because some outsider is critical before terms can be nailed down.

The game plan

Have a game plan—what you would like to accomplish at each meeting. This enables you to follow your own progress.

In a negotiation where the parties virtually must come to an agreement—as in a labor negotiation—you can maintain a strong position in your initial demands. However, where one party can run away to another source, an unreasonable demand could destroy the encounter.

Before you start, know the cost of each item being negotiated—and thus the cost of concessions. Sometimes it is advisable to price-tag every element so that compromises can be made in specific dollar terms. Thus you will be prepared to make a minor concession to gain a major point.

If something develops that calls for a change of game plan, be quick to make that change.

Procedure

It is usually most politic to start with the points on which there is most agreement. If these appear out of order in your outline, you may be able to remedy the logical outline with a recapitulation or summary at the end of the argument—usually a good idea in any event.

Some factors to consider:

1. Is there a natural time limit or do you want to create a time limit?
2. What happens if the negotiation reaches no conclusion—for yourself and for the other party?
3. Would the status quo be bad for you or for the other party? How bad?
4. What would be the penalty if you were to bluff or give incorrect information? For the other party?
5. Are there other facets you can introduce into the negotiations? For your advantage? As a diversion? As an offset for something you may have to give up?
6. Are all the assumptions you are making tenable? Are you assuming costs, attitudes, resistance which can be avoided in some way?
7. Are the facts established or will there be disagreement about them? About how much things cost? How things are now? What was promised in the past? What other jurisdictions do? Perhaps a fact-finding group should be established before the negotiation.
8. Remember that the other side has to leave the negotiations with some victories to salvage its self-esteem. If a union is involved, the leadership must account to members. If a price is involved, it must cover costs. Each side has needs—actual, psychological, hierarchical. (There is a critical boss for every-

one.) Try to negotiate problems rather than demands, which are essentially responses to problems.

Approaches

There are several approaches to negotiation. Some professionals take the attitude that they will start with their best offer—and not move. If they can hold on, this makes future negotiations easier. General Electric Company used this technique in labor negotiations for some years, but the National Labor Relations Board held this was not bargaining in good faith.

Know what concessions you can make before you begin. Sometimes you may include, originally, demands which you know are expendable.

Be aware of the costs and other problems of each of the demands. Sometimes a casual promise made in a negotiation ends up on the agreement and proves to be impossible or too costly to fulfill.

Overdemand so that you can settle for a reasonable amount. Sometimes asking many givebacks on previous contracts begins the bargaining at a lower level.

Sometimes making many demands provides opportunity for a breakthrough on some of them, while you concede others.

Strategy and timing

If you are faced with an equivocal situation or a potential problem, you must weigh whether your bringing it up to clear up the matter in advance is more advantageous than waiting for the situation to arise and fighting out the issue at that time. An important element is how damaging a work stoppage will be when the situation becomes evident.

Setting a time limit is sometimes effective in bringing a negotiation to a forced end. This is common practice. But there is no real reason why most time limits cannot be extended, sometimes by just stopping the clock.

When to state your own minimum position is a delicate decision. This is best withheld as long as possible. An important skill is learning to listen. Sometimes a negotiator begins with a position so far out that it is best not to respond to it at all.

Other negotiators make their first offer very wide of the anticipated settlement on the theory that if they meet their opposition halfway they are still ahead. This allows the opposition to cry "Unreasonable demands!" and appeal to "the public." Or it may lead the opposition to run away.

Discussion depends largely on reaction and interaction, on the arguments and emotions expressed. If A insists on discussing an unreasonable point, B might introduce a point which A would resist even more firmly, where B can make concessions.

Where possible, seek out a friendly negotiator in the opposition and concentrate on him, hoping that he will influence the others.

Basic behavior

Avoid drinking. If you smoke, don't make it "nervous smoking." Get as much rest as you can. Relax emotionally, but not mentally or physically. Take off your jacket if others do, but not your shoes. Don't put your feet on the table. But watch the tone of the meeting for how far you can go. Don't be late for meetings.

Look at the people who are talking. It is a sign of respect, and may reveal more than is said.

Courtesy and mutual respect are essential. Not holding a door could make a negotiator feel affronted and more than necessarily negative.

Your demeanor is important. Don't respond with a fast agreement or act pleased with a proposal. Act as if the terms of a victory were what you expected.

To get your image in proper focus, you may want to make a minor concession without argument.

Don't keep worrying about the effect a negotiation will have on you personally. Try to be objective, think in terms of the agreement.

If you can, remain cool at all times; it helps keep your mind clear. If you can't keep cool, don't show your temper; it is a sign of weakness.

Be prepared to lose a deal rather than accept conditions

that will compromise your long-term position, e.g., the lowering of the quality of the product or a long-term loss.

Remember that some people are especially sensitive about certain areas, such as their past or their affiliations or their color or ethnic background. Such sensitive spots when probed can lead to major antagonisms. Often it is a good idea to explain why you are asking a question. Always try to avoid putting the other side in a bad spot personally. And don't ask a question that can bring out an unfavorable point about yourself. One attorney put it this way: Don't ask a question to make a point unless you know what the answer will be.

Emotion is useful in a negotiation but it must be displayed carefully and only to move a point. Avoid threats and insults; they are counterproductive.

Make sure you are saying what you mean—and that it is not misunderstood. Groping for a word may be perceived as a pause and change the meaning.

Appear sincere. From time to time appraise the other side's opinion of you, but don't rely fully on your own appraisal. Be especially cautious of what you say if your credibility has been questioned.

Admit it when you're wrong.

The best advantage in winning an argument is to be right.

Stick to what's right, not who's right. Personalities involve deep-seated prejudices that cloud logic.

Avoid emotional, challenging, or put-down language. Be objective, factual. Avoid a win-lose, right-wrong confrontation. *Not:* The supervisor backs me up 100 percent. *But:* The supervisor says my production is at average or better.

Selling yourself as a person—reasonable, important, successful—goes a long way in winning acceptance. Enter into a negotiation with confidence, or at least the appearance of confidence.

Pick out the strongest points in your presentation—those most likely to satisfy the real needs of the other party, perhaps, and dwell on them.

Sell with restraint. Overselling an idea may have a positive effect at the moment, but as the discussion (or operation) develops, the overstatements become evident and there is a net loss.

Don't make an issue of how good *you* are. Bragging turns people off. They are tempted to put you down. But if others brag, listen. Try never to interrupt a speaker.

Avoid "I told you so." People will know if you've been right.

After each meeting, try to give a positive note to what has taken place.

> "We are making progress . . ."
> "We have a better understanding of the issues."
> "The issues have been clarified."

Avoid discrediting a member of the opposition—even if he or she is dead wrong. There is a tendency to fight those who put others down, a tendency to solidify opposition. Don't embarrass a member of either team.

Try to keep the opposition relaxed, comfortable, friendly. Be pleasant, not belligerent, even when you are aggressive.

Don't express opinions that are unrelated to the issues involved. You only antagonize those who have contrary ones. Don't denigrate any group. Telling a Polish joke, for instance, could alienate any ethnically conscious negotiator.

Don't be too heavy-handed. Pushing too hard and too far can break up a negotiation or delay it considerably.

Appreciate concessions made and hardships endured. Give credit to others for good ideas.

Tactics

Tactics and timing are important in all phases of negotiation. One expert lists eight methods:

1. *Forbearance.* Hold back the threat of negative action until the effect will be greater; hold back further talk when the sale is made or the party convinced.
2. *Surprise.* Shift approach or tactics suddenly.
3. *Bland withdrawal.* Deny everything. Say you were misquoted or the quotation was taken out of context or the deed was not authorized.
4. *Apparent withdrawal.* Deny the appropriateness of the

meeting or the authority of those present or the
jurisdiction of an arbiter—and walk out.

5. *Fait accompli*. Do what you are planning to do, then
negotiate afterward. For example, a company would
use a nonunion supplier; send a bill at a higher
price; change the work rules.

6. *Reversal*. Change the terms at issue or the issues to be
negotiated; approach the problem differently. For
instance, don't raise the price, decrease the size of
the portion. Attack on a different front.

7. *Feinting*. Appear to make plans to avoid the issue.
Management could investigate moving the plant,
changing the product line, etc.

8. *Limiting*. Place a deadline on the negotiation. Cancel
the negotiations if no agreement is completed at the
time set.

When negotiations are to be undertaken with two or more
parties, negotiate first with the weakest so that settlement
may be used as the basis of the next settlement.

Where you are forced to negotiate first in a series, require
a "me-too" clause that will guarantee a better settlement if
any other party negotiates one.

Argue from the point of view of the domino theory: if the
same demands were made on others in the same position,
the results would be ruinous.

Where several units are in the same position you are in,
consider joining to negotiate as a single unit. Where the
opposition consists of several units, consider negotiating
with all together.

Where competition with other parties is involved, wait
until all other terms have been declared, i.e., try to be the
last to negotiate.

When a unique or prestigious element is involved as one
of the parties, argue the prestige involved in such a connec-
tion. If the argument is offered, explain that even with the
prestige, the deal must be economically viable.

If a major concession is required, break it down to small
pieces at each negotiation and decrease the period of the
contract.

Placing the opposite side on the defensive is often an effective procedure. An applicant for a franchise who comes to be sold on a project is made to justify his or her ability to handle the business. An applicant for a study course is given a questionnaire or test to prove her or his capability of handling the study material. A prospective purchaser of a lot is required to give personal and character references. Take the attitude that you are not trying to sell your product or service but to accommodate the other party who came to buy.

Sometimes you are in a position where no price is indicated. If you make an offer, it may be more than the seller expects. Often the seller is in the same position. "Give me your best offer," he will say. Or he will start with an outlandish price. The response can be an outlandishly lower one. Don't just offer half. In this type of situation, don't give your best figure until you are very close to it in the bargaining. Try to find out the area which the other side expects—perhaps by determining cost or previous sales of similar property.

Don't misstate facts. The other side has probably done its homework. Bring facts, documentation, charts, photos, other evidence. Make the folders thick to seem impressive, but don't be impressed by thickness. Make sure you get back all the papers that you have out for examination—and that you have another copy if the original should disappear. Don't accept every bit of data presented as fact. Some of it may be sheer fabrication. Check.

Judge from the files that are not presented and the people who are not present where some weakness may be.

If data has to be collected, don't place the burden on the negotiators; they will resent the added burden. If you want to win acceptance for a point, offer to do any detail work involved; small chores may be a big deterrent to a negotiation.

Watch out for flattery, good-guy approaches, snow jobs, procrastination, innate antagonisms, provocations to anger.

Much of what goes on at a negotiation is not contained in the actual words said. Much is conveyed by the way in which it is said. Sometimes something is introduced incidentally:

"By the way . . ."
"Let me be frank with you . . ."

These are devices. The matter introduced casually may be a major point, well discussed in advance and introduced in this way to deemphasize it.

Set up examples from selected areas to prove your point. (If a poll is to be taken, select the areas most friendly to you.) If necessary, arrange that some areas will bear out your contention.

The term of a contract can be adjusted to make the ultimate price higher or lower by adjusting the year-to-year (or month-to-month) variations. In such cases the longer the increases are delayed, the lower the price.

Where economic factors are only one aspect of a long-term contract, allowance may be made to reopen this facet of the negotiation under specified circumstances.

The way in which things are said plays an important part in their meaning.

"You know, John, that is not true!"
"Mr. Smith, you know that is not true!"
"You know that is not true, Mr. Smith."

An increase in physical movement, coughing, facial expressions, even blinking is significant in exhibiting tensions. There are opportunities for taking advantage of these tensions and times when you should be very careful of them.

Remember that sometimes an objection is only a problem subject to a solution.

Sometimes a statement by the opposition is too strong, in error, or a tactical blunder. Hold back definitive judgments in areas where you are not fully knowledgeable, but try to take advantage of the other side's mistakes.

Don't be impressed by titles or aura of success. Sometimes they are unearned, sometimes they are phony.

Keep your guard up all the time. A nod of the head to even a single item, which may not even be clear to you can lose the whole negotiation.

On the other hand, to win an important point, wait till the other side is tired and make a seemingly reasonable offer in which your point is made.

Keep your argument on a positive stand. Stress what is to be gained rather than what is wrong with the argument. For instance, if an employer wants to counter a request for a wage hike, which would necessitate a hike in the price of his product, he might say:

> "Keeping the cost of No. 2 widgets low would enable us to beat Steel's price by four cents and double our sales. We could have jobs for seven more men on the big lathe alone."

When demands seem unreasonable, ask the opposition to explain how they think you could operate if you acceded to their demands.

Changing negotiators is helpful if bargaining is not proceeding favorably. Substituting a woman for a man, a young person for an older one—a radical change—may give the negotiation a new turn.

Changing the level or area of negotiation—from one district to the whole city, from one department to the whole organization—can give a fresh start to a bad negotiation.

Changing the opposition—e.g., going to the president of a company or to the employees over the head of the negotiators—can offer a new pressure.

Using questions

Questions can be an important factor in negotiations. They can be used to elicit information, to secure attention or divert an issue, to make a point delicately, to press an issue obliquely. They can be used to emphasize a point or just maintain interest by forcing someone to wake up to answer and they can help end a discussion.

> "Now, how many members of the union are actually involved with Saturday work?"
>
> "Would you agree to such a provision if you were part of management?"
>
> "Don't you think that kind of privilege would lead to abuses and thus demoralization of those who do not abuse it?"

Even:

> "Don't you think we ought to go out to lunch now?"
> "Will you please clarify that point?"
> "Do you mean by that . . ."

"Can you see what that would mean in terms of person-hours and increased costs?"

"Did you know that there are seven thousand people in that category?"

"Isn't it time we finished with this discussion?"

How you ask a question often makes a difference. One incident involved a priest who asked, "Is it all right to smoke while I am praying?" The immediate response was, "Of course not." But when the question was put, "Is it all right to pray while I am smoking?" the response was: "Of course." When you ask a question, make it in the way that elicits a positive answer. Try a few easy ones first so that the habit of saying yes is developed.

Responding to a question

Responding to a question poses some interesting ways to avoid an issue or advance your point of view.

You may avoid the issue by answering with another question or answering a question that was similar but not asked, or by changing the subject.

"As I understand your question . . ." (and ask your own question).

You may say you do not know or that someone else is better qualified to answer, or respond with a generalization.

You may use a false analogy.

You may say the answer is not material or pertinent, personal, privileged, classified.

You may suggest several alternative answers without committing yourself.

You may state that the question cannot be answered unequivocally.

You may comment on the subject enthusiastically without responding.

"Yes, that was a lollapalooza of a meeting in which a great many subjects were discussed."

You may tell a pertinent joke or pass a compliment.

You may ask an accusing question.

"Isn't that a matter that your security people should know about?"

You may answer with a partial or inaccurate or patently false response.

Diversionary tactics

To delay a decision that seems to be going against you, create a diversion. Raise a point of procedure that must be explored, have a poor speaker explain a complicated point, get hungry and ask for a recess, introduce a new suggested tack, ask for an explanation of a complicated point, replace a member of the negotiation team, introduce a large batch of detail, ask for a committee to be appointed to study a problem, change procedure. Or you can cause a distraction in the meeting or appear to be distracted yourself by talking heatedly with someone else.

Unless you are seeking a diversion, keep the negotiation on course after it is started. There is always someone who wants to digress. But don't stop someone from releasing his own tensions with a personal story.

When tension gets tight, inject a bit of humor—even a ridiculous suggestion. Or change the subject. Try discussing a less difficult issue. Avoid a confrontation at this point.

If necessary, adjourn the meeting. But try not to adjourn it on a negative note. Before you adjourn, set the time and place for the next session.

These principles are not limited to labor negotiations. They may be applied to any arm's-length transaction, any adversary activity: the purchaser of an automobile or paper for a printing job, a lawsuit or the sale of a product.

Sometimes, all else failing, it is necessary to disrupt a meeting. There are a number of ways to go about this:

Several people start talking at once. There are points of personal privilege, points of order, questions thrown at the speaker. The speaker is accused of lying. The chairperson just adjourns the meeting. Or one or two key people walk out. The speaker rules that no quorum is present.

Several outsiders appear. Or many friends show up to provide vocal or, if possible, voting support. Or some of the opposition is not allowed into the meeting.

The chair may divide the problem into parts and assign subcommittees to study each point.

Question the jurisdiction or the purpose or the qualification of those present at the meeting.

Adjourn the meeting to get more information or certain other parties to attend.

Solutions

There are several approaches that may be taken: an arrangement of weighed priorities of the problem; a piecemeal approach, eliminating the easiest problem first; an offsetting approach, where one thing is granted in consideration for dropping another issue; a total approach, when the amount of money available is negotiated and the cost of each of the issues left to be assigned.

The solutions are usually a compromise where each side gives a little. Sometimes one side yields; sometimes no solution is reached and each side goes its own way without the cooperation of the other.

If you are in doubt about accepting a settlement, delay an answer. Caucus your people. Sleep on it to collect your thoughts and think through the effects of the proposed settlement.

The impasse

Comes an impasse. What can be done?

You can adjourn for a cooling-off, for lunch, to caucus.

You can make it:

> "That's just about the best we can do under the circumstances."
> "Let's go on to another issue."

Sometimes a question is best put obliquely:

> "My colleagues would like to know . . ."
> "How do the other members of the committee feel about this?"

Sometimes it is desirable to appoint two negotiators from each side as a committee to try to resolve the unsettled issues.

Shifting the level of discussion from individual items to a total dollar package to be divided as desired can change the pattern of a negotiation.

Look for other alternatives. Reexamine the basic needs and see if they can be satisfied in another way. Make sure that all members of the negotiating teams understand each step and how it was arrived at.

One professional negotiator describes his technique for forcing a decision as follows: Decide beforehand how far you want to go and how far you can go. Then get an agreement for round-the-clock bargaining. You negotiate for six, seven, eight hours. At an appropriate time you indicate that you must caucus. Recess for two or three hours, using the time to sleep. Resume and repeat. Eventually the opposition wears down. It becomes too tired to hold to a position. Then you can make your deal. Of course, both sides can play at this. Who wins what may then become a matter of physical stamina.

Where a conclusion is not reached, the negotiators may agree to put the matter up to a third party (arbitration) or ask a third party to help them reach a conclusion (mediation).

The agreement

Whatever agreement you make, make it specific, unless you have a public relations problem. A minimum-maximum settlement will almost always end up at a maximum. (A minimum-maximum settlement provides for a range of wages, etc., of not less than one figure and not more than another, particularly for situations that may arise in the future.)

Concede trivia for a major point. As soon as a point is conceded, change the subject. (The salesperson who talks too much can undo the sale.)

When you reach an agreement on a point, clarify it, make it specific immediately.

When a point is left open for investigation, make sure the point is not forgotten—unless you want it to be.

Correcting any mistake weakens your position. If you are not sure of an answer, delay, say you will find out, or caucus.

If you have made a bad, unacceptable mistake, don't wait until closing to retract it. Bring it up as early in the negotiation as you can. Otherwise it could break up any agreement.

When the agreement is summarized make sure all points (in your favor) are covered. If not, be prepared to refer to notes or to renegotiate.

Don't chastise yourself if you blunder. Everyone makes mistakes, especially in a negotiation. Just try to rectify them. Analyze how they came to be made and avoid them thereafter. They may even have resulted from a trap.

Make sure all members of your team share the credit for coming to an agreement.

Check the final draft carefully.

HOW TO WIN AN ARGUMENT

Argument, or debate, is a common portion of everyday life, involved in negotiations and selling, in law, politics, and even friendly discussions. Whatever you are doing with words, if you are trying to move people toward doing or believing something, you are likely to have a discussion, a debate—well, an argument.

Although argument comes in all degrees, from discussion to war, there are essentially two types: one is to convince an opponent to believe and/or do something, the other is to convince an unprejudiced third party of the justice of a viewpoint. The tactics are sometimes radically different. Logical and emotional appeals are used in different ways.

There is a strong opinion that no one ever wins an acrimonious argument. The animosities created are often more costly than a wrong decision. Moreover, many, if not most, opinions are so strongly held for a long time that the utmost logic will do little to move a made-up mind. The common attitude has been poetically expressed:

> In matters controversial
> My perception's rather fine.
> I always see both points of view:
> The one that's wrong and mine.

There are, however, ways to penetrate the most obstinate, as we shall see.

To be persuasive, it is, first, important to know exactly what you wish to accomplish. That determined, it is wise to think through how you plan to accomplish this: by logic, emotional persuasion, demonstration, testimonial? By selling yourself, your knowledge or experience; by selling the benefits—emotional or practical—to your audience?

A personal, prewritten outline will help, not only in presenting your points but also in organizing your own arguments, gathering detail, recalling and marshaling facts. In the end, it will save both you and your reader time—you by avoiding editing and rewriting, and the reader or listener by making the points clear without necessity of rereading and reassembling the facts.

In setting up your outline, you must consider not only the logical order of your points, but also in what order they will be best received. Starting with highly controversial material will turn off your reader or listener, and create a resistance that will color acceptance of the points that follow. In general, you start with the most acceptable, least controversial points, the easiest facets to have accepted, and move on to more debatable issues.

The stone wall of belief

Before you start trying to convince anyone of anything, understand this: much of our thinking is the process of justifying beliefs we already have, and justifying actions we have already taken. When we are afraid to speak up, we justify it by saying it would do no good anyway. We believe what we want to believe—and that is usually what we think is best for us.

The rational mind is beset with irrational traps. But people always think they are rational. Occasionally, after thinking about it, they realize that most of our thinking is affected by a huge mass of subconscious instincts, prejudices, suppressed memories, base emotions, and automatic reflexes. The mind abhors conflict. An idea, a wish, a perception that conflicts with a need, a desire, or a previous conclusion tends to be banished into the subconscious and comes out at a later time in disguise. We tend to forget disturbing ideas, to rationalize by finding or inventing reasons for believing as we do. When we do something or hear something that conflicts with a religion or any set of ideas that we accept, we tend to rationalize it away. We set up separate spheres for separate beliefs: an otherwise honest man may accept cheating a telephone company or the government, lovers do not see each other's faults, and so on. When we find it difficult to accept an idea which is accepted by everyone, we find some excuse for what we do. We develop opinions and refuse to accept facts which do not fit in with these preconceptions.

Right or wrong

To begin, then, in almost every situation, the best way to win an argument is to be right from the start. If the answer to a problem is equivocal, or you are in the wrong, the next important thing to do is to make yourself as right as possible by modifying, adapting, compromising, or adding to your position. Then you must tell yourself that what you are presenting is the most correct position practical under your circumstances. For most people, trying to convince others of an idea in which they themselves do not believe is a very great handicap. In addition, winning an argument on an issue on which you are wrong can be more costly than losing it: first by setting in motion actions in the wrong direction, and second in losing a friend.

Truth is not simple, even though we think in simplistic terms. Not all men are created equal. We are not descended from monkeys. Our enemies are not all bad, nor our friends all good.

We generalize. We simplify our thinking because to do otherwise would clutter our minds, make precepts incomprehensible to many, and incommunicable to most. Even in historical terms people are heroes or villains—until we read their complete biographies.

The two approaches

There are two approaches to an argument: (1) to convince by logic and reason. This is the predominant approach if an objective reasonable third party is to make the decision; (2) the additional use of emotional appeals and pseudologic, where the primary purpose is to produce a conviction or an action by the opponent. Both techniques are used—albeit sometimes unconsciously—in every argument.

It is always an advantage to have the discussion on home ground—psychologically as well as practically—because information, illustrative material, personnel, and decision makers are more easily available.

Often, *who* says something is more effective in changing a viewpoint than *what* is said. In a difficult personal situation, having a third party intervene can be effective, particularly if it is someone with the image of authority and/or good will. A doctor telling your daughter she must lose weight will outweigh countless appeals by a mother. On the other hand, some intervention can have negative effect, stimulating aggressiveness and resistance; e.g., a policeman telling a young person to "move along now."

In any case, the listener must be able to respond favorably to the question: "Does he know what he's talking about?"

The logical approach

Logical thinking is part of the natural heritage of all mankind, like breathing. As in all things, some develop the capacity more fully than others.

How do we approach the problem of convincing? First isolate the issues—what are the objections, the differences of opinion, the noes about?—not necessarily the ones raised, but the underlying objections.

> *Not:* The price is too high.
> *But:* It isn't worth the money to me.
> *Not:* Well, I don't want to do it right now.
> *But:* I'm not convinced.

Then put down on paper your own points. If they are complicated, use shortened versions. These are easier to manipulate in your own mind. Put them in order. If your case is strong, put them in a climactic order, the strongest last. If your case is weak, put the strongest point first, to break the film of resistance. Planning will help you organize your points better and help you think of more. For instance, here is a list of reasons you might give to get a customer to place an order now instead of later:

1. I can see that you get the best deal now.
2. You can be using the machinery all the time.
3. Delivery time will be longer later.
4. Prices will be higher later.
5. Your competitors will steal your customers with better prices and service while you wait.

Then consider what objections could be raised and how you will respond:

1. *Objection:* I'm short of cash.

   Responses: We can arrange time payments.
   Selling your obsolete equipment will provide a down payment.
   Savings will meet your payments.

2. *Objection:* My volume doesn't warrant the investment.

   Response: You need to produce only x number of units to pay for the equipment in two years. If production is only y units, you'll get your money back in three years.

3. *Objection:* There will be a new, better model out in a year.

   Response: This equipment incorporates major changes, the result of ten years of research. It takes ten years to develop a new model.

The basic device of logic is the syllogism. This is made up of three parts:

A major premise: All men have two feet.
A minor premise: John is a man.
Conclusion: John has two feet.

There are 246 variations of the syllogism and few of them are used consciously. Usually only the conclusion is stated. In an argument, deductions are made without thinking too much about the technical procedures, one following the other as a matter of course.

Of course, the mere making of a syllogism is proof of nothing. There may be disagreement on the major premise, on the minor premise, or on the conclusion itself. Sometimes it is necessary to accept a premise "for the sake of argument" to follow out the logic and see what follows. If you assume a conclusion—a hypothesis, logicians call it—you should remember that this is only a probability, not a certainty.

Facts, figures, and statistics

Facts, the basis of logical argument, are necessary but often boring. A politician who tried to explain logically how he could fight inflation would lose his audience in minutes. The subject is highly technical and to be really relevant must be filled with ratios and statistics which would be difficult to get across to an audience unfamiliar with economic theory. So facts have to be presented graphically—with pictures, charts, examples, anecdotes.

Facts are not always themselves simply facts; there are shades of truth and falsity in every situation. The truth is mostly grays, not black and white. And sometimes many other colors are mixed in. This is especially true of expressions which contain "all" or "none."

Some so-called facts are value or taste judgments, and these are particularly likely to be unjustifiable, since they are not objective. The idea that women should not vote was almost universally believed a century ago, for instance, taken as a fact when, of course, it was merely a widely held opinion. Values vary from time to time, place to place, and person to person.

Figures. In many instances, facts are figures—or supported by numbers. Figures can be used convincingly or logically, or they can be distorted in the ways they are compiled, selected, or presented.

Figures, especially figures that are not rounded, add an aura of precise knowledge, sometimes to very inexact calculations. Look at statistics with a jaundiced eye. Look for bias in the person who gathers them and the person who presents them. Look for suppression of unfavorable data or explanations or limitations. Look to see if the figure means what it purports to mean. Look for the improper standard of measurement (use of mean, median, or mode can be misleading, for example). Look at the authority quoted. Is he an authority in the right field? Look for who says so and how does he or she know, how big a sampling was used, and how it was selected. Look for extreme cases in the sampling that throw the figures out of the ordinary. Look for special conditions. And watch particularly that the conclusion comes logically from the figures themselves.

Misuse of statistics is both a device and a pitfall. The failings are many. Here are some typical ones:

Generalizing from the wrong base (i.e., drawing a conclusion from wrong or irrelevant evidence):

> Everyone in town will vote for him. He won a large majority in the national polls.
>
> He was not very popular. Almost half the stadium was empty when he spoke.

Generalization from a small base:

> All of the Ainus I know [two] have red noses all the time.

False extrapolation:

> Life expectancy has increased by 30 percent in the last century. By the year 2200 we may expect men and women to live to an average age of 138 years.

Misapplication of the sample:

> Statistics show that 50 percent of adolescents who have acne eat chocolate. Therefore, eating chocolate causes 50 percent of all adolescent acne cases.
>
> If one pill is good for you, two will be better.

Misconclusions:

In an argument you often deal largely with probabilities rather than certainties, and this always leaves room for differences of opinion. Even the most reliable statistics can be made to prove a variety of conclusions:

> The study shows that students with low grades smoke 38 percent more than students with average grades. Therefore, smoking is a cause of low grades. (But no, perhaps it is students who have low grades who smoke out of frustration.)

Misuse of averages:

> Average wages paid in a company were $80,000. (The president draws $200,000, two others get $20,000 each.)

The use of averages as a kind of evidence is particularly

dangerous because averages are subject to gross misinterpretation. A platoon of cavalry drowned in a stream that *averages* two feet deep (they went under in the part that was ten feet deep).

About averages. The word average itself can mean three different things: the mean, the median, or the mode. For most people the average is attained by adding all the figures and dividing by the number of figures. This is the *mean average.* For others it is the figure which is halfway down a graduated list, the middle figure, with half the figures larger and half smaller. This is the *median average.* When one figure is the most widely applicable, it is the *mode,* also acceptable as an average. In some cases, which figure is used may not be important; but in some cases the "averages" may be radically different.

Depths of Maple River
in feet at one-mile intervals

44	
36	
20	
20	mode—most frequent
20	
20	
20	
5	median—in the middle
4	
4	
3	
3	
2	
1	
1	

$203 \div 15 = 13.53$ average or mean

Often, taking an average is itself meaningless. If you manufactured dresses only for the average-sized woman, say size fourteen, all those who wear larger or smaller sizes would be out of your market. The same applies to many other facets of life, e.g., making laws based on the average conditions, or policies based on average intelligence or reading capacity or any other "average" condition in man.

Sampling. All statistics based on samplings must be suspect because samplings depend entirely on the selection of the audience. Few samplings are taken from a truly representative audience so a probability of bias exists in all such surveys. Old-timers remember the 1936 *Literary Digest* poll that predicted Landon would defeat Roosevelt. The survey was taken from a telephone list at a time when only a special stratified economic group had telephones.

Even the kind of people who ask the questions, the time of day when the question is asked, the clothing worn by a questioner, or the purpose of the poll itself can bias a survey.

Often factors other than those that appear in a statement affect the statistic. "The average income of Harvard graduates of the class of '59 is $51,428." The statement implies the benefits of a Harvard education. It ignores the fact that many Harvard graduates have investment income, that many come from families that offer extraordinary opportunities, or that statements of income gathered by surveys are extraordinarily unreliable. The answers from a sampling would also be biased by the fact that those who had lesser incomes would be more difficult to find, less likely to respond, and more likely to lie.

Sometimes the number in a sampling is too small to be meaningful. Try a hundred surveys of tossing ten nickels in the air. Overall there may be close to 50 percent heads and 50 percent tails. But in only one of the tests, the heads could well be 8 out of 10.

The standard of measurement. Often the standards on which a test is made are misleading. Given a verbal I.Q. test, an artistic or mechanical genius might fail miserably. Sometimes the entire measuring system may be inaccurate. Most scientific charts indicate a probable margin of error (e.g., plus or minus ten). But many readers take it for granted that figures are accurate merely because they are published figures.

Another form of distortion is comparison in dollar terms. The value of the dollar changes so much from year to year that almost all statistical charts are invalidated for direct comparison unless a stable dollar is used as a base. A man who received a 5 percent wage raise every year from 1967 to 1979 was earning less in real terms at the end of the period than at the beginning of it.

Differences. Sometimes small differences can be an issue, but more often they are of no real significance. But much ado may be made of this by making comparisons with many others. For example, in a list of low-tar cigarettes, one must be on the bottom of the list, even if all are within 1 percent of each other. The manufacturer can then proclaim in truth: "Of ten low-tar cigarettes Smoothy was lowest in tar content."

Percentages. Percentages are particularly adaptable to manipulation. One failing is in the use of different bases. During the Spanish-American War recruiters made much of the assertion that being in the Navy was "safer than living in New York City." The statistic was based on comparative death rates: nine per thousand in the Navy, sixteen per thousand in the city. No one bothered to mention that the Navy was made up of physically screened eighteen-to-twenty-four-year-olds. By this reasoning, statisticians can prove that the Sunbelt is more healthful than New York— the age at death is higher because people move there at a later age—or that it is less salubrious because the rate of deaths per thousand is so much higher. (An old saw is that beds must be unsafe because more people die there than anyplace else.)

A misuse of percentages often occurs because the base figure is not stated. For instance, usually a profit is figured based on cost. Something bought for $75 and sold for $150 shows a 100 percent profit. But some calculate on selling price, and find that 50 percent of the selling price is profit.

Defining profit. The word profit is particularly subject to equivocation. How much the officers of a corporation or the partners of a partnership take out as salaries, how much is taken for depreciation or reserves for various contingencies, how much is spent for repairs and maintenance, how much is spent on improvements, and many other factors may distort a reported profit.

By changing the base another type of distortion is accomplished. A change of profits from 9 percent to 10 percent is a 1 percent increase in profits or a 10 percent increase in the rate of profit (since 1 percent is 10 percent of 10 percent).

Manipulating the base. The same ignorance of base applies to the importance of any mix. The merchant who sold chopped meat of rabbit and horse meat might say, "I mix them equally: one rabbit and one horse." In this area there are special pitfalls in averaging percentages.

Selecting the proper base period for all comparisons is essential to any evaluation. Comparing current prices with 1932 prices will show a huge percentage increase, while comparing prices with last year's will show a relatively minor increase.

A common form of statistical deception arises from the use of "more." A device that gets "10 percent more production" should immediately stimulate the questions "more than what?" and "under what conditions?"

If there are fewer airplane accidents than car accidents, you must add another factor: How many passenger miles were traveled by each means of transportation? Carried to its extreme, one could conclude that travel to the moon by rocket is safer than traveling on a city bus.

Adding an adjective to the description is usually permissible. "The rate of increase in profits was a remarkable 10 percent over last year." But often the adjective is unjustified.

Which side do you take? Taking a negative view of a positive statistic can be very enlightening. If 80 percent of the homes have running water, that's good. But if 20 percent don't have running water—the homes of 42 million Americans—that's bad.

Graphs. Because figures tend to be boring, they should be presented pictorially wherever possible. There are many devices, of which the most common are graphs, bar charts, and pie charts.

Graphs that vary width as well as height can be particularly deceptive. A pictorial figure that increases 100 percent in size has four times the impact, because it is twice as high and twice as wide.

A graph can be made to show a slight rise or fall or a large rise or fall merely by adjusting the indices.

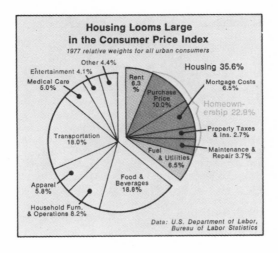

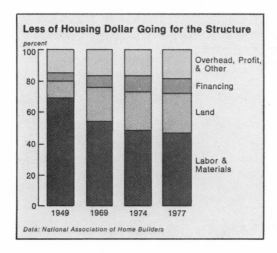

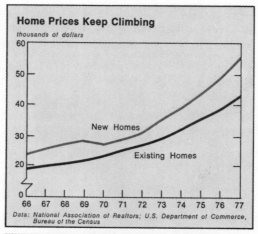

Home Prices Keep Climbing

thousands of dollars

New Homes

Existing Homes

Data: National Association of Realtors; U.S. Department of Commerce, Bureau of the Census

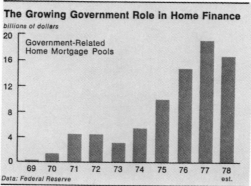

The Growing Government Role in Home Finance

billions of dollars

Government-Related Home Mortgage Pools

Data: Federal Reserve

Putting figures down on a graph is often misleading. Compare these two graphs of the same data:

1978

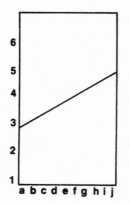

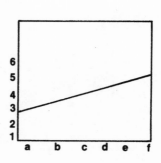

The different result is obtained by changing the proportions of the ordinate (vertical coordinate) and the abscissa (horizontal coordinate).

Similar effect can be attained through truncating the graph:

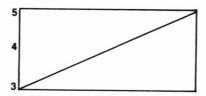

This technique can be used with bar charts or any other graphic device where proportions can be changed.

Words

Vocabulary can do or undo a great deal for you. The choice of the level should be one that fits your audience. Al Smith, who won election for governor of New York State four times, used to say, "I never use a three-syllable word if a two-syllable word will do." On the other hand, the use of technical terms or a university-level vocabulary is almost essential if you are to convince a sophisticated, knowledgeable audience of your authority.

Many words and expressions carry an emotional association or connotation which affects their impact: "red," "abortion," "dole," "Vietnam," "welfare." Such highly charged words must be chosen judiciously and you should be aware of their sometimes less than rational use when others sprinkle their arguments with them.

Many of us draw conclusions merely from the title of a person, product, or organization: "Americans for Peace and Justice," grade A, choice beef. Some words are used loosely, without being defined: "Democracy is guaranteed by the Soviet Constitution"; "All men are created equal." Any society may assume virtually any name, grade A could be fourth-rate when AAA and AA and A+ are also measures. Choice beef is inferior to prime beef. All men are created equal in what way? What is meant by democracy? Don't make judgments based on terms unless you know exactly what they mean.

The choice of words can add a great deal to emphasize your point, but some words can create deep antagonisms because they hold an association or stigma beyond their definition. For some blacks, "colored" is denigrating. Other people respond badly to "socialistic," "fascist," "childish," "Nazi," or an *-ess* added to a male profession (e.g., sculptress), etc. Such prejudices can easily get a meeting off course, into a discussion of what was meant:

> Let's not have another Vietnam!
> Watergate should never have happened.
> Communism must be stopped from getting a hold in Europe.

(Sometimes even wearing a shirt and tie or sending a letter on official-looking paper is enough to stimulate either a negative or a positive reaction.) The logic in each case is subordinated to the emotional response of the audience. If used effectively, emotional appeals can get attention, create a desired acceptance, or make a logical point.

Defining terms

One of the first steps in presenting an argument is defining the terms and the problem. A large portion of all disagreements arise from different understandings of the terms and the basic set of facts. The definitions should be precise and accurate.

You may find it to your advantage to restate the proposition in a different way:

> The question is not how many seats were empty, but how many were filled.

> The question is not whether the value of the portfolio increased or decreased in value. The question is how it increased or decreased in comparison with the averages.

> The problem we face is not too many people but too few jobs and too little increase in productivity.

Arrangement

Present your reasoning step by step. Organizing your points makes them more understandable. Organizing them in an effective way—climactic (strongest point last), anti-climactic (strongest point first), or some other suitable order—can make them more potent. Here is an argument that leads step by step to a logical conclusion.

> Increases in the cost of living have reduced the real wages I receive.
> In terms of what I produce, the output has increased in dollar value.
> In addition my productivity has increased by reason of my experience and added knowledge.
> Others with comparable productivity are being paid more.
> Rewarding my increased productivity will encourage my further efforts; conversely, it will be difficult to increase my productivity if such increases are not appreciated.

Balance an unfavorable aspect with a favorable one.

> True, I come in late every Monday morning, but I have to work late four days a week to take care of the four-o'clock deliveries.

Break it down

Break down the situation into parts and argue each of the parts.

> The problem is not just one of rising costs. It is a problem of six different kinds of costs.
> It is labor costs. We can cut these costs by installing a BX 2 machine which will reduce the number of employees by 18 percent. It is material costs. We can substitute plastics for steel and save 16 percent.

Offer alternatives

Break a subject down to alternatives, showing the advantages and disadvantages of those not recommended:

> We can either abandon the market or we can decide to spend enough to make a major impact.

> If we choose to confront our enemies, we face the danger of an attack; if we retaliate, we are virtually certain to bring about a bellicose reaction which we are not now prepared to meet. Our

obvious choice is to delay and prepare to negotiate from a position
of strength.

Present alternatives which are all unacceptable:

> We cannot afford to keep prices at the present level 'without
> major savings in product. We can cut the size of the package but it
> would then be smaller than our competitor's. We could reduce the
> chocolate content, but this would change the taste radically.

Don't accept as fact that only two alternatives exist. It is a
common misunderstanding to think that because one statement is false its contrary must be true. For instance, here are
two statements that contradict each other:

> That's John coming down the street.
> No, that's Bill coming down the street.

These viewpoints are contrary, but because one is wrong
doesn't necessarily make the other right; neither may be
right; it may be Tom or Sam or Joe coming down the street.
Beware of black-and-white either-or statements like "You're
either for us or against us" or "He is either a wise man or a
fool." Always consider the middle-ground answer, which is
frequently overlooked in discussions. By doing so you will
avoid oversimplification—and perhaps also avert the accusation that you are being stubborn.

Parallels and analogies

Arguing from parallel cases is a common and effective
method.

> John Brown, who does the same work I do, gets 20 percent more
> money.

> China, with large areas not suitable for agriculture, could learn
> from Israel how to make the desert bloom.

The analogy is commonly used to prove a point—and
often misused. Things that are similar in some respects are
not always the same in all respects.

One use of the analogy is to prove a point by taking it out
of a personal emotional setting. The Bible (II Samuel
12:1–6) cites Nathan's use of analogy to convince King
David of his error in sending Uriah to his death in order to
take Bathsheba:

And the Lord sent Nathan unto David. And he came unto him, and said unto him, There were two men in one city: the one rich, and the other poor. The rich man had exceeding many flocks and herds, but the poor man had nothing, save one little ewe lamb, which he had bought and nourished up; and it grew up together with him, and with his children; it did eat of his own morsel, and drank of his own cup, and lay in his bosom, and was unto him as a daughter. And there came a traveller unto the rich man, and he spared to take of his own flock and of his own herd, to dress for the wayfaring man that was come unto him, but took the poor man's lamb, and dressed it for the man that was come to him. And David's anger was greatly kindled against the man; and he said to Nathan, As the Lord liveth, the man that hath done this deserveth to die; and he shall restore the lamb fourfold, because he did this thing, and because he had no pity.

Then Nathan pointed out that David was like the rich man.

However, analogy is fallible. A person learning English, for instance, who uses it to determine the pronunciation of the letter combination "ough" will find that "ough" is pronounced one way in "although," differently in "through," and yet a third way in "slough." The plural of house is houses, but the plural of mouse is something not analogous.

The false analogy is one of the pitfalls of argument. Be alert to it in your opposition. Remember that not everything similar is the same. Here are two examples:

Everything that goes up must come down. His career has been a series of constant rises: he is sure to have a sudden drop in popularity.

Just as the OPEC nations have created a monopoly in oil, every developing nation will organize to raise the price of all raw materials.

In the first, there is a false analogy of a career to a physical object. While objects are subject to the law of gravity, obviously a career is not. In the second, developing nations are erroneously compared to OPEC nations, even though their situations are not really the same.

Testimonials

Enlist outside support. Quote an authority:

E. F. Hutton says: . . .

I agree with Lincoln that . . .
According to Hoyle . . .

Implication

Imply things which you do not explain.

> The course on which we are now engaged will lead to a situation no one can foresee.

Extension

Carry out the thesis to the absurd:

> Soon women will be invading the men's toilets.

> If taxes keep increasing at the present rate, our entire salaries will go to the government.

Prove a point by showing that denial of the principle leads to a contradiction or obvious falsehood:

> If you believe that reducing salaries is a practical means of stopping inflation, consider what would happen if salaries were eliminated entirely.

Shifting

Shifting the burden of proof to the other side can sidetrack an opponent's argument. This is often done by establishing a point and challenging the opposition to disprove it.

> You decry high taxes! Can you deny that higher taxes would be anti-inflationary and thus help protect the income of every worker and retiree?

Truisms

In an argument, the statement of a basic truism (or at least a widely held belief) that is not easy to refute can be effective. To refute it is sometimes dangerous, particularly in times of crisis:

> All communists are a threat to the nation!
> Moses was God's messenger who brought basic ethics to the earth.
> When he runs out of food supplies man will disappear like the dinosaurs.

Using opposites

Sometimes you can combine opposites, often paradoxically to prove a point:

> The best defense is an offense.
> The way to ensure peace is to prepare for war.
> If giving to the poor is a virtuous act, how then can taking from the rich be bad?

Questions

Questions can be used in several ways in presenting an argument:

1. Create a doubt:

> Does the support for this measure come from the underworld personalities who have taken millions from gambling in other areas?

2. Ask a rhetorical question and answer it:

> Do you expect a fair day's work? Of course you do. Then why not pay a fair day's pay?

3. Ask what a reasonable person or your opponent would have done in similar circumstances.

> There I was faced with Midland's offer of $5,000 more than I was making at Digital. What would you have done under such circumstances?

Indirection

Sometimes a direct attack would arouse resentment. You may pretend to ignore something that you affirm. Here's an example quoted from Queen Victoria's letter to Sir Henry Ponsonby:

> The Queen is no partisan and never has been since the first three or four years of her reign. But she has most deeply grieved over and has been indignant at the blind and destructive course pursued by the opposition which would ruin the country.

Repetition

Repeat your argument in different terms.

Much in advertising depends on this type of repetition to establish consumer cognizance. The fact that we have heard the name of a product over and over again seems to make it more acceptable—regardless of who said what about it. Repetition creates reputation.

Feedback

If you want to get long-term results, feedback from a message is an important factor. If the receiver of the message is convinced, the sender has an opportunity to speed effective follow-up and action. If the receiver is not convinced, there is an opportunity to find out why and follow up with further arguments. In other words, find out as frequently as possible how the person you are trying to convince or are arguing with is reacting to your efforts at persuasion so you can gain a psychological edge. One very simple way would be just to say:

> Don't you agree that this is a reasonable statement of the facts?

Or less obviously:

> You must agree that the other side has a point there, don't you?

Foresight

It is always a good idea to anticipate your opponent's objections and acknowledge them. Give reasons against you and destroy each in turn:

> You say they are cheaper. But the material is obviously inferior.
> You say they are stronger. But the material is crude steel and consequently heavier.
> You say they last longer. But they go out of fashion within two years.

Your message should then contain some inoculation against counterpropaganda.

Even when you do not expect counterarguments to be made, a message that seems to reflect two sides of a problem receives more favorable reception:

> Annie dear, I really don't want to tell you what to do. The decision has to be entirely your own. I am just pointing out the facts and the logic which should be in evidence if you are in a position to make a decision in this highly emotional period of your life.

Anticipate a point to prevent its impact:

> You will undoubtedly say that women live longer than men and should pay more into their pension funds. But women work fewer years and consequently receive smaller pensions for each year they work because vesting eludes them.

Refutation

How does one refute an argument, valid or fallacious? These are a few of the techniques.

1. Attack the evidence by reducing an example to its ultimate absurdity:

> Increasing the time in school is ridiculous. You might as well keep children sitting there twenty-four hours a day for the first thirty years of their lives.

> If pumping money into the economy stimulates business, let's issue another $100 billion in currency and let everyone be prosperous.

2. Or by saying it is old-hat:

> That was in the same report in which the committee urged cutting out all school athletics to balance the budget.

> Your statistics were outdated when the census was taken in 1960. New York is no longer the largest state in the Union. The big markets are no longer in the northeast.

3. Attack the sources:

> On that committee was the same James Johnson who last year urged cutting salaries for all town employees—a measure which would have caused a disaster for Hometown.

> The same measures were suggested by the Fascist *National Voice.*

4. Use analogy:

> There is no end to demands. If we were to respond to another demand for more money by our employees it would be pouring water into the ocean.

5. Use experience or history as evidence:

> To say you will hold the line on wages in the face of inflation is a benighted stand, reminiscent of the nineteenth-century industrial barons.

6. Restate the argument in different, less favorable terms:

It is not a question of more money for the poor but less money for the middle class who pay for welfare, the creation of a new class of underprivileged.

7. Reject a point as insignificant:

Of course I make personal phone calls on the company line. Who's counting nickels in this multimillion-dollar sales effort?

8. Concede a point as unimportant to present a more important point:

Yes, we expect more of our employees, we work them harder. But we pay better wages, give greater job security, and I think we bring them more contentment than most companies in this industry.

9. Assume the opponent is correct in his premise, but come to a different conclusion.

Yes, Tom Johnson is over sixty-five. But he is not in his dotage. He has the kind of background and experience and range of friendships which a younger man could not have.

10. Reject a point as impertinent or obviously false:

You don't really believe that all these new accounts came in over the transom without sales effort. It just doesn't happen that way. Every account has to be sold.

11. Admit something candidly and explain why it happened:

Yes, we did hold back wage increases during the past two years to keep our costs in line. Otherwise we would have lost our customers.

I cut production because raw materials were cut off by the blockade.

12. Attack a trivial weak point in an argument, and hold that the whole argument is equally vulnerable:

The opposition says that this project will cost $6 million and destroy 62 farms. The copy of the 1970 census in my hand notes that there were only 52 operating farms in the entire county of Ulster which covers ten times the area affected. Are my opponent's statistics all as reliable?

You say you require longer paid vacations. With the seven-hour day, twenty-two holidays and four weeks off, there are hardly any days left for working.

13. Pass over the point quickly:

I see no need to dwell on the disadvantages of DDT. It works effectively to kill mosquitoes and that is our immediate problem.

14. Quote the Bible: Almost any viewpoint can find support in this volume.
15. Quibble:

You say the prices have gone up 8 percent this year. Most authorities hold that maximum increase during the past twelve months is 7.2 percent. The guide you have been using is obviously unreliable. Reliable statistics come only from the Bureau of Labor Statistics.

16. Talk around a subject difficult to argue:

Wages should not be your primary concern. You should be worrying about the survival of the company, about increasing productivity. Ultimately your wages depend on these factors, and without my company's survival, your wages will be nil.

17. Digress:

You say the law is unconstitutional. The Constitution was made by human beings in the eighteenth century, a century when the industrial revolution was changing the economic nature of the world. The industrial revolution was . . .

18. Divert:

Why are you asking me to pay my old debt now? Remember the money I made for you in the Sandford deal. By the way, what ever happened to Sandford?

The founders of our nation would turn in their graves if they knew about the taxes we must pay today! After all, it was taxation that brought about the American Revolution and was the chief issue of that war. [Of course, it was taxation *without representation* that was the issue.]

19. Evade questions:

You ask me if I would fight to defend my country if it were invaded. That's a silly hypothesis. We will never be invaded.

Another way to evade the question is to shift the argument to "who is in the opposition?"

Public housing is the basic tenet of the Communist Party.

Or you can disparage your opponent:

> Who is this so-called expert in human frailties? He is a twenty-one-year-old high school dropout who has read four books on psychology and presents himself as the ultimate authority.

Or you can give an irrelevant answer to a point you cannot defend:

> The PCB which flows into the Nostalgic River as a result of making Whatnots doesn't spoil the environment; deer, rabbits, even bear still abound.

A joke is another diversionary device often useful when you cannot refute an opponent. In an 1860 debate on the Darwinian theory, Bishop Wilberforce asked Thomas Huxley whether it was his grandfather or his grandmother that claimed descent from a monkey. Huxley's response was that he preferred descent from a monkey to descent from a man who used his intellect to distract attention from the point at issue with "eloquent disgressions."

Subliminal argument

Arguing by suggestion is essentially a matter of creating a climate. If you are asked to spend the night in a house reputed to be haunted, you will undoubtedly hear strange noises. If you are at a meeting with someone reputed to be the most powerful person in the city, you are likely to accept what he has to say and to be intimidated by his threats, even those very much veiled. If the speaker is a physician of renown, you will probably even accept his ideas on the effectiveness of the President of the United States. An audience will tend to believe such a person because of who he is, not what he says.

Another form of indirect, subliminal argument is constant repetition. Any statement which is constantly repeated leaves a film of suggestion. If you say "everybody believes" such and such often enough, everybody will. This is a form of hypnotism which is hard to offset.

You can use suggestions effectively in many ways. You can avoid falling prey to it by recognizing that "belief" is not fact, and that suggestion is what it is, not logic.

Emotional devices

The real issues in an argument are quite often decided by emotions and prejudices. Rational argument is often a façade, only the framework in which the arguments are presented.

Although they have no place in logic, appeals to emotion can be as effective in negotiation and argument as they are in selling. Some techniques:

1. Appeal to tradition: We have done it this way for twenty years . . .
2. Appeal to religion: The Bible recommends . . .
3. Appeal to loyalty: We must stand shoulder to shoulder with our brother workers.
4. Appeal to pity: He has a wife and six children to support.
5. Threaten consequences: A no vote ensures disaster for the entire project.
6. Appeal to the sense of fairness: Suppose you were in my position . . .
7. Appeal to patriotism: My country right or wrong.
8. Appeal to anger: These acts are an insult to the American flag.
9. Ask the opinion of listeners: What would you say if the problem were put to you?
10. Flatter: All of you are too smart to be misled by this propaganda.
11. Attack the character of the opposition: He has fought every progressive measure since he became a member of the board.
12. Promise good fortune: This deal will make a million dollars for you.
13. Become indignant: That statement impugns my honesty, sir. *Or:* When you question my figures you are attacking either my intelligence or my integrity.
14. Associate your opponent's opinion with something negative: That is the line the robber barons took in 1870.
15. Appeal to competitiveness: The Russians will get to Neptune before we do.

16. Appeal to envy: They belong to the best country club because they pay half the rent you do.
17. Appeal to friendship: After all, how can you turn me down after all the years we have been friends?
18. Urge your listeners to get on the bandwagon: Everyone is doing it.
19. Threaten rejection: If you don't come around, you'll just be left behind.
20. Provide testimonials from celebrities (the testimonial is a basic argumentative device; see above). Although all of us know that those who endorse products or provide testimonials are paid—and often substantially—for their statements, we accept these testimonials—subconsciously perhaps—as evidence of the value of a product, notwithstanding the obvious fact that many of those who vouch for the quality of a product or the justice of a particular point of view are in no better position to judge it than ourselves.

Even an honest testimonial may be selected from among a thousand complaints. Or it may be taken out of context like some three-word quotation:

> One of the best [of the ten worst pictures of the year?]

A variation is "what the newspapers say." People believe what they see in print, almost regardless of the knowledge, intelligence, or prejudice of the medium or its staff or whether the product is highly advertised in the medium.

The use of fallacy

As we have noted, the basic logical syllogism goes this way:

> All men are mortal. I am a man. Therefore I am mortal.

But try it this way:

> All Cadillacs are cars. I own a car. Therefore I own a Cadillac.

The illogic is evident; we recognize it is so. But unless we can find the failure in the formula, it is difficult to disprove the conclusion.

Not everything that sounds true is necessarily true. A whole set of books could be written on specious argument:

Every argument can be misused. Here are a few widely accepted mislogics:

1. You or your opponent may say that a thing that happens after another happens because of it:

> Notice how the weather pattern has changed since we exploded the hydrogen bomb.

> Whenever an economic depression occurs, the hemlines of skirts drop so that the demand for textiles will be greater.

> Since Marshall became mayor, crime has gone up.

These are examples of *Post hoc, ergo propter hoc* (after this, because of this), a fallacy well known since ancient times. The fact that one thing follows another is no proof that one is the result of the other. The fact that a depression followed the election of a new President does not necessarily mean that the new President caused it. The eclipse of the moon did not necessarily cause the earthquake that followed it. There were depressions before the election of the President, earthquakes when no eclipses preceded. (Superstition is often built on this type of logic.)

To avoid this type of fallacy, examine which element mentioned causes which; what elements could be the common cause of both; and evaluate the possibility of chance correlation.

2. You or your opponent may generalize from limited examples:

> The city is as safe as any in the world. I have walked the streets of New York for forty years and never seen a mugging.

> Major crime has gone up. I was mugged only last week.

> The Finns are musical people. Sibelius was born there.

> My wife's uncle shopped there last month and couldn't find what he wanted. That store never has anything worth buying.

3. You or your opponent may beg the question by assuming the truth of the proposition before the discussion even begins:

> Everybody knows that businessmen are more interested in money than in service.

Mark Twain tells of a discussion between Adam and Eve as the animals were paraded in front of them. They get along fine until they come to one animal which has no name.

"Call it a horse," Eve suggests.

"But why a horse?" Adam asks her.

"Well," says Eve, "it looks like a horse, doesn't it?"

4. You or your opponent may be reasoning in a circle:

> Your handwriting is hard to read because it is illegible.

> "God exists. Doesn't the Bible clearly state this?"

> The Cheshire Cat: "Oh, you can't help that we're all mad. You're mad. You must be or you wouldn't have come here."

> Low-cost public housing can never be successful because the construction must be cheap.

5. You or your opponent may argue that something is true because it has never been proved false:

> There is no experience that indicates that production in a four-hour day would, with the added energy available, not prove as productive as a seven-hour day.

> I never heard of a bad museum.

> There is no record of settlers in America before Columbus.

6. You or your opponent may assume the conclusion:

> As the best player in town, Tom Brown can be depended on to win for us. [The unwarranted assumption is that Brown is the best player.]

7. Or use false analogies:

> Don't vote against the President. You don't change horses in midstream.

> I was offered a better job but I believe a rolling stone gathers no moss, so I'm staying.

> The students should not determine what the curriculum should be. You wouldn't tell a doctor what medicine to prescribe.

8. You or your opponent may be drawing conclusions by association:

> Vote for Joe Brown. He is a native son.

He was Lyndon Johnson's right-hand man. He knows what he's talking about.

He must love music. He went out with Toscanini's granddaughter.

9. You or your opponent may be oversimplifying:

Better dead than red.

Prohibit the sale of alcoholic beverages and you will save the thousands of lives which are taken by drunken drivers.

It is better to take a size too large so the shoes won't pinch.

10. You or your opponent may be using non sequiturs, statements that do not follow logically from previous ones and are irrelevant:

The show has a cast of more than a hundred. It should win a Tony Award.

Fascism was good for Italy. Mussolini made the trains run on time.

11. Similarly, you or your opponent may provide irrelevant evidence:

The measure has the complete support of John Wayne and my mother.

Dr. Jonathan Milhaver, the famous surgeon, is wholly in accord with the viewpoint that Sidney Brown is the best candidate for sheriff.

12. You or your opponent may use the "when-did-you-stop-beating-your-wife" technique. The respondent can answer neither yes nor no without admitting the validity of a statement that has not been proved:

Are you a Democrat and for the common man?

This technique is frequently used by prefacing a question with "why" or "when":

Why are women so much more concerned for human welfare than men? [The question already assumes that women *are* more concerned than men, an unproved generalization.]

Here's a practical application:

> To a customer who has not made up his or her mind: "Shall I wrap it for you, or will you have it delivered?"

SPEAKING IN PUBLIC

Like almost everything else, a speech has a beginning, a middle, and an end. But before beginning, you should decide what you want your speech to accomplish. Then decide what you will say to reach this result. Many speeches are just "saying a few words." Their objective is to entertain or to make friends. More often, however, a speech is made to inform or convince.

In either case you should outline what you are going to say. You may even write it out and memorize it. But don't, if you can avoid it, read your speech or recite it. If you need them, prepare notes as reminders. If it helps you avoid having a complete speech at hand, use file cards with key sentences on each.

It is important that you find out what you can about your audience, its prejudices, likes, attitudes, age level, sophistication, education. Write as you would speak to a single person in that audience.

The basic chronology of preparing a speech is:

1. Determine your purpose.
2. Analyze your audience.
3. Establish a rapport.
4. Establish the image you yourself wish to present.
5. Gather material on your subject.
6. Present the facts you want to discuss.
7. Make the points you want to make.
8. Outline an introduction.
9. Present any visual material.
10. Provide an anecdote or two.
11. Outline an ending—conclusion, summary, spur to action.
12. Outline how you get from 8 to 11.
13. Induce audience participation.

14. Summarize.

15. Get the audience to do what you want it to do.

If you have written an outline or a speech, read it as if you were one of the audience and gauge the reactions in that light. Will they like you? Believe you? Do what you ask? Is there some phrase or element that could offend someone? Are you asking too much? Or too little?

Everyone is at least a little nervous when he or she faces an audience. Don't worry about it. Concentrate on what you want to get across. Speak vigorously. If you can start talking with a "grabber," you will get yourself and the audience on the right path. Don't allow yourself to think "How'm I doing?" or about any special people in the audience. Keep eye contact with one person at a time, but change people. You will gather reactions almost subconsciously in this way. At the very least, know exactly what you plan to say for the first minute of a speech so as to give yourself time to get your bearings and think the situation through.

If you tend to be nervous, try to get yourself enthusiastic. When you do, the ideas will pop up easily in words. If you have concrete ideas, facts and figures will flow out as they would in a private discussion.

Home television playback gives you an opportunity to see yourself as others see you and helps you eliminate distracting fidgets. Similarly, tape recorders will help you monitor your voice and inflections. Equipment may be rented.

If you think you may be called upon for an extemporaneous speech, have a story ready for the occasion, an idea of what you want to say, even if it's only an expression of pleasure at being where you are.

Consider, too, the purpose of the meeting. Sometimes a strong speech is out of place. Business talk doesn't generally fit into a social meeting. Some subjects just don't go at a women's study group, etc.

In delivering your talk:

1. Make certain you have the subject matter well in mind. Be prepared to answer questions.

2. Get yourself enthusiastic about what you are doing.

3. Respect your audience. Don't talk or act down.

4. Don't talk the subject to death. Don't talk any point to death.
5. Enunciate clearly. Talk at a conversational pace in conversational language.
6. Vary the way you talk; in voice quality, type of sentences, type of material, the pace. Pause.
7. If you fumble, don't fret.
8. Feel confident. Look confident.
9. Relax.
10. Move your arms and body.
11. Watch your audience for clues on their reaction.
12. Try to be useful in providing answers to pertinent questions by entertaining your audience, by inspiring, by awakening enthusiasm.
13. Stick to an outline the audience can follow.

Watch your language. Don't use Cadillac prose on a working-class audience. Don't use slang or what would be considered improper language to a ladies' auxiliary. Do try to use colloquialisms, even foreign expressions familiar to your audience; an Italian phrase, a Yiddish expression is helpful in establishing a rapport with Italian or Jewish audiences for instance.

Your body itself can be useful in conveying and emphasizing ideas. Use of arms and hands, facial expressions, head movements, a pointed finger, a clenched fist, a nodded yes or no emphasized by arm movements are part of an almost subconscious body language. A forward step emphasizes an appeal to action. Lateral movements signal a new point. A backward step indicates a conclusion. But gestures should be spontaneous and natural or they appear stilted and are counterproductive.

The makeup and emotional condition of your audience can be a factor in what you say and how you phrase it. A tense audience needs some humor. An antagonistic audience needs both humor and buttering—pointing out what you have in common.

My parents were born on Balsam Street right here in Reading . . .

Three years ago, when I last addressed the BPOA . . .

But don't urge a temperance group to temperance or talk to an Audubon Society on the need to safeguard birds. Tell a group that agrees with you what *more* they can do.

An apathetic audience, probably more difficult to deal with than an antagonistic one, needs an emotional, do-it-now speech, full of crises, horror, anger, etc. to stir it up.

It is not wise to use the same speech for every audience, nor to repeat it too often. It may not be appropriate for everyone, and if you are tired of it, this will be reflected in the way you deliver it.

Watch your audience's reactions. Sometimes a faux pas you have committed becomes evident on the faces of your listeners and can be corrected quickly. On the other hand, sometimes enthusiasm may encourage you to follow further along a certain path.

Be aware that your status, how you dress, how you are introduced, are part of what you communicate.

When you are making a point, even when it is directed at one person, encompass the whole group with your eyes.

If a point is complicated, outline it first, even in short remarks.

For a toastmaster

If you are toastmaster for an event, eat early and nibble at the dinner served so that your eating will not interfere with the timing of your remarks. Often a toastmaster will be responsible for the physical attributes of the dinner, keeping it on schedule, and sometimes for the air conditioning, music, and relations with the kitchen. But the main problem is to recognize some of the guests, usually with some humor. In fact, humor is the key to being a successful toastmaster. You should have an ample stock of anecdotes and jokes appropriate for the situations that will occur. Here is an amusing story about a toastmaster:

> There is the appropriate story of the toastmaster whose wife died two days before the convention dinner. He wired the president of the association: "Regret death of my wife makes it impossible to join you. Can you provide a substitute."

If you are often asked to be a toastmaster, it might be wise to write out appropriate stories and quotations that will be helpful for impromptu speeches, for getting over difficult moments (disputes, embarrassments, antagonisms, critical comments). If you must improvise, describe an incongruous absurdity of the event ("If we were having this dinner on the moon . . ."), pun, exaggerate, redefine the name of the organization, be sarcastic, create an epigram, parody the purpose of the event, etc.

Many books offer a variety of jokes and anecdotes specially designed for situations in which speakers may find themselves.

Stories and jokes

Some people listen to be entertained. Some people listen to learn about a subject. Some people listen to be emotionally aroused. A good speaker provides something of each of these. That is why a speech usually starts with a story to break the ice for the speaker, relax those in the audience who are tense, and sometimes lead into the subject.

> "A funny thing happened to me on the way to the conference . . ."

Never read a funny story. Tell it as if you were telling it to a friend. Personalize it by applying it to the interests of the audience—persons, places, things they know about. Don't telegraph either the fact that you are going to tell a story or the punch line. Make the story short. And if the audience doesn't laugh, drop it. Don't explain. And don't criticize the audience for not laughing.

Be careful to tell only stories that are appropriate to the audience, and try to have them appropriate to the occasion. (Using names of prominent members may help.) But remember that humor can hurt people's feelings.

The lead-in to the joke makes it more appropriate. Here are some common ones:

> On the way to the hotel this morning . . .
> Last time I was at an Owls meeting . . .
> Just before Bob Somers asked me to be toastmaster today . . .
> At breakfast yesterday my wife . . .
> When the Retirement Committee met last night . . .
> Joe Jones grabbed me by the collar last night to give me an important bit of information . . .

I am reminded of the story about the lawyer who was approached by an eighty-four-year-old woman who wanted a divorce from her eighty-seven-year-old husband. "Why, after sixty-two years of marriage?" he asked. "Sixty-two years is enough," she told him. "Enough is enough." So I say, "Enough. . . ."

Several good books are available to provide jokes or anecdotes for various situations or material adaptable for a variety of situations. Those who speak frequently make arrangements with professional writers who create timely gags or publish newsletters with timely humorous material. (Orben's Current Comedy, Comedy Center, Inc., Wilmington, Delaware, is one.) A joke may form a bond between speaker and audience by indicating a common problem.

> If we are what we eat, the Post Office cafeteria must serve a lot of escargot.

> Death is nature's way of telling you the F.D.A. was right.

Extemporaneous speaking

It can happen that one day you will be called upon to speak with little or no warning. Don't panic. Spend a few seconds to think about the audience and the occasion and tell how you are honored to be there and how good they are. Quote one of the acknowledged geniuses. (It is a good idea to have a few ever-appropriate quotes on the tip of your tongue.) If you can, tell an appropriate story. Tie the talk together. Then sit down.

Don't apologize or say how unexpected this is.

Preparing the speech

The conventional steps in presenting a speech are (1) gathering the material, (2) deciding what you want to accomplish, (3) arranging the material, (4) putting it together into a whole, and (5) saying it.

In arranging your speech don't try to cover too much ground. Keep a unity to your speech. One test: can you summarize it in a single paragraph?

Selecting a title

The title of your speech should be selected primarily: (1) to motivate an audience to come:

> "How to Live to be 100."
> "How to Become Rich Slowly."

(2) to tie in with the occasion:

> "Teaneck's Next 100 Years."
> "The School Situation Today and Tomorrow."

or (3) to tie in with the audience.

> "Building Bigger Profits in the Plumbing Business."
> "Why Teachers Must Learn."

Openings and beginnings

Beginnings of speeches have a very special function: to establish rapport with the audience, to get the audience in a good mood, to bring up the subject. The most common way of doing this is with an anecdote, a joke, a bit of poetry, a quotation, a reference to what the group has been doing or to a prominent member of the group.

The beginning of a speech may be a story, a quotation, a thank-you, an explanation of a common experience, a compliment, or it may be more interestingly a personal experience, a tie-in with a timely event, or a dramatic statement.

One device is to precede the address "Ladies and gentlemen" with: "My good friends, Chairman John Brown, and Tom Collins, etc." Sometimes you add: "My fellow Americans" or "My fellow Rotarians," etc.

Before beginning, pause for five seconds. Then you can start with a story or a quotation.

> When I was a young man in India, I used to report criminal cases for the newspaper that employed me. It was interesting work because it introduced me to forgers and embezzlers and murderers and enterprising sportsmen of that kind. Sometimes, after I had reported their trials, I used to visit my friends in jail where they were doing their sentences. I remember one man who got off with a life sentence for murder. He was a clever, smooth-speaking chap, and he told me what he called the story of his life. He said: "Take it from me that when a man gets crooked, one thing leads to another

until he finds himself in such a position that he has to put somebody out of the way to get straight again." Well, that exactly describes the present position of the cabinet.

—RUDYARD KIPLING

Establishing yourself

Sometimes the speaker has to establish himself and his credentials with the audience. The first step is to make certain that the person who introduces you has a full background, even some set paragraphs of what you have done. Thereafter you can allude to them, indirectly if possible.

> While I was preparing an exhaustive study of birth control in Tunisia for the Ford Foundation . . .

> I am a political scientist by training, a lifelong student of economics by inclination, and a steelmaker by profession. That's why I'm delighted at the opportunity to meet with you and discuss our common problems. I feel that our international trade problems in steel, for example, are deeply rooted in the historic political decisions our nation has made over the past thirty years. We've got nobody to blame but ourselves for the fix we're in.
>
> What I am going to try to demonstrate, however, is the idea that some of the gravest problems facing us can reach a far speedier and satisfactory solution if we can identify them correctly.
>
> —GENE DROSSEL

Sometimes a complete introduction is necessary:

> Mr. Chairman, members of the board, my name is Martha J. Sara. I'm an Eskimo. I was born and raised in Bethel. I'm a junior at the University of Alaska. My major is sociology and I plan to go on and become a social worker.
>
> On behalf of the Theata Club, which is an organization of native students on the University of Alaska campus, and on behalf of myself, I would like to say that I'm grateful for the right and am happy to take the responsibility on behalf of the Native Land Claims.
>
> —MARTHA J. SARA

Sometimes two elements can be combined:

> That was a very nice introduction. I only hope I can live up to all the nice things he said about me. There are some flattering remarks that should be taken with a grain of salt, but what our friend said about me—well, I like it.

If the audience is strange to you, try to get some information about it from the person who invites you to speak. If you can, strike up a conversation with one or two of those who will be listening and get an idea of how they think.

Recognize the audience

Recognize that this audience is special, that it is important. Incidentally, indicate your own qualifications lightly if the toastmaster has not done so.

When practical, mention the group, the occasion or something that compliments the group you are talking to:

> It is always a pleasure to talk to the Jamestown Rotarians because . . .

> I first met Johnny Johnson seven years ago right here in this room, when he was not the famous . . .

> You of the Seventh Night Juniors honor me with the privilege of speaking to you on this fiftieth anniversary because . . .

Acknowledge the invitation and express your pleasure at being asked:

> Thank you, President Yankee, distinguished guests, parents, students and graduates. I am happy to have the opportunity to share this milestone with you; to be with you at an event marking the end of one point in your search for education, and to be with you as you start down a new road.
>
> —JOHN D. SELBY

> Good morning. It's good to be with you this morning. For one thing, I expect to learn a great deal. More on that later. For another thing, the spring equinox is at hand. It has been a long cruel winter for railroads everywhere. At Rock Island, we prayed for the Ides of March—and hoped that T. S. Eliot was wrong, all wrong, about April.
>
> —JOHN W. INGRAM

Break the ice

You may refer to a previous encounter:

> Eight years ago it was my painful duty to present to the House of Congress an unexaggerated picture of the general distress pervading the whole land. We must all yet remember some of its frightful features. We all know that the people were then oppressed and borne down by an enormous load of debt; that the value of property was at the lowest point of depression; that ruinous sales and

sacrifices were everywhere made of real estate; that stop laws and relief laws and paper money were adopted to save the people from impending destruction; that a deficit in the public revenue existed, which compelled the Government to seize upon, and divert from its legitimate object, the appropriation of the sinking fund, to redeem the national debt; and that our commerce and navigation were threatened with a complete paralysis. In short, sir, if I were to select any term of seven years since the adoption of the present Constitution, which exhibited a scene of the most widespread dismay and desolation, it would be exactly that term of seven years which immediately preceded the establishment of the tariff of 1824.

—HENRY CLAY

You may make a dramatic statement or a startling forecast:

Joe College is dead. The era of reversible topcoats, porkpie hats, yellow chrysanthemums and football weekends is now just a memory. We have pressed them all between the pages of time alongside our lost youth, and our bright hopes.

College life when I enrolled at Fordham University in 1939 organized itself around weekend spectaculars—football games and fraternity dances in the autumn, pilgrimages to nearby girls' colleges for "mixers" in the winter, and dates downtown in New York during the spring. It is a sweet-sad exercise to think back on those days.

—WILLIAM J. McGILL, 1969

Or use a strong story or quotation:

Let me begin with a modern parable that portrays the plight of a public health regulator in an age when a technological revolution is producing synthetic organic chemicals made of the materials of life but never before encountered by living systems, when analytical chemistry is routinely detecting substances in parts of parts per billion, and when regulatory decisions affecting the production and distribution of such compounds often involve monetary losses in the tens or hundreds of millions of dollars.

—DONALD KENNEDY

Ladies and gentlemen: "Let him who desires peace prepare for war." Sound scary? It is. But this time-tested Roman advice has served nations well through the ages.

—PAUL LAXATT

Nostalgia can provide an interesting opening:

Once upon a time in the not so long ago in a rolling land washed by aquamarine waters, cloaked by green forests, and caressed by a warm sun, the people worked and played, but something was missing in their lives. By and by certain among them recognized that there was no place to broaden their intellects . . . to quicken their minds . . . or to challenge their spirits. "How do we brighten our lives in this beautiful land?" they asked. And they were puzzled, but by and by a small voice said, "Let's build a university." . . . and presently another voice said, "Let's" . . . and the few voices became many . . . and the many became a rising chorus.

And lo and behold they did . . . and after much planning and building and work, the little university on the hill in the forest by the river near the sea nestled snugly among the pines, close by the aquamarine sea, beneath an azure sky. They chose the school colors for themselves and all those to follow after them and it was natural to choose blue and green, for blue and green were everywhere. And they were happy with what they had wrought, and it was the beginning of the beginning.

—ARTHUR H. DOERR

Take the viewpoint of the audience to get it involved:

You've worked hard for this moment and now you're anxious to get on with the rest of your lives. But before you step out on square one—or whatever square it is for those of you who are already past square one—I want you to take a few minutes with me. Not because I pretend to have the answer to any searching questions you may have, but because we share a common identity and in our mutuality we may both find answers.

—ALAN K. CAMPBELL

Or refer to a common experience:

In his famous Gettysburg address, Abraham Lincoln described government as "of the people, by the people, and for the people." Nearly 115 years later, we understand the "of," are willing to tolerate the "by," but tend to forget the "for." And if government is indeed "for the people," then we as federal employees have the obligation to keep the people informed.

—DAVID H. BROWN, 1978

Talking to you today is a sentimental journey. I'm a local boy. I grew up around here, and once even had dreams of playing on your football team. But I must confess that one exposure with the greats of the Marshall Goldberg days was enough to send me to the less strenuous athletic life up at Grove City.

—J. PAUL STICKL, 1978

When you face an antagonistic audience, humor is a helpful ally.

Perhaps I should have prepared a bit more thoroughly before getting onto this platform this evening. Perhaps I should have done what a speaker friend of mine did a few years ago. He was to speak in a small town where public speaking was more or less frowned upon.

He told me a man entered the only grocery in the town and asked the grocer to sell him all the stale eggs he had in stock. The grocer thought it a peculiar request and asked, "What do you want with all the stale eggs? Are you going to throw them at the speaker tonight?" "Sh-sh!" hissed the buyer. "I'm that speaker."

—ARTHUR L. KASER

Get to the point
Then introduce your subject:

What I'd like to discuss with you today has the potential of tearing our country apart at the seams.

There's a new 'war' raging in the United States. It's a war that has caused considerable concern—and a great deal of interest—on the part of serious observers of the American scene.

—STEVEN R. HURST, 1978

State the problem and the questions you propose to answer:

Colleges and universities are deeply concerned about their institutional roles. How much of the traditional function of higher education should be preserved? What sort of accommodation should be made to the demands that colleges serve more fully the social needs and aspirations of the community? What type of orientation can and should be made to a rapidly developing urban society? How can communities be brought more fully and meaningfully into the mainstream of educational experience? Should the administrators accede to the pressures for an active institutional participation in politics? Should the requirements for admission to colleges be relaxed, or done away with? How can the colleges help to improve the quality of American life? These are but a few of the questions affecting the expanded role which colleges and universities are expected to serve. Higher education is launching forth on a new mission.

—WILLIAM H. BIRENBAUM, 1969

The middle

The middle of a speech tells and persuades. It offers facts, figures, charts, photographs, other evidence. It arouses emotions. Perhaps it enlists audience participation. It builds images of what will happen if . . .

If you have to lead an audience to your way of thinking, start with the points where you agree:

> You are absolutely right in taking a stand on . . .
> But I would go even further . . .
> Let us approach the problem in this way . . .

If you have several points to make, enumerate them:

> I want to make several points on this project: First . . . Second . . . Etc. . . .

It is a good idea to outline your points so that the audience can follow your thinking in a more organized way.

> Some in the audience know my long-standing interest and concern with instructor preparation; that might have been one area for special discussion.
>
> There were, and are, many additional possibilities: (a) parent involvement in driver education; (b) pedestrian education; (c) affective skills for traffic safety education; (d) evaluation.
>
> —CHARLES H. HARTMAN

You may wish to name the points first and discuss each at length, or you may summarize each point in one or two sentences.

Some material may not lend itself to "points" but to another logical order: the past, the present, and the future; America, Europe, and Asia; the rich, the poor, and the middle classes; and so forth. Or start with a description of a problem, how it grew, how it affects the audience, how it can be solved, what the audience can do. If there is another point of view, you may want to mention it.

If your speech has to do a selling job, check the section on sales letters in this book and use the same formulas. But don't wander. Stick to an organized outline or you will flounder.

Don't be declarative throughout. Ask rhetorical questions. Use exclamations!

Here are some examples of the effective use of the enumeration of points and outlining:

> I would like to sketch five forces for change in America—some more familiar than others—that have very significant implications for marketing the years immediately ahead.
>
> These forces for change are:
>
> 1. The new demographics;

2. The rising level of education;
3. The new values;
4. The new economic realities;
5. The growing poverty of time.

After reviewing these forces for change, I will then suggest several increasingly important consumer orientations that are emerging as a result. In short, I plan to be true to the title of this speech.
—LEONARD L. BERRY, 1978

The ending

The end of a speech does two things principally: it summarizes and it presents a plan of action and requests action. And it might include a catchy slogan.

Not all speeches are effective. Most of the foul-ups are due to: (1) bad material, (2) bad organization (number your points), (3) bad delivery, (4) bad explanations, (5) talking too long or not enough, (6) speaking over the head of the audience in material and/or vocabulary, (7) patronizing your audience, (8) not establishing acceptance, or (9) not specifying the action desired.

Here is a closing that clearly states and summarizes the speaker's points and plan of action:

Finally, a strategy that I feel holds the highest potential: to press for tax incentives as the best way to achieve goals of regulatory agencies.

Environmental and safety regulation activity has tended recently to eclipse the regulatory effect of IRS rules. Yet, I believe a case can be made that the Internal Revenue Service is the greatest regulator of all, even though regulation per se is not intended.
—JOSEPH P. FLANNERY, 1978

Close with a summary of the points you have made:

In summary:

There have been two broad parts to this presentation. In the first part, I sketched five forces for change in America that I believe hold very significant implications for marketing. The forces for change reviewed were:

1. The new demographics;
2. The rising level of education;
3. The new values;
4. The new economic realities;
5. The growing poverty of time.

These are, of course, related forces for change. For example, educational gains are contributing to the emergence of the new

values and the new values, in turn, are giving new meaning to a
variety of time-using activities . . .
     In the second part of the presentation, I suggested four . . .
                                        —LEONARD L. BERRY, 1978

Keep in mind how you began your talk and get back to the point—especially if you have rambled a bit:

That observation permits me to close by returning to the point
which, at the outset, I labeled as my subtheme: the corporate lawyer,
in his role as director, counsel, and draftsman of articles, bylaws,
incentive compensation plans, and in myriad other ways, has a
crucial choice. He can be the mechanic—a highly skilled but
essentially nonprofessional technician—and thus a perpetuator of
the problem. Or he can choose to bring to bear his broader vision
and his sense of responsibility to both the corporation and the
board. Corporate leaders, and those who advise them, including
many in this room, must realize that each issue cannot be treated as
a discrete, narrow case, but rather must be seen as a part of a much
larger pattern in the mosaic reflecting the relative roles of the
public, government and business—and of board and management—
in our private enterprise system. We are now mounting pieces of
that mosaic. If the corporate community, including its counsel, does
not like the picture at the end, it should begin by blaming itself.
                                        —HAROLD M. WILLIAMS, 1978

No, tomorrow will not be an easy time; but it will be a fascinating
time! And it will be a particularly rewarding time for those who
truly understand that the mission of business, and of our other
institutions, is to serve people, not to use them.
                                        —LEONARD L. BERRY, 1978

And urge action on the point you are making:

Let's force more balance into our education policy today, so that
our leaders tomorrow have our system in better perspective.
     The attitude of many public officials toward business verges on
righteous hysteria.
     They kiss off the free enterprise system in favor of small special
interest groups.
     We are all in business . . . we are in a position of influence. I
respectfully suggest that we have a great responsibility to help turn
this thing around.
     We have a magnificent country. A powerful free market econ-
omy. A great mass of citizens. Let's preserve it.
     There's so much at stake. Together we can get something going
. . . let's get with it.
     Thank you.
                                        —J. W. MARRIOTT, 1978

But, with your help and that of labor across the nation, there is much that we can accomplish. Every American worker can, in effect, serve as inspector, consultant, and monitor of safety in the work place. Organized labor can preach the Gospel of prevention and protection. And we can advance the idea that safety in the work place is an investment, not just an expense.

With efforts like these, I have no doubt that we will write, in our crusade for a safe, healthier working environment, a record of vigilance—and victory. Thank you.

—JOSEPH C. CALIFANO, JR., 1978

You may end with an appropriate story:

May I close, as I began, with a story which I think will sum up perhaps the way we might feel about this program for the coming year.

One of the participants in this conference told me that as he was coming down Pennsylvania Avenue from the station, he went by the National Archives Building. He saw carved on the front there, as you may have seen many times, the phrase: "What is past is prologue." He said to the cab driver who was one of these intellectual cab drivers that we have in Washington who is supposed to know about quotations and such, "What exactly does that mean?"

The cab driver said, "That is just another example of this government jargon that you hear about. What it really means is you ain't seen nothing yet."

—ARTHUR LARSON, 1978

An emotional ending can also be very well remembered:

A wealthy man took a poor boy from the slums of a great city to his lodge high in the mountains. The boy awakened in the morning. The sky was illuminated with the red and gold of the rising sun reflecting on the ice and stone of the rocky pinnacles and blazoned across the sky. The boy rubbed his eyes in wonder and a great fear filled him. Looking at the flaming splendor, he knew he had burned to death. Terrified, he screamed, "Please, sir, wake up! Something awful has happened, the whole world is on fire." His wealthy friend opened his eyes and, seeing the flame pictures of the Great Artist on the tapestried skies, replied, "Don't be afraid, my boy, everything is all right. The world is not burning up. It is just the dawn of a new day."

The world is on fire, but it need not be the holocaust of destruction. It can be and it must be the flaming dawn of a new day.

—LUTHER W. YOUNGDAHL, 1978

It calls up the indefinite past. When Columbus first sought this continent—when Christ suffered on the cross—when Moses led Israel through the Red Sea—nay, even when Adam first came from the hands of his Maker; then, as now, Niagara was roaring here. The eyes of that species of extinct giants whose bones fill the mounds of America have gazed on Niagara, as ours do now. Contemporary with the first race of men, and older than the first man, Niagara is as strong and fresh today as ten thousand years ago. The Mammoth and Mastodon, so long dead that fragments of their monstrous bones alone testify that they ever lived, have gazed on Niagara—in that long, long time never still for a moment, never dried, never frozen, never slept, never rested.

—ABRAHAM LINCOLN, 1863

If you can end with a memorable key phrase, people will remember much of what you have said:

We must acknowledge that Japan's success is not a temporary phenomenon. There has been a tendency in the past to think that when Japan matures and their wages catch up to the rest of the world that they will lose their cost effectiveness. A number of noted authorities on Japan do not feel that way, because of the many inherent advantages of their system which I have touched upon. Edwin Reischauer, U.S. Ambassador to Japan, 1961–1966, feels their system may be the wave of the future.

And now, I will give you my three M's: Monster—no, Miracle— yes, Message—we can learn from the Japanese.

—PHILLIP S. HYATT, 1978

I have one more thought that will put my remarks in perspective. It's a quote from Malcolm Muggeridge, the British writer and social critic, who once said, "There is no such thing as darkness; only the failure to see." We in the business community are playing not to lose, instead of playing to win. Let's play to win.

—DAVID MAHONEY, 1978

Sometimes you must admit you're wrong. This is one approach:

I must admit that I was strenuously opposed last year to any projects advocated by Bill Jones. I know that Bill and I have had some serious differences at many of our meetings, and some of them have been pretty bitter. But tonight I am going along with Bill. I am going to vote with him for the resolution before the house.

In this respect I feel something like the sixteen-year-old-boy who laughed at every suggestion his father made. Everything the old man said was wrong. In fact, in the lad's mind, the old man was just plain dumb. When the boy reached the age of eighteen, his viewpoint towards his father changed. But one thing perplexed him. He couldn't figure out how his father had learned so much in two years.

(Pause.)

I'm not admitting that I'm trying to figure out how Bill got so smart in a year, but I'm going along with him on this resolution.

—HUGH LINCOLN

Assessing your effectiveness

In making your speech, try to talk to your audience, not at it or about a subject. Make believe you are having a conversation with one person in the group.

In presenting a talk to a group, you may feel a tenseness. The best protection against this is to feel confidence that you are thoroughly familiar with your subject, able to answer any questions that may come up. (If you can't, you may try to fudge an answer, but it is better to say you don't know.)

The test of a good speech is simply: Did it bring the results you tried for? What was the effect on the audience? How lasting will that effect be?

Special kinds of speeches

Speeches of introduction should be brief, complimentary and informative about the speaker, the subject, and sometimes the occasion. It can be humorous. Don't dwell on the speaker's speaking ability: the audience will soon hear for itself. Then present the speaker: Mr. John Doe, who will talk to you about: "How to Listen to a Speaker."

A welcoming speech serves two purposes: (1) it expresses the good wishes of the audience and (2) it honors the person welcomed. The speech must sound sincere and friendly. It should be in a light vein, as original and apt to the person welcomed as possible, and brief. Don't get extreme, flowery, or emotional, unless the occasion specifically warrants it.

A speech of presentation should: (1) pay tribute to the recipient, (2) give credit to the donor, (3) explain the reason for the presentation, (4) honor the sponsoring organization. Make sure you know the whys and whats of the occasion; a mispronounced name is deadly. It may also be wise to mention the runners-up, the losers. Be brief; sound sincere.

The **reply to a speech of welcome or honor** must express: (1) the appreciation, (2) modesty—noting those who share the honors of the accomplishment with you: "I accept the award on behalf of all those who worked to make the project successful"—and (3) acceptance with thanks. Avoid dwelling on your accomplishments, "I don't deserve the honor," and "I can't thank you enough."

A **eulogy or encomium** is especially difficult to prepare because it should encompass a great deal of detail about accomplishments. It may be for a living person (as in nominating someone for office or even in honoring someone), or it may be for someone who has died. Such a speech requires preparation by talking to those who know or knew the subject well, who have special feelings for the subject. Sometimes small details or incidents help to illustrate character. Such a speech may be emotional but should not be flowery.

An **after-dinner speech** is similar to a speech on any subject, except that the subject and the tone is lighter, the material contains more humor (but it should not be just a series of jokes), the presentation more colloquial. The conclusion need not be formal, maybe a joke that summarizes the feeling of the event.

Questions

If there is to be a question-and-answer period after your talk, announce this in advance. Allow at least ten minutes for questions. In a large audience repeat each question or paraphrase it so that everyone has heard it.

If a question is loaded, defuse it by interrupting to correct false assumptions which are made. If one person tends to monopolize the questioning, point out three or four members of the audience who want to be heard. Don't wait till questions peter out. Make it "We have time for just two more questions" while the audience is still enthusiastic.

Try to anticipate what questions will be asked and prepare either an answer or a way to avoid answering. Some speakers ask for questions to be submitted in advance. To get an audience—and yourself—started well, plant one or two questions with friends in the audience. (Few things are so much a dud as the audience that has no questions. Sometimes no one wants to be first.)

Don't try to answer a question before it is finished. If you need time to think, use: "I am glad you asked that question . . ." Then repeat the question. (This is also a good idea if the hall is large and not everyone might have heard the question.)

Make the questioners look good. Don't become angry or try to lecture a questioner or indicate that he is stupid or that you have already answered the question. Don't allow the questions to lead you off the subject.

> I would like to discuss that subject at length, but time does not permit it."
> Our subject tonight is . . .

If you don't know the answer, admit it. Someone in the audience probably does. You may want to ask.

Scatter the questioners—some from the front, some from the back, some from the left, some from the right, some women, some men, etc.

Feedback

After a speech or a presentation, you will want some feedback. But don't ask, "How did you like it?" You will get a more effective response if you ask a multiple-choice question: "Was it too long or too short?" "Did we get the main point across?"

If you ask for evaluations after every meeting, make it a formality with a purpose.

Chapter 6

The Business Side of Personal Life

INTRODUCTIONS

Letters of introduction involve a number of situations, varying largely with the amount of enthusiasm you wish to display and how well you know each of the parties involved. You are sometimes obliged to write a letter for someone you do not know because someone you do know will ask you to. Sometimes you are obliged to write for someone you know only too well, but cannot refuse. The best procedure is to be frank and open and yet tactful, explaining how well you know the person introduced. Here are some variations:

Dear John,
   This note will introduce to you Jonathan Jones, who is visiting Tulsa for a few days.
   Jonathan is an old friend of a dear friend of mine, Sidney Blank, of whom you may have heard me speak.
   If you can be of any help to him, I will consider it a personal favor.
   Thank you.

Very sincerely,

Dear Sandra,
   Two very dear friends, Tim and Sylvia Roberts, are moving to Tulsa next month and don't know a soul in town. Tim was assigned to handle the Tulsa office with two weeks' notice.
   Sylvia has been active in the Great Books Club here and is one of the nicest people in town. She collects butterflies and old dolls and cooks a mean pasta.
   I know you'll find the Robertses interesting people and I'd appreciate it if you could invite them over and shepherd them around a bit when they get there.
   I expect that they'll arrive about the 22nd, so expect a call from

them about that time. They don't have an address yet, but Tim's office is in the Woodward Building.

Love to you all,

Affectionately,

Dear Jim,

This is Tom Collins.

He popped into my office this morning and asked if I knew you—and I said I did.

Tom is a college classmate, a nice guy, and he wants something from you.

This letter is to break the ice or get past your secretary or something of the sort. I hope I'm not imposing.

Regards,

Dear Mr. Roberts,

Mr. Jonathan Smith, with whom we have been doing business for the past twenty years, has produced a new widget which he feels has special application for your industry.

He is making a presentation of the device in Minneapolis this week and asked if I might introduce him to you so that he could have an opportunity to show it to you on the same trip.

From my long experience with the Smith Company, I can assure you that they are substantial, ethical people. Their engineering staff has been effective in meeting the problems of my company on several occasions. I am sure that, at the very least, you will find Mr. Smith an informed and interesting businessman.

I hope you will have time to have lunch with him while he is in town or at least give him an hour of your time.

Very cordially,

Dear Sam,

Barry Cornell, who is presenting this letter to you, is an old and trusted friend, so I am undoubtedly prejudiced in my opinion of him.

However, when he told me he was going to Pikes Peak I immediately thought of you and how well you two would like each other.

Barry is an avid student of ornithology. I used to call him a bird watcher till he set me straight. And I know how keenly you appreciate the wonders of nature.

That is why I've asked Barry to drop in to see you when he gets to your town. I hope you'll have him to dinner to meet that charming wife of yours and set him straight on the ways of the birds in your area. I'm sure that if you know some other kindred spirits, you'll see that Barry gets to meet them.

Sandy sends her personal regards to you and Merle and the kids.

Very cordially,

Dear Sam,

My cousin Jim Robsham will be in Topeka next week for a convention, and I am urging him to give you a call for lunch or dinner.

Jim has a lot in common with you and I have wanted you two to meet ever since you told me about the book on ornithology you were writing. He is president of the local bird watchers group here and head of the Bird Sanctuary. Moreover, he considers himself an authority on several species of woodpecker.

Jim will probably call you, but in any case, he's at the Quality Inn. Try to get together, will you?

My best to Sandy.

Cordially,

The other side

In addition to a letter of introduction to be carried, it is wise to forewarn the recipient. In this case, you wish to limit your responsibility:

Dear Mr. Roberts,

Some time next week you will probably receive a call from Mr. Sim Thomas of this city.

Sim is an old friend who thinks he has some good ideas for you and asked for the letter of introduction which he is carrying. We went to school together, parted company some five years ago when Sim went into the Air Force, and he has recently been working with Sandman Co. of Chicago.

I can't vouch for the ideas Sim is presenting, but he himself has been a moderately successful promoter. So I think the time you spend with him will be enlightening at the very least.

I do hope the interview will be mutually profitable.

Very cordially,

Dear Sandy,

Within the next few days, you should get a call from Cynthia Brown, a school chum of mine and a very delightful person.

Cynthia will be spending several weeks in Jamestown on a series of interviews for a national survey and I gave her your number to call. While she is in town, her evenings will be free, and she will probably be lonely, so I hope you will take her to your bosom for a few of the days. You will enjoy her company, I am sure.

Give my love to those three brats of yours. I think of them often.

Love,

FAMILY BUSINESS LETTERS

Personal and family business is carried on at a level that usually only remotely resembles the pressures of business. Although the basic principles remain the same—saying what you want to say clearly and in a way that will achieve the purpose—the tone of a family business letter is generally friendlier, less incisive, more direct, franker, and more related to personal considerations. Moreover, interfamily relationships dictate a more careful, long-term outlook.

As in all business letters, an important factor is giving all the necessary facts. Leaving blanks in the information makes for additional time wasting and expensive correspondence that is often embarrassing. It makes mistakes and misunderstandings more likely.

The following are typical of the letters the members of a family may be called upon to write:

Making reservations

Gentlemen:

Please reserve a twin-bedded room with bath for the nights of Tuesday and Wednesday, June 6 and 7, for Mr. and Mrs. Thomas Murdock. We will arrive before 6 P.M.*

We would prefer the minimum-rate room facing the ocean.

Will you be good enough to confirm this reservation and indicate the rates.

Thank you.

Very truly yours,

*If you will arrive after 6 P.M. a deposit may be required.

Excuses for schoolchildren

Ms. Amy Bright
Public School 6
106 West 79th Street
Pittsburgh, Pennsylvania

Dear Ms. Bright,

Sandy Murdock was ill with a sore throat last Thursday and Friday, May 21 and 22. As a precaution for her and safeguard for the other students I induced her to stay at home.

She seems better at this time. Will you be good enough to see that she receives the assignments given to the other students and any

other material which will help her catch up with work she missed.
Thank you.

Very sincerely,

Dear Ms. Spencer,

I know that Samuel has been as much as half an hour late several times this week and I do apologize for any disruption to the class this may have caused.

Our household has been very much upset during the past month due to a fire in the attic on January 7. As a result our electricity has been turned off, our electric clocks have become unusable, and the normal routines have been thrown entirely off balance for all of us.

We have now managed to arrange for a few manual clocks and hopefully our electricity will be operative within a week, so Samuel should be on time from now on.

Please be understanding of our family's difficulties.

Very sincerely,

Dear Ms. Amiable,

Sandy Murdock will be traveling with us to London next week to visit our relatives in England.

For this reason she will be unable to attend classes between March 17 and March 25.

I will appreciate it if you will excuse her absence. If possible, could you provide her with study material and assignments for this period so that she may be able to keep up with her class, at least to some extent?

Thank you for any cooperation you can give.

Very sincerely,

Dear Ms. Lacy,

Samuel Murdock, who has his home room with you, has had a bad fall which injured his knee and ankle.

Our family doctor is permitting him to attend school but asks that as little weight as possible be placed on his right leg.

Will you be good enough to see that a pass to use the school elevators is issued to Samuel for at least the next six weeks, the crucial healing period. It is only with this privilege that he will be able to get from classroom to classroom.

Thank you.

Very sincerely,

Paying a bill

A letter is important for your records beyond the returned check. It is important for the receiver to note what the check is for and the account number involved so that it will be posted to the proper account. An acknowledgment is sometimes requested to make sure the check was received and properly applied.

> Gainsborough National Bank
> Gainsborough, Massachusetts
>
> *Gentlemen:*
>
> Herewith is my check amounting to $479.50 for interest of $179.50 and principal of $300.00 on account of my loan number 487654 with your institution.
>
> Please confirm receipt of the check and provide me with a statement showing the balance. Thank you.
>
> Very truly yours,

> Personal Loan Department
> Gainsborough National Bank
> Gainsborough, Massachusetts
>
> *Gentlemen:*
>
> Enclosed is a check for $250.00 representing January payment due on my loan from you.
>
> I understand that February and March payments are past due, and I hope to be able to pay one of these next month, leaving myself three months in arrears. The arrearages will be made up during the next eighteen months.
>
> Some temporary financial difficulties occurred last month as the result of my marriage two weeks ago and a change of positions from Data Processing Corp. to Honeywell Manufacturing Co.
>
> I trust that you will be able to adjust my payment schedule so that the three months arrearage will be payable in equal instalments next July 1, December 1, and the following July 1.
>
> If this is satisfactory please let me know and confirm this rearrangement to Tom Murdock, 1401 Main Street, Gainsborough, who has guaranteed my account.
>
> Thank you.
>
> Very truly yours,
>
> Copy to Tom Murdock

Asking for advice—and giving it

> *Dear Uncle Tom,*
>
> When Pop was alive, I remember how he would call on you from time to time to "brainstorm" a problem, as he would say. Pop had a great respect for your judgment. He always felt that there were times when we ourselves are too close to a situation to see it clearly.
>
> I learned a lot from Pop and one thing I learned was to ask for advice when I am not sure about a decision. So I am imposing on you for a bit of your time.
>
> Uncle Tom, you know I plan to get married next June. I am

earning a reasonable living and Jane feels that with our two incomes we can support a house and live comfortably in a suburb near the city.

Although I have old-fashioned ideas about wives working, particularly because I want to raise a family, I can see that two incomes will be necessary for a few years at least. By that time I hope to be earning enough to get along on my income alone. That seems like a sound and steady course of action.

However, one of my co-workers has come up with an idea for a new valve that could save people a lot of money on natural gas. It may have other uses, but he showed me how it works in his house. I saw that his gas bills dropped 30 percent after he installed it himself. Uncle Tom, I am completely sold on the device.

Jim has saved up $10,000 and I have about $5,000 in the bank. He would like me to go partners with him on a fifty-fifty basis, with our moneys to be put in as loans.

We have worked out a manufacturing budget, including patenting costs, marketing plan, and gone through all the preliminary steps the textbooks recommend. Our plan calls for neither of us to draw salaries for four months, which both of us can manage, as we will stay at our jobs for most of this period.

The Liberty National Bank has promised us a line of credit to finance our accounts receivable after production is underway and we think we can borrow $10,000 more if we need it.

Now I understand the risks inherent in any business, so I do hesitate. But I don't want to be an employee all my life, and I am tempted to take the chance to become independent.

Can you suggest anything that will help me make a wise decision?

Affectionately,

Dear Sidney,

I read your letter carefully several times and slept on it for two nights. So don't think I delayed answering for any personal reason.

First, you must understand that I have no way of knowing th practicality of Jim's new valve or the problems in its use or production or its cost and possible selling price. These are just a few of the factors you should discuss with some engineer besides Jim, someone you can trust. Your father's good friend Stanley Saunders might help you on that score.

But even before that, I think you should discuss with Jane the whole idea and the risks involved. After all, your money and your future will be hers as much as yours and she is entitled to a voice in the decision.

When you have gone through these two hoops, you will have to face up to the problem of raising more capital. Most new projects fail for lack of this, and $15,000 is hardly enough to get started in a new business these days. I might suggest that you protect your development by a patent application, then try to enlist one of the larger manufacturers who have already been established in your market, to take over the manufacture or marketing or both for you. You might even be better off with a licensing or royalty agreement that would eliminate most of the risk.

Whatever you do, Sidney, please keep in touch with me and let me help in any way I can. Don't feel it is an imposition. I am, after all, family. And I find pleasure in helping and am flattered that you seek advice from me.

Affectionately,

To borrow money

Dear Uncle Tom,

It was good to have a chance to have a long talk with you last month at Grandma's. I see you so seldom that I often forget I have family.

I know that if you were sitting here, you would say, "Come to the point, John." So I will.

You know that I received my master's degree in computer science from New York University last June. Since then I have been working for a large computer company in one of the suburbs. My salary is adequate, but it is apparent to me that any real breakthrough in a substantial raise will come only if I have a doctorate.

I have thought of trying this on a nighttime basis, but as far as I can determine, getting a doctorate at night might be a matter of eight to ten years. At my age this seems almost half a lifetime and I feel I might very well give up before I could complete the course.

I am willing to invest the four years which I think would be necessary, working part time and using my savings of about $6,000. But being realistic, I know that this will not see me through. Although I can earn my subsistence from part-time wages, tuition and other university costs will require $20,000 even with scholarships and deferred payment plans after the first year. Assuming a tight budget, and not figuring the added costs which will result from inflation, I will run short about $10,000 during the four years.

I know it is an imposition on you and that you have many obligations to your own children, Uncle Tom, but as a practical matter, there is no one else I can turn to. I have great confidence in myself and my ability to pay off any loan soon after I graduate, but this confidence is not a bankable commodity, as you know.

What I need, Uncle Tom, is a loan of $5,000 now and assurance of a similar sum eighteen months from now.

If I can get my degree in four years, I should be able to earn twice as much as I do now and be able to make substantial payments to return the whole amount within three years.

I know you will say that within seven years I will want to get married and will need all the money I can get. But nowadays wives do work, and if I should get married I don't think it will make much difference in my ability to pay. Besides, people do get married late in life these days, and I have no immediate prospects.

As a business deal, I realize that a personal loan is not the best investment. But I will pay the current interest rate and sometimes you do get a return in what you used to call "good-will dollars." You are known in the family as a hard-headed businessman, Uncle Tom. I'm sure you will appreciate that the loan is a good investment from the family point of view, and offers little risk.

Please?

Thanks for at least thinking about it.

Affectionately,

Response to a request for a loan

Dear John,

You made a strong appeal in your letter and I have given the matter of the loan a good deal of thought.

You know, John, that I do have a great respect for you. Your record in college was most commendable and I feel strongly that you will go on to make a name for yourself. I know, too, that the best way to lose a friend, even a friendly relative, is to lend him money.

In the family, John, many look to me as a rich man because I have a business and most of my brothers and in-laws are salaried people. But business is a tricky thing and a $10,000 commitment is no small matter.

After a lot of thought, I have come up with a plan which will serve your purpose and make it practical for me to say yes. I have arranged with the Gainsborough National Bank to establish a credit for you on which you can draw up to $10,000 during the next four years at the bank's regular terms. Needless to say, I have guaranteed the bank against any loss, but they will have some other protections from federal insurance. The pressure to make payments to the bank when they are due may be greater, but I know you would not want to duck this responsibility. In the end, I am counting on my faith in you to come through with the doctorate, the greater earning power, and the willingness and ability to repay the loan.

If you find this solution satisfactory, come up to Gainsborough anytime after you have registered and I will help you complete the arrangement.

Affectionately,

Dear John,

I wish it were easy to say yes in response to your letter asking for help. But, John, you know I don't believe in lending money, particularly to friends and members of the family.

Under other circumstances, John, I might have been tempted to break my own rules. However, my own situation is such that an additional commitment of even $10,000 would be a real hardship. Because of constantly rising prices and the custom of selling far ahead in my business, it is necessary to keep a large inventory of materials on hand, and this stretches my resources to the limit.

If I may make a suggestion, there are some institutions that do make substantial advances to students under federal loan guarantees. Joseph Johnson of Ninkoma was able to borrow his entire tuition from such loans and I am sure he would be glad to tell you about procedures and how he did it.

John, I am sorry if I disappoint you in this, but please don't think too badly of me for it. I am sure you will find another way.

Very cordially,

When the debt is not paid

Dear John,

All of us here were delighted to hear of your new job and your wedding to Nancy Lowell. I hear she is a real beauty. Martha and I regretted very much missing the wedding, but you know it is very hard for me to travel these days.

Yesterday I received a note from the bank that your January payment was not made and is now ninety days overdue. With all the excitement of preparing for the wedding, this may have been overlooked, and if so, I hope you will get a check to them to bring your account up to date.

Or have the trousseau expenses left you broke? If that is so, I suggest that you borrow against your future salary and keep your record with the bank clean. It would be a real hardship on me to undertake to make your payments at this time.

Please let me know that you have sent off a check, or if not, what you plan to do.

Affectionately,

POLITICAL MAILINGS

Political mailings often fail because they ignore the basic common sense of communication. The letter should say more than "Vote for me." It should make the reader aware of who the candidate is, what he or she stands for, and why becoming involved is important. It must sound sincere. It should be designed specifically for each group to which it is mailed, groups selected for their interest and for the size of donation or amount of help expected. It should be part of an overall selling package, preferably started before, and lasting after, election day. It should seem as personal as you can afford to make it. It should be timed properly and prepared long before mailing time. It should give a convincing reason for contributing. It should suggest amounts. It should be easy to respond to. And it should not appear shoddy.

Laws regulating fund raising include requirements for registration, limitations on fees, written consent for use of names used in the mailing piece, contracts with organizations for whom you are soliciting, and prohibition against some telephone solicitation, among others.

Dear Fellow American,

As you know, on November 20 I announced that I will seek the office of President of the United States. I am writing to you today to explain why I made that decision.

It is a decision which I did not make easily, but it is one to which I am totally committed.

After months of close consultation with friends and others who are deeply concerned with the future of our nation and that of the Republican Party, I have concluded that if we are to maintain our free society we must change the role which government plays in our lives.

We must again look at the world realistically so that we may understand the grave responsibilities which we must face as the leader of the free world.

I am convinced that 1976 will be a year of decision for our great nation. Events of the last several years—indeed, of the last several decades—make it absolutely necessary that changes be made if we are to survive.

The majority of American citizens still believes in what those in Washington too often refer to as "old-fashioned" virtues and attitudes. Plain, everyday morality is still the bedrock of the typical American's life.

Self-reliance, pride, dignity, and just plain "horse sense" are still vital parts of the ideals of most Americans, despite the fact that those in Washington continue to take more and more of our honest and hard-earned dollars for every conceivable pseudo-social purpose.

The sad fact today is that most of our problems originate in Washington. Too many of those chosen to lead are unable to do so because they have been in Washington so long they have become a part of the problem instead of being a part of the solution.

[Etc. for five pages]

If you believe in our cause, then I ask you to send your contribution today. If we are to succeed in the early primaries then I will need your immediate support.

Whatever you can send will be sincerely appreciated and wisely spent. Your dollars may well spell the difference between success and defeat.

I know I can count on your help in this critical effort. Thank you.

Sincerely,

Ronald W. Reagan

P.S. The early polls which I have seen are very encouraging. I am confident that with enough financial support and volunteer effort we will achieve the victory the citizens of our great nation want and need.

Few people run for President. But candidates run for all kinds of offices—and they always need money. To be effective the appeals must be made to very special lists and each list should have its own personal approach. Here is a typical appeal:

Dear Mrs. Murdock:

We need your help, now!

One of our fellow NAEM members, Glen A. Knapp, exposition manager of the Eastern Mining and Industrial Exposition, has been nominated by the voters of Kanawha County (Charleston), West Virginia, for a seat in the West Virginia House of Delegates. Glen will be a candidate in the general election to be held this fall. He needs our help and support now in the form of a financial contribution to conduct an aggressive and thorough campaign.

Glen has been in exposition work for over ten years, is one of the charter Certified Exposition Managers and has been a member of NAEM since 1968. By helping to elect Glen, we will be electing a legislator who knows our industry's potential and problems. He will speak effectively on our behalf with his fellow public officials in any of the states in which we operate. Glen will be a real asset to each of us involved with expositions in dealing with governmental agencies in promoting the exposition industry. We need to get behind his candidacy and give all of the moral and financial support possible— any amount you can give will be very appreciated and put to good use.

West Virginia law does not permit corporate contributions; thus please make your personal check payable to the Glen A. Knapp Campaign Fund and send it directly to Glen in the enclosed envelope. Political contributions are deductible on your federal income tax return.

Thank you for your financial assistance. If you have any questions regarding the campaign or Glen's political views, please call him at his office (304) 744-4681 or at home (304) 925-9186.

Very sincerely,

To stand out from the pile of mail, an attention-seeking device may be used. Here the letter looks like a tax bill:

Taxpayer's Liability Index (prepared by)
National Taxpayers Union
325 Pennsylvania Avenue, S.E.
Washington, D.C. 20003

STATEMENT OF ACCOUNT

TAXPAYER NAME AND ADDRESS

315

N. N. MAGER
11 WARREN ST.
NEW YORK, NY 10007

TERMS:
You just keep paying

YOUR ATTENTION IS DIRECTED TO AMOUNTS DUE AS INDICATED BELOW

DEBT OR LIABILITY ITEM	GROSS COST	YOUR SHARE
Public Debt	$ 721,000,000,000	$ 9,012
Accounts Payable	$ 80,000,000,000	$ 1,000
Undelivered Orders	$ 332,000,000,000	$ 4,150
Long Term Contracts	$ 15,000,000,000	$ 187
Loan and Credit Guarantees	$ 209,000,000,000	$ 2,612
Insurance Commitments	$1,733,000,000,000	$ 21,662
Annuity Programs	$5,900,000,000,000	$ 73,750
Unadjudicated Claims International Commitments & other Financial Obligations	$ 43,000,000,000	$ 537
TOTAL	$9,033,000,000,000	$112,912

Dear Friend,

That's quite a bill, isn't it? Better take another look because this bill's no joke. And it has a lot to do with your other bills and why it's so hard to pay them. You see, a study by the National Taxpayers Union (based on official Treasury Department figures), reveals that U.S. taxpayers are now on the hook for at least $9 trillion.

Your personal share is over $113,000. While you've been working to make ends meet, politi-cians have been wracking up debts and liabilities which you'll have to pay.

An appeal by the Democratic National Committee uses this approach to bring you onto the team:

Dear Friend and Contributor:

I want to take this opportunity to personally bring you up to date on our plans and prospects for the 1978 midterm elections . . . which, as you know, are only about 90 days away.

We face some tough fights:

—The extreme right wing is using inflammatory rhetoric and emotional issues to raise unprecedented millions of dollars to defeat Democratic candidates;

—Republican candidates across the country have given up the hope of selling their basic philosophy to the American people—so they are simply promising massive and irresponsible programs which would produce substantially higher inflation and budget deficits;

—And, of course, it is always easier for the party out of power to criticize the way things are than for the incumbents to defend them.

I think we have made some real progress during the past eighteen months. 6.4 million new jobs have been created since the Republicans left the presidency, and total employment is at its highest level in history. President Carter's administration cares about people. The President has appointed a record number of women and members of minority groups to high office. And we have a foreign policy which identifies Americans with struggles for human rights everywhere—from Rhodesia to the Soviet Union.

Nevertheless, our work is cut out for us.

[Etc.]

To be an effective lobbyist you must make it easy for the person you are soliciting to act. Many appeals suggest the gist of a letter you could write to get action or enclose a postcard ready to mail. The original, personal letter is, of course, more effective in influencing a legislator. But the response to the original appeal is substantially greater if the reader merely has to sign and mail something. Two postcards were enclosed in a letter urging a vote against the Panama Canal treaty:

Dear Senator:

Please vote *against* President Carter's treaty to give away *our* Panama Canal Zone.

I completely agree with the four former Chiefs of Naval Operations who wrote Jimmy Carter:

"Loss of the Panama Canal . . . would contribute to the encirclement of the U.S. by hostile naval forces, and *threaten our ability to survive.*"

Under no circumstances should the U.S. surrender its rights of sovereignty to the demands of Gen. Omar Torrijos, a Marxist friend of Fidel Castro.

Sincerely,

Dear Congressman Hansen:

I agree: "Loss of the Panama Canal . . . would contribute to the encirclement of the U.S. by hostile naval forces, and threaten our ability to survive."

☐ I have expressed that view to my two U.S. Senators.

☐ I have enclosed my contribution to the PANAMA CANAL DEFENSE FUND of the Council for Inter-American Security.

☐$20   ☐$25   ☐$50   ☐$100   ☐$250   ☐$500
☐$1,000 $____(other amount)

Fill in name and address below only if label on envelope is incorrect.

NAME_____
ADDRESS_____
CITY_____STATE_____ZIP_____

Make check payable to "CIS"

FOR THE PUBLIC GOOD—CIVIC AFFAIRS

Not everything we work at is entirely personal or entirely business. A good portion of a balanced life should be devoted to religious, philanthropic, or public affairs work for community, church, charity, or politics.

Although correspondence for a public purpose usually follows the techniques of business writing, it is inhibited by a restraint and etiquette that grows as the community gets closer to home. A letter for your Rotary Club must be friendlier and more personal than a mass mailing for a business. Tact becomes more important if you will probably meet your opponent at a mutual friend's dinner table next week. Here are some suggestions for typical situations.

Proposing a member to a society

Dear Mr. Solsky,

It is my privilege to propose for membership in the Owls Society Mr. John Josephs, who has been my business associate for the past seven years.

Mr. Josephs is well known in the community. He has been active in many worthwhile civic projects and has been a substantial donor to our Community Chest.

The Owls Society would be the richer for his membership and I am honored to be his sponsor.

Very sincerely,

Responding to a proposal

Mr. Sidney Solsky
2 Washington Avenue
New York, N.Y. 10010
Dear Mr. Solsky:

Your name has been proposed for membership in the Owls Society of Saratoga Springs by Mr. James V. London.

It is our great pleasure to extend to you an invitation to join our Association, which is dedicated to the improvement of living conditions among indigent children.

If you will fill out the enclosed form, I will be pleased to present your name to our membership committee for affirmative action.

Very sincerely yours,

Nomination by a committee

Dear Miss Witherspoon,

It is a pleasure to advise you that you have been selected by the nominating committee of the Owls Society to be the official candidate for the year beginning next January 2.

It was the unanimous opinion of the committee that you were outstanding among our members suitable for this office and that you would serve with distinction during the two-year term.

Please advise us as soon as possible of your willingness to serve during this period.

Very sincerely,

Accepting a nomination

Dear Sir:

Thank you for your gracious invitation to act as the official candidate of the nominating committee to serve as president of the Owls Society.

I consider it an honor and a privilege. I look forward to serving for the two years and to leading the society to even greater service.

Very sincerely,

Declining a nomination

Dear Sir:

Thank you for your kind invitation to serve as the official candidate of the nominating committee for the office of president of the Owls Society.

It is with great regret that I must decline to run for this office. The pressures of business and certain family obligations make it impossible for me to serve at this time.

Believe me, I appreciate the great honor of this invitation, and it is only after careful consideration that I must reluctantly say no.

Very sincerely,

Begging off

Saying no is often a difficult and unpleasant necessity in business and particularly in civic affairs, even to strangers and particularly to friends.

Sometimes you can claim you lack the authority. You may have to defer to a boss, to a committee, to company policy, a government regulation, a trade practice, etc. Sometimes you can plead pressure of time, health, other engagements.

Here is an approach you may find useful:

I am forced to curtail my speaking engagements to the barest minimum. When I receive an invitation to speak to a group as interesting and influential as yours, it becomes particularly difficult.

Resigning an office

Jonathan Gred
Chairman, Board of Directors
The Owls Society
23 West 23 Street
New York, N.Y. 10012
Dear Mr. Chairman,

It is with deep regret that I find I must tender my resignation as president of the Owls Society effective at the end of this month.

For the past few years I have found the responsibilities and pressures of the position an increasing burden and a threat to my health.

Under the circumstances, on my doctor's advice, I have decided to take an extended vacation to recuperate from my recent illness.

If, when I return, I feel capable of again becoming active in the work of the society, you may be assured of my willingness and intention to do so.

Very sincerely,

Letters to the editor

Sometimes it is important to take a stand on an issue that concerns you. You may write to newspapers which often publish letters to the editor. The techniques for this are self-evident: you refer to an item in the publication or to an event, and make your points, indicating any correction in the facts, an elucidation, or an argument for or against. You send the letters on an appropriate organizational letterhead if you can. And you indicate your special competence either in the signature title or in the letter itself.

This is a typical approach:

To the Editor:

I listened to the President's speech in Georgia carefully, hoping to hear a clear interpretation of our foreign policy. Instead there was rhetoric about supporting our commitments with military power and dealing with unrest in countries that have new regimes and ideologies. The speech had a decidedly political tone; an attempt to mend fences rather than to present a master plan.

I think we would be wise to try to solve the multitude of problems in our own country before we dissipate our efforts in the international field. We all yearn for peace, with honor for all concerned, which can only be achieved by wise leadership and respect for our historical background. . . .

Carola Warburg Rothschild
Boca Grande, Florida
Feb. 20, 1979

FUND-RAISING LETTERS

Making an effective appeal for funds for a philanthropic organization is always a difficult letter to write. It has to tear at the heart yet not be too corny. Most people part reluctantly with funds for nontangible gains. Your mailing list of previous contributors or contributors to a similar cause is most important. The names on the letterhead (which lend credibility to the cause) and those who sign the letter are also extremely important.

The following letters have been effective. Many of them are substantial in length. If the letter is a single page, the reverse side sometimes carries the message in pictures and graphics.

> Dear Mr. James,
>
> During 1968 your past contributions have been at work. Teen-age gang warfare has disappeared almost entirely from the areas in the city where the Police Athletic League now operates.
>
> While juvenile crimes are down from last year, there still remain many areas not now covered by PAL. We need your help again to keep this worthwhile program alive and growing.
>
> [Etc.]

In framing a fund-raising letter select the part of the work being done that has the most human appeal—love, pity, patriotism, responsibility, self-interest, self-preservation. Then tell a story or illustrate the problem in human terms.

Some fund-raisers lace their appeal with unordered merchandise: stamps, a pen, a calendar, a ruler, a pad, an appropriate gadget. This seems to place a moral—though not a legal—obligation on the receiver to send a contribution.

Sheets of Christmas Seal stamps have been used by the National Tuberculosis Association since 1907. Easter Seals are part of an annual mailing by the National Society for Crippled Children and Adults. Boys Town and the National Wildlife Federation have built programs around stamps. Sheets of household labels are a free premium of the Epilepsy Foundation. Religious groups such as St. Anthony's Guild distribute quotations from the Bible. Miniature license plates with your license number on it have been sent out by the Disabled American Veterans organization.

In most cases the use of the free premium is self-evident, but one organization includes this paragraph in its letters:

> The stamps, as always, will add an extra touch of beauty to your cards and gifts. Please accept them and use them. A contribution is always welcome and helpful in our wildlife programs, but please do not feel you are under any obligation.

For those who feel resentment at receiving unordered merchandise, this is, at least, a palliative.

Select your list carefully. If you have a big list of previous donors, or if you want to extend your list, create a profile of your donors. Then go out to find a list that approximates this profile.

Some experts feel that photographs make a letter look like a circular and decrease its effectiveness. But in fund raising the graphics in a letter hold much of the appeal, and circulars tend not to be read.

Here are some more fund-raising approaches that have been effective.

Photographs of children have a special appeal. Here's how a CARE letter puts it.

> This Thanksgiving these children need your help.
> Won't you provide them with a lifeline today . . . for a road to a better tomorrow?

> *Dear Friend,*
> A time to share. A time for thanks. A time for compassion . . . that's the meaning of Thanksgiving . . .

The self-interest appeal is effectively used by the National Wildlife Federation.

> . . . for the first time since 1972, all dumping of toxic chemicals by large companies has been stopped off the New England Seaboard. Also . . .
> . . . NWF continues to demand that federal dams and channelization projects consider fish and wildlife planning plus good water quality standards in areas such as Louisiana's Atchafalaya River Basin, Florida's Big Cypress Swamp, and others.
> . . . NWF is conducting citizen action workshops to educate the public on solid waste management and water pollutants. And this is just the beginning . . .

The sale of cookies, Christmas cards, calendars, prints, religious objects is a quid pro quo approach. It is used extensively by UNESCO and on a real commercial basis by museums with the sale of artifacts. This ties in with the text:

> YOUR GIFT TO PAL IS THE BEST WAY TO HELP A CITY
> CHILD
> *Dear Friend:*
> It's not easy for children growing up in many New York City communities to look to the future with hope and enthusiasm. Living

in poverty and in an environment which breeds crime and violence, drug addiction, and false values leads to wasted lives for many. These youngsters desperately need a chance to get involved in worthwhile activities; to learn discipline, respect and cooperation; and to get the guidance so many are not getting in their homes or in school.

PAL gives kids that chance. Your support makes it possible.

—Police Athletic League

An attention-getting opening is very important. Here are some that immediately grab the reader's interest and make him want to read on.

We can't guarantee you that a Chicago Boy Scout won't stick up a grocery store, shoot heroin, or turn into a bum. But we'll give you odds.

—Chicago Boy Scouts

Dear Fellow American:

Why do you suppose twelve of the most powerful union bosses in America would get together and launch an all-out attack on our charitable foundation, filing what they call "the largest multi-union legal action ever undertaken"?

I'm sure you know the answer.

[Etc. for four pages.]

—National Right to Work Defense Foundation

HUNGER IS DISASTER PROLONGED

Dear Friend:

A hungry child dies a slow death. The effects of semistarvation and malnutrition facing over 300 million children in poorer countries today are disease, blindness, mental retardation and stunted growth—unless short-term and long-term aid can be provided—*by UNICEF and you.*

—UNICEF

Dear Friend:

Do you remember when you were very, very young how difficult it was to tell left from right . . . or how often there seemed to be more buttons than buttonholes? It's that way for most children and perhaps more so for those who are blind or have a severe visual impairment.

—The New York Association for the Blind

Dear Friend,

When the snow was knee-deep in the streets this winter, didn't you dream about summer vacation?

Youngsters can't wait till school lets out this summer. But soon the novelty of being able to play outside all day wears off . . . suddenly there's nothing fun about hanging out on the streets well into the night.

You've seen the pavement heat up until it bubbles.

Apartments are stifling. Public pools are overcrowded and rough. Kids are left to open up the fire hydrants or play on fire escapes. Stoop weather they call it.

No school and nothing to do for relief except spray hydrants at passing buses.

That's not your summer, it shouldn't be theirs. Vacation time means going away to the country. And missing out on green shade and sweet water swimming really hurts for a city kid. Seeing it on TV and billboards and magazines is no substitute.

YMCA-YWCA camps are located on 1,000 rolling acres in the beautiful Southern Catskills, just 90 miles from the city. Out of 5,319 Y campers last summer, more than one-third were on full or partial scholarship—enjoying the three lakes, program centers, cabins, and athletic facilities for every sport from tennis to volleyball.

But, in order to make the camping opportunity a reality to more boys and girls—and to provide them with all the advantages of a rich summer experience—additional funds are necessary. Turn to the back of this letter to see what happens to the youngster at camp.

Every gift is welcomed. A full two-week scholarship costs $220. A week in the outdoors for each camper adds up to $110. You may even wish to sponsor a deserving boy or girl on a daily basis which costs $15.70. In any case, do your own mathematics and decide if you would like to send a boy or girl to camp . . . and for how long?

So won't you pitch in *now* and help us send kids to camp from your borough.

Sincerely,

P.S. Remember, today's action will put a child in camp tomorrow! Please mail your generous check—TODAY.

—LANDON K. THORNE

Dear American:

Winning is an American tradition.

And there is no better testimony to this than the achievements of the many fine American athletes who are able to represent our country at the Olympic Games through the generous help of individual citizens like you.

—UNITED STATES OLYMPIC COMMITTEE

A photograph with an emotional appeal usually appears at the top of this fund-raising letter:

Dear Friend:

Once the streets of New York were full of hope for those who wanted to get ahead. But yesterday's opportunities are harder to find in today's more complex society.

For poor children today, summer streets are dangerous places. The only recreation is often to be found in littered lots and gutted buildings. This summer, The Children's Aid Society will offer 1300 boys and girls an alternative at Osborn Day Camp on Staten Island and in Home Camps at our neighborhood centers and playgrounds. And for 400 handicapped youngsters for whom summer would otherwise be a time of lonely confinement, CAS's Wagon Road Camp will offer a month in the country for fun, growth, and relationships with other children.

For many teenagers, summer streets are where pent up energies from idleness and boredom often trigger violence and crime. As in the past, CAS will work this summer to defuse the rage and despair that threaten so many of New York's neighborhoods by . . .

. . . employing some 700 teens in their own communities with work that will offer them both spending money and practical skills they will need for the job market.

. . . providing thousands of children, teens, and families with all forms of recreation including play streets, sports tournaments, trips to state parks and beaches, arts and crafts, and street festivals as well as keeping our centers open on weekends.

. . . giving hundreds of youngsters remedial tutoring, and the opportunity to visit museums, theatres, and other places of cultural interest to broaden and enrich their lives.

With more and more social service cutbacks by the City, your gift to The Children's Aid Society for $10, $20, $50, $100 or the most you can afford is urgently needed this summer to serve more than 12,000 youngsters and their parents in our camps and neighborhood centers.

Only you can change their despair into hope this summer!

Many thanks,
Victor Remer
Executive Director

VR:C

P.S. For a total picture of our many services and programs serving children throughout the year, please see the other side of this letter.

One organization sends a letter of thanks to newspapers that draws attention to a suggested editorial:

Dear Editor:

At this holiday season, we want to thank members of the American press for their excellent coverage of CARE programs which help destitute people throughout the world. Your cooperation in publishing the message of CARE's work is invaluable in maintaining much needed support from the American people. Their support enables CARE to continue helping millions of people lift themselves out of poverty in 36 developing countries in Africa, Asia, Latin America and the Middle East.

—CARE

A bright new penny is pasted at the top of this letter:

There is hope for these children . . .

And for the estimated 4,000,000 children and adults like them.

Hope as bright and shining as this new-minted penny . . .

Hope and help that *you* can provide . . . for only pennies a day.

All these people suffer from epilepsy—which is *not* contagious, *can* be controlled, is not usually, by itself, any impediment to a normal, happy life.

And grants from Epilepsy Foundation of America right now are supporting long-range research which may finally lead to a cure for epilepsy.

Meantime, other research . . . your understanding . . . your pennies a day can provide *help* right now.

Help for thousands of children who kill time, dully, alone. Because a playmate's mother whispered:

"Don't play with him. He's not right."

Help for the child who may have an attack in school. Information and instruction for the teacher . . . so that a child can get at least the same care and attention and respect as any child who becomes ill in school.

Help for a man who wants to work . . . who rots on relief, because superstition whispers: "Epileptic."

$2, $3—invested in research, public education, or training will help many thousands of epilepsy patients.

$5, $10—or more—would represent a major contribution to our work.

Please say you want to help . . . place your contribution in the enclosed envelope and mail it *today*. Thank you.

HALF THE WORLD'S CHILDREN SUFFER FROM MALNUTRITION!

WON'T YOU PLEASE JOIN CARE'S 1978 FOOD CRUSADE AND

HELP THEM TAKE THEIR FIRST STEP TOWARDS A HEALTHIER LIFE?

Dear Friend:

Today in Asia, Africa, Latin America and the Middle East CARE feeds and helps more than 25,000,000 men, women and children.

Most in need are the children who are unaware that the future holds the same bleak outlook for them as it does for their parents.

Poor nourishment, inadequate food, too few jobs, little education, a lack of clean, fresh water, untreated sicknesses and diseases.

This is a brand of poverty that can carry these little victims deeper and deeper into the web of helplessness.

Without caring hands, your hands, their hope is dim, indeed. CARE's feeding projects therefore are geared to help destitute people work their way out of poverty and into healthier more productive lives. Poorly nourished people have little strength to help themselves. So CARE's nutrition programs are targeted primarily to the vulnerable groups—infants, young children and pregnant and nursing women.

Building up weakened bodies is CARE's first step in making self-sufficiency possible.

The next step is integrated community projects and self-help programs which include food-for-work projects. These contain strong built-in incentives for poverty stricken people to work their way out of poverty and into more productive lives. . . .

—CARE

Dear Friend of Planned Parenthood:

As you read this letter, a teenage girl somewhere in the United States is giving birth to an unwanted child.

This year, 300,000 teenagers will give birth to children they do not want. That's about 800 every day. One every two minutes.

That's just *one* reason why Planned Parenthood needs your support this year.

Last year, we gave counseling and contraceptive services to 1,100,000 people in the United States—including 340,000 teenagers. But despite the efforts of Planned Parenthood and others the epidemic of teenage pregnancies goes on, touching one out of every ten American girls. Especially heartbreaking to me are the 30,000 pregnancies each year among girls 13 to 14 years old.

A teenage pregnancy can do lasting physical and emotional damage to both mother and child. It can force a girl into an unwise marriage, can put an early end to her education, or condemn her to a lifetime of dependence on public assistance.

We *can* prevent this. The means to eliminate most unwanted pregnancies are available. But too many adults would like to pretend that teenage sexuality doesn't exist. The result: young people are not prepared to deal with their sexuality and often find it impossible to handle in responsible, understanding ways.

In previous years you supported Planned Parenthood. But we have not heard from you recently. I'm writing to ask that you renew your support for Planned Parenthood so that we can redouble our efforts to stop unwanted teenage pregnancies *before* they happen.

Planned Parenthood is responding to this crisis with a strong teen program. Not only are we giving special help to our own clinics, helping them to reach more teenagers; we are also working with schools, counselors, and youth agencies to give teenagers and their families the information they need to deal with their sexual responsibility.

[Etc. for two pages]

Make sure you send an acknowledgment and thanks promptly for each contribution. Publicizing the donor makes friends in most cases—though some donors do not wish to be identified.

Dear Friend:

I gratefully acknowledge your generosity and thoughtfulness in the contribution which you have sent to the Police Athletic League.

Thousands of youngsters who are benefiting from the work of the Police Athletic League in every area of our city, through the 35 PAL full and part time Centers, through the playgrounds and the playstreets send their especial blessings.

I know that we may look forward to your continued cooperation and support.

Cordially yours,

Acknowledgments of contributions and services

Every courtesy, financial or in terms of service, should be acknowledged:

Dear Committee Member,

What a splendid job you did. Your contributions made the festival the greatest one ever.

The professionalism all of us demonstrated was remarkable and certainly showed we learned from our past experiences.

As you know, the reports from the public as well as the press have been superlative and should give you a great deal of satisfaction.

Next year will come soon enough so we hope you'll give it some thought. Remember, we're committed to expand in both time and space. Jot down your ideas and when we meet again we'll be well on our way to another exciting event for our city.

Thank you for all you have done.

Sincerely,

Dear Mr. Johnson,

Please accept this belated letter of gratitude for your kindness in inviting me among others of the fifty-year-service class to the luncheon, which I might add was succulent and in good taste to meet everyone's requirements for dietary conditions.

Of course the picture was excellent and topped the day for the eight men and myself who were lucky to be on hand to enjoy it.

Gratefully yours,

Chapter 7

The Social Side of Personal Life

INVITATIONS AND OTHER LETTERS FOR SOCIAL OCCASIONS

Some letters must be written because social convention, "etiquette," or just graciousness requires them. Sometimes they should be formal (but this does not mean they must be trite). Sometimes they can be informal—if they are to someone you see often on a friend-to-friend basis.

Such letters include letters of condolence, invitations to a gathering, letters of thanks, and sometimes letters of congratulations.

One element common to such formal letters: they must stick to the point. Don't mix an expression of sympathy with unrelated gossip, a letter of thanks with an unrelated funny story you heard.

Formal notes are brain savers: you don't have to think hard for proper wording. Most of what should be said has all been set down for you. In fact, the printer will probably have samples of engraved invitations, announcements, and acknowledgments. All you need to do is to select one of several variations, and change the names, place, and time.

Usually formal notes are printed or engraved on the first page of a double sheet of quality paper. If you do not want them engraved, they should be handwritten on formal stationery.

Formal invitations

The engraved invitation is usually a practical necessity for a large gathering:

Mr. and Mrs. Theodore Thorndike
request the pleasure of your company
at dinner on
Thursday, September the fourth
at eight o'clock
100 Riverside Drive, Pittsburgh

Sometimes a blank space is left where a name is to be filled in:

Dr. and Mrs. Seymour Thorndike
request the pleasure of
<u>Mr. and Mrs. Fisher's</u>
company at a dance on
Saturday, the thirteenth of September
at half after ten o'clock
Meadow Country Club
R.S.V.P.

No abbreviations are used except for R.S.V.P.

Where the group is small, handwritten invitations are more practical. They follow the same style.

In this generation, the formal invitation is reserved for very special events or events which are to be made to seem important.

To recall an invitation, the same formality is appropriate.

Dr. and Mrs. Seymour Thorndike regret that owing to the illness of their daughter, they are obliged to recall their invitation for Saturday, the thirteenth of September.

For a wedding, the best affordable engraving (or, if necessary, thermographed imitation engraving) is usually used. Paper is 7½ × 5½ inches, in a four-page folded sheet. Allow three weeks for engraving and three weeks for advance notice.

The formal invitation uses two envelopes, one envelope addressed only to the person invited without an address. In this envelope the invitation is placed. Sometimes a piece of tissue is inserted to protect the engraving from smudging. This in turn is inserted into a mailing envelope which carries the name and address of the person to whom it is being sent.

One invitation is sent to husband and wife, but separate invitations are sent to each of the other adults in the family.

Children who are invited are named on the inside envelope of their parents:

> Mr. and Mrs. John Brown,
> Alison and Peter

Invitations to adult sisters or adult brothers may be included in a single invitation:

> The Misses Alison and Ruth, or
> The Messrs. Peter and Steven

Both parents issue the invitation if they are together. Where one is dead or they are divorced, the invitation is issued by the host or hostess, unless a divorced spouse joins in hosting the occasion. Where no parents are alive, invitations may be issued by a relative or friend, or by the couple themselves when they are the hosts. The usual invitation reads:

> Mr. and Mrs. Jonathan Brown
> request the honor of your presence
> at the marriage of their daughter
> Diana Gail
> to
> Mr. Sidney Smith
> on Sunday, the eighth of October
> One thousand nine hundred and seventy-nine
> at twelve o'clock
> St. Bartholomew's Church, Philadelphia

Invitation to the reception is indicated by additional note:

> and afterward at
> Ten seventeen Cedar Lane

If not all the guests at the church are to be invited to the reception, an additional card in an envelope is enclosed with the invitation to the ceremony:

> Mr. and Mrs. Jonathan Brown request the pleasure of your company at the wedding breakfast following the ceremony at the Plaza Hotel.

For a small wedding (less than twenty people) the invitations should be handwritten on note paper (black or blue ink) and may be mailed two weeks in advance:

1012 Cedar Lane
Pittsburgh, Pennsylvania
October 1, 1979

Dear Aunt Molly,

    Diana is to be married to Sidney Smith in St. Peter's Chapel of St. Bartholomew's Church on Thursday, October eighth at twelve o'clock. We hope you will be able to be with us and to join in the reception afterwards.

Affectionately,

Friends and relatives not invited to the ceremony may receive an announcement:

Mr. and Mrs. Jonathan Brown
have the honor of announcing [or have the honor to announce]
the marriage of their daughter
Diana Gail
to
Mr. Sidney Smith
on Friday, the eighth of October
One thousand nine hundred and seventy nine
St. Bartholomew's Church, Pittsburgh

Included with the announcement there may be a smaller "at-home" card, half the size of the announcement, which gives the address of the new couple:

At Home
after the tenth of December
2764 Lafayette Street
Erie, Pennsylvania 70764

Recall of wedding invitations, when necessary, must be sent as quickly as possible after the announcement:

Mr. and Mrs. Jonathan Brown
announce that the marriage of their daughter
Diana Gail
to
Mr. Sidney Smith
will not take place

Response to a formal invitation follows the same formal style, reversing the wording. This would, of course, be handwritten:

Mr. and Mrs. Molly Montana accept with pleasure the kind invitation of Mr. and Mrs. Jonathan Brown to the reception for their daughter Diana Gail on Tuesday, September sixth at half after ten Meadow Country Club

Similarly:

Mr. and Mrs. Molly Montana regret exceedingly that because of a previous engagement they are unable to accept Mr. and Mrs. Jonathan Smith's kind invitation for Tuesday, September sixth

Friends and relatives who are not invited to a wedding usually receive an announcement. The usual form is:

Mr. and Mrs. Norman Majors
have the honour of announcing
[or have the honour to announce]
the marriage of their daughter
Alice
to
Sidney J. Manors
on Sunday, the sixth of June
One thousand nine hundred and seventy nine
Presbyterian Church
Pittsfield

Wedding announcements to the press are made by the family. They should be typewritten (not phoned in), and should follow the style of the other announcements published in the paper. Use formal names (not Liza or Betty unless they have been well established). Notices should be sent to the society editor (by name if you know it) with a date when it is to be released. You may include a recent (within a year) picture of the bride.

Formal invitations are also issued to other important or large gatherings—reception, dance, dinner, etc. They are usually engraved and they are written in the third person:

Mr. and Mrs. Jonathan Lavelle request the pleasure of your company at a dinner dance for their daughter Miss Blossom Lavelle Saturday, the fifth of May at eight o'clock The Plaza

Informal invitations

By far the greatest volume of social correspondence is informal. Although traditional practice suggests that social letters be handwritten, both convenience and legibility suggest that the typewriter can sometimes be used where it is available, especially for long letters. However, a personal letter should not carry a transcriber's initials if it is dictated, and the business-type address, if included at all, is preferably placed at the bottom left side of the letter.

Typically, an informal invitation to dinner would go:

> *Dear Mrs. Sally,*
>
> Will you and Tom join us for dinner on Thursday, February thirteenth at seven o'clock?
>
> Tim Tomkins is in town and I have asked him to join us so that we can hear about his plans for a new book.
>
> Cordially,

Even an informal invitation—and all letters of thanks or sympathy, too—must be in good taste and reflect the importance you attach to them. They should be written on plain stationery, preferably on a single page. They should be handwritten. Most important: They must be timely. A last-minute invitation is sometimes taken as an insult by sensitive people: They assume someone refused to come so that they are wanted now.

Invitations have one additional requirement. They must be explicit and complete. Check your informal note so that there can be no misunderstanding:

1. **Who is invited:** *Not:* You and your friends (family), *but:* You and John, *or:* You, John, and the children, *or:* You, Clarisse, and Sylvia.

Except in rare situations (a hen party or stag party), an invitation to an event in the evening should include both husband and wife but may be addressed to either (or both).

2. **When:** *Not:* next Tuesday, *but:* on Tuesday, January 10 at 6 P.M.

3. **Where:** *Not:* at the church, *but:* in the auditorium of the Holy Name Church on 90th Street and Amsterdam Avenue.

4. **How to get there,** if directions are deemed necessary. If an event is in a suburban home or even a public place and some guests are likely not to know the way to it, it is wise to enclose a separate card with instructions.

5. **Why:** *Not:* for Alice Farnsworth, *but:* to welcome Alice Farnsworth and her new husband on their first anniversary. If the event celebrates a birthday or anniversary, you will embarrass the guest who comes empty-handed.

Dear Lillian,

Will you and Saul join us for dinner next Tuesday, the 21st?

Peter is coming home for the holidays and we want him to have a chance to see all his old friends and also to celebrate his birthday.

We have also asked Ruth and Alan and Clarice and Teddy, so it will be quite a reunion.

I am sure Peter will have a lot to tell you about his adventures in the Peace Corps. He expands more eloquently with guests than with us, so we will enjoy the retelling as much as all of you.

Call me on Friday. I'll be home all day.

Affectionately,

Dear Miss Harris,

Will you come to lunch on Monday, June eighth, at noon?

I would like to talk to you at length about some thoughts for the Garden Club program this year.

Please call me at 787-6400 any afternoon.

Affectionately,

If the invitation is for an out-of-town visit, be sure to include instructions for getting there and if it is for a long stay, what clothes to bring.

Dear Ruth,

While the snow was still falling last week, Alan reminded me how much you love to ski. Alan and I would love to have you and Sidney join us for the weekend of December seventh. The ski runs here are in top condition and the lake is already frozen solid.

Richard and his new girl friend will be with us and I am sure he will not miss the opportunity to show us his "hotdogging" on the new skis he picked up in Sweden.

You won't need any special cold-weather clothing or skis or skates. We have closets full of all the necessities of winter weather, including mittens in all sizes.

If you drive up, use route 90 to Gainsborough, then turn west for two miles on route 17. We're about 100 yards beyond the huge red barn on the right. Ours is the white Cape Cod cottage, you'll remember.

Trains run twice a day from Pittsburgh at 9 A.M. and 1 P.M. The trip to Gainsborough takes about two hours, barring snow slides. We'll meet you at the station if you'll let us know which train you're making. Or you can phone us when you get there.

All of us are looking forward to seeing you again and updating our lives. Please phone me as soon as you decide.

Affectionately,

Responding to an invitation

Response to an informal invitation should be immediate, brief, and handwritten, with the envelope addressed to the hostess, but the letter addressed to host and hostess. If you find it very difficult to write immediately, phone your acceptance or regrets.

Don't leave your answer uncertain. If you don't know whether you can join a gathering, say no and explain the situation. Let the hostess make the decision as to whether you can accept at a later time. The hostess may wish to invite someone else and she is entitled to know how many to prepare for.

A response to an invitation should contain: (1) an expression of pleasure at being invited; (2) a definite response as to whether you will be coming; (3) if the answer is "no," an expression of regret or disappointment and a reason; (4) if the answer is "yes," a repetition of the essentials: "For Ruth and Alan, Friday, February 14, at 7 o'clock at your house." This serves as double check on the hostess's writing and your reading of the invitation. (Imagine the embarrassment if the party is on the following Friday.)

Acceptances should echo the degree of formality or informality of the invitation:

> Tom and I will be delighted to join you for dinner Thursday, February thirteenth. We look forward to seeing Tim again and might even offer a few thoughts for his project. Thank you for asking us.
>
> Sincerely,

Accepting a weekend invitation

> Dear Mathilda and Tom,
>
> Before Tom pleads pressure of business, I am going to say yes to your gracious invitation to join you for the weekend of February 10. We'll be delighted to join in the skiing, skating, or just sitting around. I'm so glad you asked us.
>
> Tom would surely prefer to take the train Saturday morning. He is afraid the snow may cause driving problems on Route 90. As soon as we reach Gainsborough we will give you a ring. Don't try to meet us; the train may be delayed and it's a shame to miss even a half hour of fun waiting for us.
>
> Both Tom and I have a lot of gossip to pass along so keep your ears clean. We look forward to seeing you after so many months.
>
> Affectionately,

Note: Don't forget to bring a house gift. Don't forget to follow your visit with a "bread-and-butter" letter.

Regrets

Regrets similarly are definite and cordial:

> Tom and I are sincerely sorry we can't join you on Thursday, February the thirteenth.
>
> Tom will be in San Diego for that week attending a seminar. We regret especially the opportunity to talk to Tim again. We always found him fascinating.
>
> Please call me whenever you have a chance to chat, particularly after you've had your dinner party.
>
> Cordially,

> *Dear Mathilda,*
>
> When I first opened your invitation for a weekend at Briar House I almost shrieked with delight. But when Tom came home that evening he told me it would be just impossible for him.
>
> As you know the paper industry has been in a supply crisis for months and Tom has been working almost every night developing new sources. Some foreign suppliers will be in town during the weekend of February ninth and Tom must get to talk to them.
>
> You can see how much I would like to join you, but I have to say no.
>
> Please accept our thanks for the invitation. I hope you will invite us again when the time is right. We look forward very much to seeing you.
>
> Very cordially,

SMALL-TALK AND FRIENDLY LETTERS

Small talk

Small talk, or plain conversation, comes with great ease to some (ask any boss about the coffee klatches in his office) and with difficulty to others. Part of this is usually attributed to shyness.

One way to break the ice is to learn a few good stories or jokes and put them in your own words. Overlearn the material so that you don't fumble it in the telling or recalling. Pick an item that intrigues or amuses you and tell it in a conversational tone. And make sure you don't telegraph the punch line. But don't tell too many stories.

Use the story as an icebreaker. And change the stories from time to time.

Another type of icebreaker is the provocative question: "Where would you go if you had no obligations?" "What would you do if you had a million dollars?" "If you were mayor?" "Where do you think the economy is going?" "Have you read the new book by Wallace?"

Or tell about something interesting you have been doing. "I've just reread *War and Peace* and it seems to be a different book from the one I read ten years ago." "The museum has a new exhibit on Queen Mary this week."

Spontaneity is important. Worrying about the impression you are making tends to make you dull and boring.

For others, monopolizing the conversation is the fault. They have to learn to be a good listener, not only opening their ears and minds but observing the speaker fully, expressing appreciation at humor or emotions. It is often difficult to appreciate those we know too well. And don't interrupt.

Don't be a one-subject conversationalist. There must be a few areas that interest you. Create a "starter" to bring up each of them.

Telling a joke is a never-ending way of carrying on a conversation. Telling one that is slightly risqué may advance your familiarity, but it is necessary to know the background and feelings of your partners in conversation before you risk this.

In general, it is best to avoid being extreme in your statements unless you are pushing an issue as a major part of your image. Some partisans never give up on a subject and become a bore or a nuisance.

Don't be dogmatic. There are always at least two legitimate points of view, and lots of gray areas. Be careful not to offend—either those present or others. Try not to be derogatory of anyone unless it is necessary to make a frank appraisal.

There are a few areas of conversation that require special care. Don't get too personal especially to someone you have just met, and especially if he or she shows reluctance to discuss personal things. Until you know a good deal about your partners in conversation avoid sex, religion, and politics. These are areas which can lead to distasteful controversy. And avoid asking the cost of things, health, or marital problems.

And if you are a parent or grandparent, please don't dwell on the accomplishments of your progeny. Above all, remember to think in terms of "you"—not "I."

When you carry on a conversation in a group, speak around the circle, but look at faces, not into the distance.

The friendly letter

The ability to engage in written small talk—as in conversation or in writing—is also not given to everyone. Many people are inhibited in talking of personal or trivial things. They just can't get a friendly conversation going in a letter.

The difficulty starts with beginnings. No one wants to sound banal. We begin by assuming that strangers are not really interested in us or what we are doing, unless it affects them, or perhaps because what we have to say is something they would have liked to do. Good friends, on the other hand, relish all the gossip with details.

A friendly letter is easier than friendly conversation because there is no person watching while you form your message.

The *trite* beginnings are easy but not very good:

> Sorry I was so long in responding . . .
> Thank you for writing . . .
> As I promised, I am sending this letter . . .
> Your letter came as a welcome surprise . . .
> As soon as I received your letter . . .

These are much better:

> The cheerful smile I last saw on your face when we drove away last Thursday is still in my mind . . .
> What a juicy bit of news I have for you . . .
> You'll never guess what's happened here to get me to write at last . . .
> It's finally happened just as you predicted . . .

Start with something interesting that will make the reader want to go on. Here are more good letter starters:

There are times when it seems everything is happening at once.

You would have stood on your head if you had been at our house last week.

The fates have been with me this week. Everything is going right.

There has not been a dull moment at our house since you left.

I just had to pick up a pen to write to you today.

It was good of you to call yesterday to tell me the exciting news.

I've become engaged! Yes . . .

Sit down! Hold your breath! You'll never guess what happened here yesterday.

No news is sometimes good news. Nevertheless, you'll want to know . . .

Even if there is nothing exciting to write about you can say something:

There are times when life is a bore . . .

It seems nothing ever happens around here, but . . .

All is quiet on the home front. Perhaps this is for the best . . .

So we've begun. What shall we write about when everything is the same?

Sam dropped in last week with a funny story.

Did you read about the sextuplets born in Australia?

I've just finished reading *War and Peace* for the fourth time.

We are looking forward to a vacation in the Adirondacks next June.

Unless you are writing to those who you know are really interested, avoid referring to your aches and pains, the children's illnesses (or even triumphs), or the negatives of life. Each person has his own. Many of us subconsciously revel in the difficulties of our friends, but you don't have to wallow in your own troubles.

In general, unless there is a reason to tell it, don't pass along bad news or complaints or derogatory statements.

If you have to pass along news of an accident or death, try to prevent the shock of sudden announcement. Lead up to it:

Not: I am sorry to tell you your son was hurt in an accident yesterday.

But: We've been doing a lot of exploring in the suburbs lately and had more than we bargained for last Thursday. A five-ton truck ran right into us at a cross section. Three of the boys were sent to the hospital, including Sandy. He is shaken up with a few bones broken, but the doctor assures us he will be okay in a few months.

Remember: Your good friends want to hear about you, but within limits. People—including all readers—are primarily interested in things that concern themselves. When you write, keep in mind your reader, his or her interests, ambitions, hobbies, friends.

Try to think in terms of the one who is receiving the letter. Start by writing about the receiver's interests. Visualize the receiver as if he or she were right with you and you were talking.

Dear Cyrus,

I just couldn't wait to get home from our trip to be able to set down all the adventures we had doing the Grand Tour of Europe. The route from London to Rome seems to have been part of the standard education of young men and women in the early part of the century. For me it was a series of excitements I shall remember for the rest of my life.

When you visit with us at Christmas I'll let you read the day-to-day diary and see the hundreds of slides I took. Then you'll understand why I couldn't take off more than the minute to send a postcard.

First, we arrived in London in the midst of a cabbies' strike and had to call our friends in Guildford to pick us up. They took us to our London hotel and then spent several hours showing us the highlights, such odd bits as the place at the Tower of London where Anne Boleyn was beheaded. But much more.

We visited Paris (including a trip through the sewers), Venice (where Pete fell into a canal trying to hop into a gondola), Florence (the art is magnificent), Assisi, San Marino (it's a little country on the top of a hill), and Rome (where the Pope gave us his blessing together with several thousand others).

There is so much to tell you that I can't wait to see you again. If I tried to put it all into a letter, I'd never get back to school in time.

In the meantime, my love to your sister, and your mother too.

Cordially,

Dear Mal,

You'll remember our talk about solar heating and its future when we met in Denver. I thought then it would be too expensive to install in homes. And I'm not sure I wasn't right.

But now I must tell you, our next-door neighbor has put one on his roof and he says he'll save money eventually. It isn't particularly pretty but it does work. It stores up heat during the day in a water heating system that creates electricity that he uses to heat at night.

The news in the family is nothing startling. Leslie is off to college next month. She had a choice of Radcliffe or Bennington and chose Radcliffe, but not without a lot of soul searching. Tom, her boyfriend, is at the University of Vermont, but mother went to Radcliffe. Tradition proved stronger than affection.

Mother has become a member of the local bird sanctuary and is studying up on the species she is likely to see.

As for me, I keep plugging along. My grades are averaging a high B, so I hope I can make honors before graduation. I'll be sending out applications for college in a few months. Any suggestions?

At any rate, I'm looking forward to seeing you during the holidays.

Regards,

Don't close a friendly letter with "I must close now to catch the last pickup" or "My date will be calling soon." Close with a sendoff:

Stay well, we look forward to seeing you soon.

Tell us as soon as you know what's really happening in your neck of the woods.

I can't wait for your call (or letter) (or visit).

Take good care of those charming kids. We love them as our own.

Here's a letter from a college girl to the folks back home:

Dear Folks,

Thank you for the wonderful package. I really did appreciate the new Durrell book and other goodies, but please don't send those tempting cookies any more. Everyone on the dorm floor had some and now they're berating me for the extra calories they have to work off.

The term is just starting but my assignments have piled up high enough to assure me of a lot of sleepless nights. All my professors are nice, but Dr. Sommers is a real martinet. He's told us our papers are due before Christmas, with no leeway, and his requirements are monstrous: 20,000 words responding to 200 questions. Nevertheless, I think I'll enjoy the work: he is so informative and fascinating in his lectures.

My new roommate is Mary Jane Tibbett from Atlanta, Georgia. She is a nice girl and a good student, and I expect that we'll get along swimmingly. We have a lot of interests in common—not excluding boys.

I'll keep you posted on how I'm getting along, but don't worry. You know I can take care of myself, scholastically and otherwise.

Affectionately,
Alice

Here are some letters to a child away at camp.

Dear Cynthia,

Mother is already complaining that she misses the third at breakfast—meaning you, of course. Your friend Sam came to call this morning. His folks are sending him to Boy Scout camp in August, but that seems a long time off to him, with you away.

Aunt Molly is due to visit us next week and she'll be staying in your room for a few days, so she's sort of your guest. Mother spoke to her last night and she sends her love. She'll also send you some cookies and some old (perhaps rare) comic books she found in the attic.

Visiting day isn't until August 1, so write soon to tell us what's happening at camp and how you're doing, especially in swimming and tennis.

Love,
Dad

Dear Johnny,

Here we are back at home at just about the same time you arrived at Tangleford. And, of course, on the way home Mother thought of half a dozen things she forgot to tell you before you left.

First, the Swiss knife you got for Christmas is packed among your socks. Mother found it in the pocket of your old jeans and slipped it into the trunk at the last minute.

Second, your allergy pills are in the first-aid kit. But please don't take them during the day unless you are sneezing or tearing badly. They do make you drowsy.

A message for you came in by phone last night from a young man named Alan Brown. He's at Starlight Camp near you and hopes to be able to come by for a visit during the summer.

Try to find time to brush up on your French. There are two textbooks and an old French-English dictionary in your trunk. Do you think you can converse with that French boy in the senior group?

We'll phone you Sunday to see how things are going. In the meantime, have fun.

Love,
Mother and Dad

Dear Jimmy,

So you are now all set in a bunk. We hope you like your new roommates for you will be spending a lot of time with them during the next few months.

Mother and I got a copy of the summer schedule—the same one you received when you boarded the bus—and it looks like a wow of a summer. You'll particularly enjoy that hike through Sleepy

Hollow. I still remember the area from the days I went to camp. It can get real spooky on an overnight.

Make the most of that beautiful lake. It offers a good chance to improve your swimming so that you can pass the life-saver test in the fall. Tom Messin wrote his mother that he passed beginners and expects to catch up with you.

Take good care of yourself. You're on your own now.

Love,

Parents are always hungry for news:

Dear Mother and Dad,

We have all finally set up in our new apartment and everything seems to be working out as we expected.

Joan and Mark have been registered at the local school and have been placed in appropriate grades after many examinations. Joan was placed a year ahead of her 5th grade rating in the Ardsley school; Mark is in the 12th grade, expecting to graduate this June. He'll be close to the top of his class, I think. Soon we will be writing for college applications.

Martha has joined the local PTA and Garden Club and has already made many new friends. Shopping is easier for us here than in Westchester; there are food markets only a few blocks away.

And as for me, I am well as usual, still too busy fixing things around the house to get out much, but in good spirits.

As soon as all the little things are nailed in place, we'll have you for a weekend. Mother can run her critical eye over the new decor and tell me how I didn't put up the curtains properly.

Love to you both,

And of course, friends always want to hear the latest:

Dear Alice,

The only news I can give you is that nothing has happened here! If no news is good news, you have it.

Actually, of course, everyone is doing his or her thing in a very proper way. There have been no heroics and no accidents. Jane is active in school student affairs and works hard on the weekly newspaper. Arthur is struggling with French and Latin, driving me to distraction with questions on long forgotten irregular verbs. "Look them up," I say pontifically, as if the dictionary had all the answers.

Mother is as well as can be expected. She gets around everywhere she really wants to go.

As for me: I continue to be active in PTA and some church activities, but essentially I'm the usual mother-housekeeper-chauffeur-cook-maid-etc. everyone expects of me.

But soon both kids will be off to college and I'll really be emancipated.

Love,

LOVE LETTERS

For most ordinary people writing anything sentimental is a heavy chore. Yet a letter expressing affection or any deep emotion must be spontaneous, an expression of the heart rather than the head. Even a serious, no-nonsense recipient likes to get a letter in which sincerity and love flow beyond logic and serious matters.

When you write a love letter, picture the recipient; even fantasize a little to let yourself go. Write as you would talk, but if presence inhibits your conversation, write to an imaginary figure.

Be careful of your choice of words. When you write a sentimental letter you may strike a chord which you don't anticipate. So after you have finished, reread your letter as if you were receiving it.

You don't have to be blunt. Metaphors, hyperbole, and other figures of speech have a special place in letters that express emotion.

The secret is really in letting yourself go and imagining yourself and the one you love in a fantasy world.

Dear Jane,

I can't thank Ma Bell enough for bringing your voice to me last night. It was like a flower garden in the middle of a desert. I can still feel that I am holding your hand across the miles that separate us.

Frankly, if it were not for your call I think I would have not been able to work today. I miss you so. When you ended with "I love you dearly" a glow ran through my whole body and all the tensions of the day seemed to fly away. All night long I continued to hear your voice in my dreams so I just hated to wake up to another morning without you.

Right now I feel I'm the luckiest guy in the world. Sometimes on the bus, I pinch myself to make sure it's really me and that I'm not just still dreaming.

I'll call you again tomorrow night when I reach Chicago. Till then, please take good care of yourself.

Love,

Dear Tom,

Your letter was just what I needed this morning to make a new woman of me. For days I had been wondering where and how you were and suddenly the mailman showed up with those cheering two pages from you.

The days seem weeks while you're gone but I realize that you must do what you are doing for both our sakes.

All is well here so there is no need to worry about anything. Mother came down for a short visit to keep me from getting the blues, but even without her I can beat it and grin because I know you'll be home soon. Whenever I feel blue, I know I can call your sister and spend an evening watching TV or take in a movie.

So please don't let my missing you so much bother your thoughts. You'll need all the concentration to finish your project.

Just remember I'm here—waiting—and loving you more each day, darling.

Devotedly,

Dear Amy,

When I used to read those wonderful letters Napoleon wrote to Josephine, I wondered if he had a Cyrano on his staff. That kind of writing doesn't come easily to me. But you know I love you dearly and miss you terribly. In my everyday terms I'd express my affection mathematically, but that looks so unromantic.

My plans now are uncertain. Everything depends on whether the company gets the contract I'm estimating on at the moment. But whatever happens I'll make certain to get back to you for at least a week next month.

It is only the happy recollections of our last few dates that sustain my morale here. I count the hours like a prisoner marking the days, knowing that when they reach the magic number I'll be free to be with you again.

All my love,

Darling,

If I were a little younger, I'd cover the pages with those magic XXX's that represent the ten thousand kisses. Thank you for that beautiful letter. I didn't need it to tell me you love me because I have always known that, but I confess seeing it in writing gave me a special thrill—as if you were here personally holding me in your arms and whispering in my ear to that old sweet music.

Needless to say, every day you are away seems endless. I try to distract myself by keeping busy redoing the curtains and rearranging furniture, but eventually the living room returns to the way I remember you in it, sitting in the big easy chair.

Mother is busy shopping for a trousseau for me, in spite of the fact that I've told her I already have everything I need. But she insists it's a family tradition, so I will probably end up with two of everything.

The Carmodys keep asking about you and send their best wishes. They want very much to remain friends with us even if we move away. If you think of it, send them a card at your next stop.

Do be careful with yourself. I'd love to be looking out for you but the best I can do from here is send you my prayers,

All my love,

Dearest,

Sometimes I curse the modern devices that make distant places so close that one can't resist getting to another city. But now there are only four left on this schedule and I will be homeward bound.

Yesterday I saw three customers in Topeka and passed my sales quota for the month. The Libens there sent their best. You'll remember them from the convention in Chicago, Mrs. Liben wore that daring red dress that shocked you so. I had dinner with them. She's still a knockout, but you don't have to be jealous. John never lets her out of his sight.

Tomorrow I'm off to Joplin, then St. Louis, Cincinnati, and home. I'll call you from St. Louis at about eight o'clock, before the children are in bed. I want them to recognize their father when he comes home.

Stay a good angel till I get back.

Lovingly,

My wonderful guy,

I didn't make up the line, but I do love you twenty-four hours more than yesterday and each day adds another few drops. Still I think I'll burst before you get home.

There is hardly a moment during the day that I'm not thinking of you. True enough, sometimes in my fantasies you're painting the garage or mowing the lawn (Johnny did it yesterday), but mostly I think of us cuddled up somewhere or doing something romantic.

Everything is fine at home. Johnny brought in his first report card yesterday with everything marked satisfactory except "conduct." There was note attached saying Johnny just couldn't stop talking in class. Put that into your computer and see if you can find the right answer for fathers. But I think he'll get over it. Last night he had to write out the Declaration of Independence as punishment.

Both of us are waiting for next Friday when you'll be back. In the meantime do take good care of yourself.

Lovingly,

HOW TO SAY "I'M SORRY"

One of the most difficult things for everyone is to admit being wrong. Having decided that you were wrong—or at least that you have to admit that you were wrong, even if you don't believe it's so—how do you go about with as much salvage to your ego as you can muster?

The easiest and probably the most tension-relieving method is to say outright: "I was wrong." If you must do some sugar-coating, you can add, "I just don't know what got into me at the moment."

Dear Maybelle,

When I'm wrong, I'm wrong—and I must admit it this time.

One of New York's famous mayors once said, "When I make a mistake, it's a lollapalooza." Though I am not in a class for doing big things, apparently I am when it comes to making mistakes.

I do want you to know that I am sorry I blew up and did the things I did. I hope you understand the pressures I am under that caused the explosion.

Sincerely,

Dear Sonia,

Sorry! Sorry! Sorry!

I am in a sorry state today over our argument yesterday. In the fresh light of morning the whole thing seems just a bit of nonsense, and I shouldn't have said the things I said or done the things I did.

I guess it was the long period of restrained tension that burst out in a moment when I let myself go. Actually, I was angry about a lot of other things and your comments just pulled the cork out of the bottle.

I didn't agree with you entirely in what you said. But I had no right to act the way I did and I do want to apologize.

Very cordially,

Dear Bill,

I tossed all night last night thinking about the letter I had sent off to you.

In the morning light I must say I really didn't mean it—at least not in the way I put it in that letter.

Although I still think I was right in refusing the invitation to Cecelia's party, I must agree I could have handled the situation much more tactfully. It will be a long time before I forget our argument over Mother's furniture. But I guess that I can't make it a cause célèbre for the rest of our lives. Materially of course the argument was not over a matter of value, but I did have a sentimental attachment to many of the things.

I'll try to restrain my temper when I talk to the north branch of the family next time. Obviously the whole thing is a silly reason to split up a family relationship, and I'll try not to widen the break any further.

Cordially,

Dear Maybelle,

You know how often you go away from a conversation and say to yourself, "Why didn't I think of saying that!"

Well, that's just the way I feel today. I realize that some of the things I said to you must have sounded selfish and unfeeling.

I really didn't mean them that way. The words just bubbled out of me with you as my emotional catch-all. Of course I do feel put upon by having all the burden of my mother's care thrust upon me, but I don't want you to feel that I resented it or didn't want to do it or expect you to give up your job to come and live with us.

You can understand that once in a while all of us get into an emotional dither, and I guess I was in one of these when we had our talk.

Please understand that I don't blame you for anything, and I really didn't mean what I seem to have meant when I complained.

Cordially,

Dear Miss Tambor,

Please accept my apologies for the delay in sending your package.

It went out in the mail yesterday by priority mail, and you should have it within the next day or so.

Frankly, the whole matter slipped my mind under the pressure of everyday chores, and it wasn't until I got the frantic call from your sister that I was nudged into finding the old letters and sending the package off to the post office. Please forgive me.

Sincerely,

CONGRATULATIONS

A man we knew made a habit of greeting friends he had not seen for some time with "Congratulations!" Most of them beamed and wondered how he knew about their recent accomplishment.

There is no paucity of reasons for congratulations: a raise, a change in job duties, a commendation from anyone, any job finished, any objective attained, any desire fulfilled—small or large—can be a reason. And the more trivial the reason the more appreciated is the compliment.

In general, letters of congratulation should show that you share the joy of the event. Sincerity, friendliness, good cheer are essentials. To a good friend, the letter should be chatty and informal; to an older person with whom your relationship is more formal, the letter should be briefer and accordingly more formal. And always make a point of mentioning the occasion.

Here are some simple beginnings:

> Joan told me the good news . . .
> Sylvia and I were thrilled to hear . . .
> You must know how pleased I am . . .
> I couldn't be more happy . . .
> It's wonderful news to hear . . .

On an engagement

Dear Cynthia,

Sylvia joins me in extending our sincere congratulations on your engagement. We've known Tim for ever so long and think the world of both of you.

May time bring you both ever increasing happiness as the years go by.

Dear Ruth,

Eunice and I were, of course, delighted to hear of your engagement.

Knowing you, we appreciate that Johnny must be something very special and we look forward to meeting him. Of course, we are prejudiced, but we think he has a real find, too.

All of our best wishes go out to you both.

Love,

Dear Norman,

As soon as Mother heard the news, she picked up the phone and passed it along to all of us in the family.

Congratulations!

Arlene is one wonderful girl. You are a lucky guy to have been able to induce her to say yes.

Sandy joins me in sending wishes for the best of the best to both of you.

Cordially,

Dear Tom,

Some of the Joneses have all the luck.

I got a peek at Michele as you were leaving the party last week. She's beautiful and she must be a wonderful girl to have pulled you out of your bachelorhood resolutions.

Sylvia joins in wishing you both the best of all good things in your life together.

Affectionately,

Dear Sandy,

Happy days!

What a joyful surprise to hear that you and Lee are going to make it official. It couldn't happen to two nicer people. All the gang agrees it is going to be the ideal marriage.

For myself, I hope—and believe—you'll be happy together always.

Fondly,

Dear Sandy,

If you could look me right in the eyes this minute you'd see that they have turned green with envy.

Tom is a wonderful guy. I've been in love with him since I was six. Now you've gone and taken him out of circulation.

You know I wish the best for both of you. And I know you're going to make the fabulous ideal couple they used to write novels about.

Love,

Dear Marlene,

We've just read of your engagement in the *Press*.

Sylvia and I extend our congratulations and best wishes to you and Tim.

We wish you many years of joy and contentment.

Affectionately,

On a marriage

Congratulations on a marriage are offered to the groom, best wishes to the bride. Even in a liberated society, we do not acknowledge the well-known fact that the woman is the one who makes the choice. But if you are writing to both— the preferred procedure—congratulations are acceptable. The message should be sent as soon as possible after a wedding announcement is received or made public.

Dear Joyce and Harry,

It was grand to hear that the two of you have joined the ranks of the married. Jim and I are delighted. We've always thought you were made for each other and that fate had brought you together.

Needless to say we extend our love and best wishes, and look forward to seeing you after your honeymoon.

Love,

Dear Sandy,

What good news!

We received your announcement yesterday and Joe whooped almost to the ceiling. We've met Tom several times during the years and know he's a really fine fellow. You certainly will be happy together.

Please let us know when you get back to town so that we can have all our friends meet the new family.

Love,

Dear Cynthia,

News of your wedding came as a spring breeze here. All of us are pleased as punch that you finally found a guy you really love.

Robert sounds wonderful. I think he has all the qualities we all love in your father—which, of course, does make him a great person.

The whole family is overjoyed and send you their very best wishes.

Love,

Dear John,

It's about the most thrilling news we could hope for!

Congratulations to you and best wishes to your new bride.

We know you will have a wonderful life together, certainly if all our good wishes for you come true.

Love,

Dear Mrs. Matthews,

All of us at International House wish to extend our best wishes to you and Mr. Matthews on your marriage. You know of our fondness for the Thomsons and the Matthewses these many years.

Very cordially,

Dear Larry,

Our congratulations to you on the big leap.

I hear you have selected a wonderful gal. She must be wonderful to induce you to make the break.

We look forward to meeting her.

With love,

Dear Sylvia and Jerry,

It was great news to hear of your wedding. Needless to say we extend the best of our good wishes and expect that this will be the beginning of a wonderful new life for both of you.

A package will be coming to you from Altman's as a souvenir of our love.

Please get in touch with us as soon as you get back to town. We would love to have you for dinner and to let some old friends meet you both.

Affectionately,

Dear Dorothy,

Sylvia and I join in extending our best wishes to you.

I can see from your choice of a husband that your waiting was well considered because I know he is just the right guy for you. We are sure that this marks the beginning of a long and happy relationship for both of you.

All of us look forward to meeting Tom when you get back from your honeymoon.

Affectionately,

Dear Timothy,

The announcement of your marriage came in today's mail and brought us great joy.

Our sincere congratulations and best go out to you both on this happy occasion.

Sincerely,

Dear Tom,

Jeffrey and I were delighted to learn of your marriage to Janet Dennis.

We extend our sincere good wishes to you both and look forward to meeting your bride soon.

Very cordially,

On the birth of a child

The birth of a child lends itself to much more informality in announcement and congratulations than any other major event in a lifetime. A response to a birth announcement should be lighthearted, sentimental, cordial, and optimistic.

Dear Cynthia,

It's grand news—and all of us share in your joy.

Janet tells me the baby looks just like you, which promises another beauty in the family.

If I know George, he must be blooming, taking all the credit. Tell him to save a cigar for Richard.

All our love,

Dear Cynthia,

Paul and I are as elated as if we had an addition to our own family. It's good to have a new boy with the Dinerstein name.

Have you decided on a name yet? We're hoping it will commemorate Grandpa, but I'm sure you have ideas of your own.

As soon as you will be receiving visitors, we'll be by to see you.

Love,

Dear Sandy,

It's just wonderful news!

Tim told me you've had a baby brother for Alison; just what she asked for.

Congratulations on the occasion and all the best for the years ahead.

Tim and I look forward to seeing you and John and the baby for a firsthand appraisal as soon as you feel up to it.

Love,

Dear Sis,

Mother called me with the wonderful news at seven this morning. I am thrilled, particularly because it's a girl and we've had such wonderful luck with girls in our family.

Mom says you'll be calling the baby Alison, which I think is charming and altogether appropriate. I know babies don't really look like anything except babies, but I'm told yours is already exceptionally pretty.

Jerry and I will be up to see for ourselves soon,

Love,

Dear Sally,

The excitement at our house that followed the news of your new baby would have led a stranger to think it was our own.

All of us are delighted at having a little man in the family at last. Susan just can't wait till he's old enough to play with.

John and I send all our best wishes and look forward to seeing you and the baby soon.

Love,

On an anniversary

Dear Margie,

Can it be that ten years have gone by since we danced at your wedding?

Tim assures me that the days have come and gone but neither you nor John seems to have changed a bit.

Our congratulations to you both on the day. May all the anniversaries ahead be as bright and joyful for you.

Cordially,

Dear Mrs. Sondheim,

Sylvia and I extend to you our congratulations on this occasion of your silver anniversary.

We have enjoyed knowing you through many of these years and look back on happy events we have shared with you.

With all of your scores of friends we extend our hopes that we may be with you on many more occasions in the years ahead. May these years hold great happiness for both of you.

Affectionately,

On a birthday

Birthday greetings are done so well and with so much variety by commercial greeting card manufacturers that your letter needs to be exceptional to be an adequate substitute for it.

If you want to be "special"—or show you think more of the birthday person than a card would suggest—you might write a bit of personal poetry, or even a letter.

The important thing is that the greetings go out. In this case what you say is relatively unimportant.

Dear Tom,

I notice that this is May 3—a special day on my calendar and yours. It's the day I repeat I'm glad Tom was born!

Affectionately,

Dear Harry,

May 5 remains a special day on my calendar because it reminds me of all the joys we have shared since you were born.

May the years ahead bring much good health and happiness to you, and many more May 5ths to reminisce upon.

Cordially,

Dear Joan,

Whether you admit it or not, you're older today than you were yesterday.

I'm not counting the numbers, but I do want to wish you many more happy days—with or without special note, as you wish. May the years bring you increasing joy!

Love,

Dear Cynthia,

Happy birthday!

I want you to know that I'm glad you were born and reached this time and this place so I could get to know you.

Affectionately,

Dear Jim,

Happy birthday!

It's a good day to say again, I'm glad you're around and that you're my cousin.

Regards,

Dear Jim,

A ton of good wishes to my favorite uncle on your birthday.

I'd deliver them myself if I could get to Smithtown, but being far away, I want you to know that the wishes are there.

Stay happy and healthy.

Your nephew,

Dear Grandma,

Happy birthday.

If I had a space ship I'd be aboard in a second to come to tell you personally how glad I am that you're around.

We think of you fondly all year round, but on your birthday, most of all, we wish we could be with you.

Love,

On someone's success

Obviously, congratulations offered immediately after a success are more appropriate and more appreciated than a later letter. Congratulations reflects your pleasure at a friend's success. The sooner it is expressed, the more spontaneous and the more sincere it seems.

Congratulations should be given briefly, usually as the sole subject of a note, with good cheer. They should be, unlike a general friendly letter, specific as to what you are congratulating for. And if they express envy, it should be expressed humorously.

Dear Jim,

"Hail to the Conqueror!"

I knew you'd make the varsity the minute I saw you in those workout clothes.

Already I see you captain of the team beating Columbia in 1982. Stay well!

Affectionately,

Dear Tom,

I heard the good news over the grapevine as I passed the clubhouse last night.

I think it's wonderful—your making Phi Beta Kappa in your junior year. I tried till my eyes popped out but never could.

Looking forward to your summa cum laude next year.

Cordially,

Congratulations on a graduation

Dear Andrew,

Congratulations on your new diploma!

I know how proud and relieved you must be at passing another milestone in your career. As you have heard it said before, commencement is just a beginning.

We hope this is the beginning of many exciting adventures on your way to a great career.

Cordially,

Dear Sidney,

It is good news indeed to hear that you have your doctorate in mathematics. All of us know the title is the result of a lot of hard work accomplished over many years.

Your family is very proud of you indeed on this day. We know it is just the beginning for you of new challenges and achievements in your profession.

Affectionately,

Dear John,

Our warm congratulations!

Now that you're on the way to college, our very warm good wishes go with you. We know you'll find the next years as exciting and rewarding as the last few and look forward to your next commencement four years from now.

Love,

Dear Jimmy:

I knew you would make it in spite of all the extra difficulties you had!

Congratulations on your graduation. You deserve all the honors you received and more. But as you know, these are just the opening wedges for your new career, which, I am sure, will bring as much success and enjoyment as the challenges of the last four years.

Affectionately,

Dear Frances,

Not so long ago, it seems, we were helping you write your name. And here it is graduation time—and with such honors.

Needless to say, we are proud as punch, as your parents must be, to see you in cap and gown, near the top of your class.

As a remembrance of the occasion, and of us at it, we want you to have the new Atlas of the World—perhaps a reminder of the world of business ahead for you.

Whatever you decide to do, I know that with the energy and intelligence you have always applied you will continue to distinguish yourself.

Good luck on your way!

Cordially,

On an honor or award

Dear John,

Congratulations and good wishes go out from all of us at the Maraneck Country Club. In a sense we feel that because we know and love you, we share in your great honor.

You deserve every bit of the awards that are coming your way. Good luck!

Cordially,

Dear Tom,

It was wonderful to hear that you had taken first prize in the state poetry contest.

Frankly, I never knew there was that kind of talent in you and I am most pleased to find that I know a renowned writer.

The best of good luck.

Cordially,

Dear John,

It seems only yesterday that you were struggling with the debating team and high school calculus.

Now we're proud to add our congratulations to you on your graduation from Yale and the many honors you have received. Sally and I enjoyed watching your progress through the years and join in the happiness of the occasion.

Your mother tells us that you plan to go on to graduate school. Whatever course you take, our best wishes go with you for successful and happy years ahead.

Cordially,

Dear Maybelle,

Cynthia just told me about Harvard accepting Andrew for early admission.

I think it's wonderful! Everyone knew he deserved it, but there is always such a chasm between our own convictions and those of others that getting the confirmation makes us doubly happy.

Jimmy joins in wishing you continuing good news.

Cordially,

Dear Tom,

I see by the newspaper that you have received first prize in the John Adams Essay Contest.

That's wonderful. I know that you richly deserve the honor and I am most pleased that your talents have been recognized. You have been a credit to your class since you joined us here at John Adams and I know you will continue to win honors for us and for yourself.

Cordially,

Dear Mr. Jones:

Our warm congratulations on your election to the Board of Governors of Presbyterian Hospital.

The tribute from your colleagues is well deserved in view of your outstanding record in hospital administration here and abroad. The hospital needs men of your caliber on its board.

I know you will serve with great distinction, lending the experience and understanding that your years in the field have provided.

All of us extend our warm good wishes.

Cordially,

On a business promotion

Dear Mr. Johnson,

It was with mixed emotions that I heard that you had joined the executive staff at National Bank: pride and pleasure at your recognition and regret that we will be seeing so much less of you now that you are in the upper echelons.

All of your friends in Springfield are wishing you success in meeting the challenge of your new position and good fortune in the opportunities it offers.

Cordially,

Dear John,

So you did get the job! Congratulations.

Needless to say, I think your new boss has himself a jewel.

Good luck. I hope this is just the first step in a long successful climb up the ladder.

How about getting together to help celebrate the first paycheck?

Cordially,

Dear Sidney,

Anita told me the wonderful news of your appointment as assistant manager at the Star Store. Congratulations!

I always said you had the stuff in you to take you places, and I see you're on your way.

The best of good luck on the new job. I expect to get another piece of good news from your corner soon.

Cordially,

Dear Harry,

Nobody asked me, but I could have told the Macy management months ago that you were topside material. I'm glad they finally got around to recognizing it for themselves.

Congratulations on your promotion, Harry. It couldn't happen to a nicer or more deserving guy.

Cordially,

Dear Jim,

They tell me you've gotten the extra stripes you deserve. Needless to say, Jane and I are proud and happy at the recognition.

Keep adding the braid to your sleeve and you'll soon find it on your cap. All of us at Homestead look forward to seeing you in your new uniform.

Affectionately,

Dear Sam,

Congratulations from the old gang at Oxford!

We're all delighted to know an Army lieutenant and guarantee that we'll show your picture in uniform to all your old girl friends in town.

Write to us once in a while to let us know a little about life in the Army and how you're getting along.

Cordially,

Dear Dick,

Sonny grew two inches when he heard about your latest promotion. He thinks—as we all do—that it's great to have an uncle with a chicken on his shoulder.

Congratulations on the promotion! We'll see you a general yet.

Affectionately,

Dear Tim,

The news today carries the story of your election as president of John Whittier Co. Our warm congratulations.

I can't say that the news came as a complete surprise. Whittier would have been wise appointing you years ago. There just isn't anyone better for the job.

Accept our best wishes for success in meeting the company's problems and your continued growth in the industry.

Very cordially,

Dear Bill:

It was great to hear the good news about your promotion.

I know you are going to knock them dead. The challenge and the company seem right down your alley.

If I knew him, I would tell Jim Dolan, the president, what a wonderful piece of luck it was for them to get you.

Affectionately,

On a business deal

Dear Bill:

Congratulations! Good luck on your new venture.

All of us join in extending our best wishes for a successful administration.

Very cordially,

Dear Richard,

Everyone must be congratulating you today on getting the new Wintertown Dam contract. Let me add my sincere congratulations and good wishes.

With your wide experience and that so-called luck you've always had, I'm sure you're going to do an outstanding job of it. At any rate, they couldn't have picked a better man.

Keep at it. We're all proud of your success.

Sincerely,

On a speech

Dear Bill:

Your speech last night is the talk of the town this morning. You certainly hit the issues head on.

Lots of people aren't going to agree with you but everyone is rethinking the feasibility of the new projects and many will certainly change their minds.

It was a great presentation and we're proud of you for it.

Very sincerely,

GET-WELL LETTERS AND CONDOLENCES

There are times in life when you wonder if the world has forgotten you—times when an illness, a death or other misfortune make you particularly vulnerable to depression.

At such times you tend to count your friends from among those who remember. If you are the fortunate friend, a note is almost a matter of obligation. If the tone and substance are difficult, you will find some help in these sample letters.

To someone who is ill

In almost all circumstances, a letter to someone in a hospital or ill at home should be cheerful, optimistic, encouraging, friendly, and, if possible, helpful. Scores of commercial cards are available to do this. But there are occasions when a letter shows a greater concern, or when it meets the needs of a special situation better. If the illness or convalescence has been prolonged, a bit of news or gossip or an anecdote is welcomed. Send flowers or a potted plant if you wish.

> *Dear Sally,*
>
> Sorry to hear you're laid up for the week. We'll be missing your cheery good-morning at the office. And Anne is already complaining about the extra work load.
>
> Get well in a hurry. We can't get along without you.
>
> Regards,

> *Dear Sally,*
>
> Your only consolation is, it could have been worse. Sorry about the accident but glad you were able to walk away from it, even with a limp. The worst of it will be over in a week or two, so cheer up.
>
> In the meantime, if you'd like to ease up, why don't you send the kids over to our house for a week or two. Johnny and Alice would love the company, and it will be a vacation for my Tim and Minna. I can manage it. It will be easy because they'll keep each other out of mischief. Just pick up the phone and say yes and I'll do the rest.
>
> Cordially,

> *Dear Sally,*
>
> Phyllis told me you're in the hospital. Sorry!
>
> Get well quickly. We miss having you around and we're counting on you at duplicate bridge May 18.
>
> Sincerely,

> *Dear Mr. Phelan,*
>
> All of us at the Sanding Club join in wishing you a speedy recovery from your illness.
>
> We have admired your staunchness and stamina through all the trying days you had, and hope the hardships did not contribute to your illness.
>
> The hospital reports that your condition is improving, so we look forward to seeing you out and abroad soon.
>
> Very sincerely,

> *Dear Sally,*
>
> So you finally decided to settle the problem with an operation!
>
> I think it was a wise decision. It made no sense carrying the irritation with you all the years when a week or so of discomfort will get rid of it.
>
> Don't rush to get back to work. We'll manage to get along, and

save all the hard problems so that you won't be idle for weeks after you get back.

But do get well soon, then take it easy for a few days.

Regards,
The Boss

After an accident

Dear John:

Sorry indeed to hear about your accident. What an unlikely thing to happen!

The word around is that you will be back, good as new within a few weeks. I hope you live up to the rumor.

So get well soon.

Affectionately,

Dear John,

What a silly thing to do—get hit by a truck, and a big one at that.

All of us at our house hope you'll be on your feet again soon. They can't hold a good man down!

Cordially,

Dear Cynthia,

We're all sad indeed at the news of your accident. Fate can be cruel, can't it?

All of us will miss you around here for the next few weeks, but the forecast is that you'll be back before the end of the month. Inasmuch as you can't do anything but leave things in the doctor's hands, just relax and let nature take its course.

If there is anything you need done in the meantime or want to have done for yourself, just let me know and I'll be the best substitute for you I can.

Sincerely,

Letters of sympathy

Most letters of condolence tend to be cold and formal, which many consider proper in the time of death. Whenever you can, however, include some personal background, an appraisal of the good things in the life of the departed, a point about your contacts with the deceased.

Dear Mrs. Mead,

Sidney's death must be a terrible shock to you as it was to all of us who knew him.

He was always so much the life of the party that his passing is unreal to us. Although he was not related to any of us, he was "family" in a very direct way. The kids called him uncle and most of our friends thought he was at least a cousin.

You have our heartfelt sympathy. We will all miss him with you.

Sincerely,

Dear Sandra,

Each of us, in our own way, shares your grief at John's passing.

He was the kind of guy who became part of the life of everyone who knew him, always offering a helping hand to anyone who needed it.

Our town is a little bit less because he is not with us anymore.

Sylvia joins in extending our sincere sympathy to you and the children.

Affectionately,

Dear Martha,

I know that nothing anyone can say can be of real comfort to you at a time like this, but I do want you to know that you have the heartfelt sympathy of all of us.

We all loved your mother, a bulwark of tradition in this changing world. I don't think any of us will ever stop missing her.

Time takes all of us in its course. We must get used to the idea that even the best things are not forever.

Accept out sincere condolences on this occasion.

Affectionately,

Dear Frank,

As we move along in life we have to expect that some people will die before us just as we know that others will outlive us.

Death has been a pretty constant companion for you these days, I know. And now this blow!

All of us at the office do wish to express our sincere sympathy.

Sincerely yours,

Dear Martin,

It must come to all men.

You know, at least, that your father had a good life, respected by everyone, and full of accomplishment even to his last days.

Everyone who knew him will miss him. So I know how hard these days are for you.

The staff at the *Record* all join in sending their sincere sympathy to you and Margaret.

Very cordially,

Dear Naomi,

My sincere condolences.

We all know this has to happen sometime but always it comes as a shock. Only inanimate things last forever, and even these have their casualties.

If it is any consolation, both you and Paul have had a full life and you do have a fine new generation to carry on.

Very cordially,

Dear Jane,

I can't begin to tell you how sorry I am about Tom's accident. It is the shock that comes from life's unreasonable events that makes you want to shake a fist at fate.

Tom was so full of life, with so much verve and joy. All of us were proud to be his friends.

Our deepest sympathy goes out to you and Mrs. Macdonald, on his loss. No one can explain why it had to happen. So let us all accept it and treasure Tom's memory.

Sincerely,

Dear Jane,

Words have so little comfort at a time like this that I wish I could be with you to put my arms around you and join you in your tears.

Pop was a great fellow, but all men are mortal.

All of us must take comfort in knowing that he enjoyed life and lived it to the full. He leaves behind a generation of fine sons and daughters to carry on his name and traditions.

Allan and I extend our sincere sympathy.

Sincerely,

Dear Sam,

Sylvia and I want to express our deep sympathy to you and the family on the loss of Mary Jean.

Her passing leaves a vacuum in the hearts of her many friends and in the community itself.

She was loved by everyone. People still talk of how she helped the Vietnamese family get set up in town and how she organized the Community Chest last year.

We all must go sometime, but few of us will leave behind the affection and respect that Mary Jean evokes in all of us.

Sincerely,

Some deaths are longed for as a release from pain, suffering, or sickness. To send an ordinary letter of condolence can be a mockery in such circumstances.

Dear Joan,

It had to come for Ted as it must for all of us. You have our sincere sympathy, not only for this difficult hour but also for the many past.

In a sense the final hour was for the best. There were years of suffering for him and trying, hopeless burdens for you. It is never easy to accept death but sometimes it is the better of two bad alternatives.

All of us loved Ted. We will remember him as the jolly, always well man who took us to school on cold winter days, who brought us cheer on Christmas day with his "ho ho."

Let us treasure the good memories together.

Sincerely,

Dear Naomi,

Death is never what we wish for anyone, but after these many months of suffering for Jack, I am sure he was happy that the end was near.

Through all this time you have had our heartfelt sympathy and you have it now. But it is time now to dry your tears and look ahead to a rearranged life with your beautiful children.

When you look back, remember the happy days and the wonderful guy that your husband was until last year. Those are the memories to treasure.

Our heartfelt condolences to you all.

Love,

On the death of a child

Condolences on the death of a child should be carefully written and brief, and the writer should be particularly aware of the special sensitivity of the bereaved. Usually the fewer questions asked, the less said, the better.

Dear Sandra,

There is no understanding the way of the world that takes a child. Our hearts go out to you in your bereavement.

It is a time to be brave to face the future for what it must be, to pick up and go on.

You have all our sympathy.

With love,

Dear Sandy,

We join you and Sidney in sorrow in these days of grief. It is hard to have courage in the face of such adversity but you must carry on bravely for the other children.

Our deepest sympathy to all of you.

Please call us if there is anything we can do.

Sincerely,

Dear Mrs. Johnson,

Word has just reached us of the death of Arnold. It is a great tragedy indeed and you have all our heartfelt sympathy.

Nothing I can say can be really helpful in your grief, but I did want you to know that we feel deeply for you and that you are in our thoughts constantly.

Sincerely,

On the death of a relative of a friend or acquaintance

Dear Mrs. Johnson,

Mother just told me of the death of your sister Alicia. Please accept my condolences.

Alicia was a fine girl and would have made a mark for herself in the world. All those who knew her loved her quiet charm and her intelligent politeness.

Please convey my sincere sympathy to your mother and brother Ben. I know how much Alicia was part of their lives as she was of yours.

Sincerely,

Dear Sam,

I was shocked to read in this morning's *Times* of the death of your Aunt Celia.

You spoke of her so often, I feel I, too, knew her. She was so much more than just an aunt to you that I know her death must bring you a great deal of sadness.

Please accept my sincere sympathy. Call on me if I can be of any help.

Sincerely,

In case of a suicide

Dear Martha,

The tragic news of Tim's death stunned us all here. Our deepest sympathy goes out to you.

If there is any way in which we can be helpful, please have someone call us.

Affectionately,

Dear Louise,

How terrible for you! I can't begin to express the sorrow we feel at your tragedy.

You know you have our deepest sympathy. If there is anything we can do to help, please have someone call us and we'll be there on the next flight.

Love,

Acknowledging condolences

Letters of condolence should be acknowledged with hand-written notes, but the pressures of the time and numbers force many to use engraved cards. These may be sent to all those who attend the funeral.

Because condolences usually come in bunches to a person in an abnormal emotional situation, the usual acknowledgment is an engraved or printed card with a message like:

> The family of John Smith acknowledge with thanks your kind expression of sympathy.

The handwritten acknowledgment should show that you have read the letter of condolence; make a mention of it if there was anything distinctive about it.

The minimal note is:

Dear Martha,

Thank you for your kind expression of sympathy. I appreciate your thoughtfulness.

Sincerely,

Dear Cynthia,

Thank you so much for your comforting note about Uncle Ted. It was nice of you to write.

Thank you, too, for the offer to come to stay with us for a while to help out. Ordinarily we would be delighted to have you here with us, but Anita says she would prefer to be alone for a while. Perhaps in a month or so she will feel more like being with others.

Please give our love to your mother and Beth.

Affectionately,

Dear Mr. Murdock,

Thank you for your kind condolences and the nice things you said about Frank.

All of us miss him greatly, of course, but we do have many pleasant memories of life with him to console us.

Affectionately,

Dear Sandy,

Thank you very much for your kind letter of sympathy.

Indeed, Frank had many friends and tried very hard to do his part to make ours a better town. He mentioned you often and had a great respect for your judgment.

We will miss him very much and I know you too will find he leaves a gap in all our lives.

Sincerely,

THANK-YOU LETTERS

From early childhood we are taught to say thank you. Common courtesy requires it. As we grow older, seemingly, situations arise that make it not so simple. A thank-you note, however, can cement a relationship. Any gift and most courtesies (including congratulations) require an acknowledgment. Most new relationships, such as the opening of a new business account or receipt of an order, offer an opportunity to say thank you.

The essence of a good thank-you note is when you send it. A note delayed becomes an unpleasant duty to the recipient of a gift or favor, and a reminder of lack of courtesy to the one receiving the thanks. Only the newly married couple off on a honeymoon, or the bedridden, or a new mother, has a good excuse.

Thank-you notes are important not only as a courtesy. The sender of a gift needs to know that it was received. Often it is sent by a store and could go astray. The sender holds the receipt for a reasonable time; after that tracing a package becomes more difficult. But whatever way it was sent, the receipt of a gift should be acknowledged. The proper way is with a thank-you note.

Thank-you notes should express sincere pleasure at the receipt of the gift, favor, or hospitality and the thought behind it. Be sure to mention what the thanks are for, and the occasion.

For a gift

Dear Aunt Tania,

How nice of you to go to the trouble of finding just what I wanted for my birthday!

I've struggled for months trying to save up enough money for a good microscope, but each time I thought I almost had enough something happened to deplete my funds.

Your choice was terrific! It will certainly help in my schoolwork and the experiments I am making as part of the Science Day competition.

Aunt Tania, you're a peach!

Love,
David

Dear Janet,

I wish you had been here to see the look in Johnny's eyes when he opened your Christmas package!

It took us ten minutes to get him to let the mechanical man go on its way before we could go on with the rest of the evening, and half an hour to drag him away this morning.

You're a darling for the thought, Janet. Johnny sends you his love.

Martha

Dear Mr. and Mrs. Sandstone,

What a fantastic gift! The two books are just gorgeous; I don't know which one is more beautiful. Michael and I will treasure them. Thank you so very much.

Sincerely,
Elizabeth

P.S. Please forgive the late arrival of this note. There was some confusion retrieving the package from the country post office.

Dear Sandy and Bill,

How am I ever going to be able to dissuade you from sending such an elegant Christmas present? The contents I can cope with, but the decanter is so lovely that it far surpasses what's in my liquor cabinet. The only answer I can think of is to drink it quickly so as not to put the rest of the stock to shame.

Thanks and happy New Year.

Sincerely yours,

Dear Sandy and Bill,

Mein Gott! Another of those superb decanters of brandy! You overwhelm me, as usual. Coming on top of that spluzzy lunch at the Forum, I can only stammer: "Thanks."

Happy New Year,

For a favor

Dear Sam,

A million thanks for your kindness to my son Don last week. He wrote to tell me how much time you spent with him and the sound advice you provided about job hunting in Chicago.

As a result of your suggestions, he has made contact with half a dozen prospects and has interviews scheduled with three of them.

I am sure Don will keep you up to date on his progress as soon as he knows a little more. At the moment he is staying with friends, looking for a small apartment.

It is good to have a wise friend in high places.

Don joins me in wishing you the best.

Cordially,

Dear Sidney,

"Thank you" expresses only a small measure of my gratitude for your courtesies to Sandra while she was at Princeton last week.

Sandra tells me she would have been lost without your shepherding and chauffeuring. After all the fuss, Sandra has decided that Princeton was not for her and has decided to enroll at Radcliffe, her mother's alma mater. Sylvia cannot yet accept the fact that Princeton is coed and so is a bit relieved.

All of us look forward to your next trip to New York and hope we will have an opportunity to spend some time with you.

Cordially,

Dear Ned,

Thank you so much for the wonderful event. It is very easy for most people to write letters of complaint but this is a letter of appreciation.

You, through your organization, did everything possible for the dealers and public in regard to the Columbus Day Fair. The publicity was good; the posters were excellent; the dates on posters were changed promptly; block captains were ready and helpful; etc., etc.

Every dealer understands the risk of inclement weather and must be prepared for it. We took our chances last Sunday. We were miserably soaked three or four times. But we did sell a lot and we consider it a real success. If we have the merchandise and the know-how, and the backing such as you give, we will always come out all right in the long run.

I look forward to continued cooperation between us.

Sincerely,

Dear Mary,

Thank you for your lovely letter.

It came as a rainbow amid the shower of complaints.

Very cordially,

Dear Lina,

Now that I am home again and able to put pen and paper together I want to say thank you for your many messages of encouragement and the beautiful flowers you sent while I was in the hospital. Both helped brighten the gloom of monotonous days and dreary nights.

Your thoughtfulness and concern is a constant encouragement to me.

I look forward to being out of bed and out of the house, to the time I can join in your meetings once again.

Cordially,

Dear Sam,

    I am at a loss for words when it comes to writing a thank-you note to you for your splendid cooperation. I am reminded of the very nice liturgy which we recite on Passover night in the Haggadah, which I paraphrase in the following manner:

    If you had provided us with the information and mailing lists free of charge, it would have been enough.

    If I had gotten the photographs within a very reasonable time, it would have been enough.

    How much more gratitude do I owe you when you are doing so much work free of charge and I get back proof almost before I sent the copy. Which only proves that when you give, you give with an open heart and open hands.

    Thanks a million.

Sincerely yours,

Bread-and-butter letters

    A letter of thanks after a dinner or overnight stay is a social must. It should be sent within two or three days after you return. Bread-and-butter letters are the touch that assures your host and hostess that you enjoyed your visit with them—an evening of bridge, dinner or a weekend. Some hostesses are very sensitive on this point. If you cannot write, at least telephone.

Dear Mathilda,

    It was wonderful seeing you and Tom again. We had a grand time and that not-Thanksgiving dinner was so reminiscent of Grandma's homecoming parties, I almost cried. You must give me the recipe for the orange-cranberry dressing.

    Now that we're back to the humdrum life of workaday living, I am insisting that Johnny get out to the skating rink more often. He enjoyed the exercise so much at Gainsborough, but he never seems to find time to skate here in town.

    I told Maryann about your beautiful garden. She is quite envious of all the space you have.

    Please call us when you plan to be in Hometown. We would like to see you again and perhaps have a local reunion at our house.

Affectionately,

Dear Mrs. Murdock,

    Thank you very much for the delightful weekend in the country. It was a real relaxer and a great chance to improve my tennis.

    It was most gracious of you and Mr. Murdock to invite me and I sincerely appreciate your hospitality.

Cordially,

Dear Joan,

Annette and I want to thank you for the wonderful weekend at Journey's End.

It was good to have an opportunity to see you all once again before we leave for Europe. We particularly enjoyed the reminiscences and those photographs of the old days. Did we really ever look like that!

As soon as we get back—probably in mid-October—we'll call you to get you updated on our own experiences.

Cordially,

Dear Clarice,

You must know how very much Sylvia and I enjoyed the splendid day at the seashore with you. We were delighted with the swim in your calm inlet, the lovely decor of your new home, and especially the conversations with your friends.

Most of all it was good to see you and Sam and the children again and to compare notes about all our mutuals.

Good luck in your new house!

Love,

Acknowledging good wishes

Dear Jane,

If, by some chance, I should forget, I can depend on your annual good wishes on our anniversary.

Thank you for remembering and bring back the fond memories of the days when . . .

Affectionately,

Dear Tom and Mary,

It required only your timely greetings to make our anniversary celebrations complete.

It was nice of you to remember and to send such a happy greeting. We wish you yourself could have been with us.

Affectionately,

Dear Mr. and Mrs. Johnson,

It was great to get the annual Merit Award but even more rewarding were the good wishes of old friends like you.

Thank you for the good wishes. I do hope indeed that your nice forecasts come true.

Cordially,

Dear Miss Carlyle,

Your announcement of my winning the Tennalton Science Award was a most pleasant surprise.

Please express my thanks and gratitude to the Screening Committee, and my admiration for their excellent judgment, I might add.

Rest assured I will cherish the medal and try to prove myself worthy of it in the future.

Very cordially,

Dear Mrs. Porter,

Thank you for the lovely and sentimental remembrance of my birthday.

Much as I hate to count the numbers, I relish the good wishes of my old friends like you and treasure the memories of the good times they recall.

Please continue to remember!

Affectionately,

Dear Sam,

Take four giant steps for the lovely card—and do take them in our direction.

We look forward to your flawless memory of our "occasions" to keep us informed where you are and that you are well as the years go by. It is good of you to remember and to take the time to write.

Affectionately,

Thank-you letters in business and public life

In business, the thank-you letter is equally important.

Dear Mr. Kandel:

May I, as president of the Community Committee, thank you for the contribution of a spot in your exhibition.

It was a gift of many facets. It gave the Community Committee a new project, a new source for earning monies for the museum and an opportunity to bring the museum to the attention of a large new audience.

The project was successful in every dimension for us. We hope you will consider it sufficiently productive from your viewpoint so that you will want us to continue this as an annual event.

Sincerely,

Dear Mr. Johnson:

Your article on the Community Committee was first-rate, a real eye-catcher. The article certainly touched all the bases without wasting a word.

Our sincere thanks. Just let us know if we can give you a lift on any future project.

Very sincerely,

Dear Sam . . .

Usual thank-you letter omitted . . . at the suggestion of the Society for the Suppression of long thank-you letters!

Sincerely,

P.S. They tell me people don't read lengthy letters anyway . . . and the chances are you don't need to be reminded that we appreciate this order.

Dear Sandy and Bill,

In advance of the election on Tuesday next, both Bette and I want to thank you very much for your encouragement, assistance, and support—and in particular for your willingness to permit us to use your names in the endorsement ad which appeared last week. I was honored.

We have every reason to feel optimistic, but whether or not our joint efforts turn out to be successful, we both know and appreciate how important everyone's help has been.

I just felt that you should know that, win, lose, or draw, it is just great to realize we have friends like you.

Thanks for everything . . . ·

Sincerely,

Dear John,

I want you to know how deeply I appreciate the editorial entitled "Everyone Should Join Revenue Sharing Fight" which appeared in the March 9 edition of the *Record.*

It is through this kind of thoughtful and responsible journalism that your newspaper has served the public employee so well during more than three decades of publications.

Revenue sharing, for which I am fighting so strongly, is, indeed, the concern of every citizen of our state. By urging support of this concept you have served the best interests not only of all civil servants but of the general public as well.

With warm regards,

Sincerely,

Dear Sidney,

Not many nice people like you are around but that is why you count so much in counterbalancing the elements of human nature— why some of us have that constant optimism and faith in the Good, à la Plato or Maimonides.

Always,

A certificate of appreciation adds another dimension:

On behalf of the United States Customs Service it gives me great pleasure to present to you at this time your CERTIFICATE OF APPRECIATION awarded to you by Acting Commissioner of Customs Lester D. Johnson in appreciation of your outstanding contribution to the success of the Anniversary of the United States Customs Service.

Sincerely yours,

Index